Teaching Adolescents With Autism

Practical Strategies for the Inclusive Classroom

WALTER KAWESKI

Foreword by Kathy Gee

CORWIN
A SAGE Company

CORWIN
A SAGE Company

FOR INFORMATION:

Corwin
A SAGE Company
2455 Teller Road
Thousand Oaks, California 91320
(800) 233-9936
Fax: (800) 417-2466
www.corwin.com

SAGE Ltd.
1 Oliver's Yard
55 City Road
London EC1Y 1SP
United Kingdom

SAGE India Pvt. Ltd.
B 1/I 1 Mohan Cooperative Industrial Area
Mathura Road, New Delhi 110 044
India

SAGE Asia-Pacific Pte. Ltd.
33 Pekin Street #02-01
Far East Square
Singapore 048763

Acquisitions Editor: Jessica Allan
Associate Editor: Allison Scott
Editorial Assistant: Lisa Whitney
Production Editor: Amy Schroller
Copy Editor: Brenda Weight
Typesetter: C&M Digitals (P) Ltd.
Proofreader: Scott Oney
Indexer: Sheila Bodell
Cover Designer: Michael Dubowe
Permissions Editor: Karen Ehrmann

Copyright © 2011 by Corwin

Printed in the United States of America

Library of Congress Cataloging-in-Publication Data

Kaweski, Walter.

Teaching adolescents with autism : practical strategies for the inclusive classroom / Walter Kaweski.

p. cm.

Includes bibliographical references and index.

ISBN 978-1-4129-9529-0 (pbk.)

1. Autistic children—Education—United States. 2. Inclusive education—United States. I. Title.

LC4718.K39 2011
371.94—dc22
2011006846

This book is printed on acid-free paper.

11 12 13 14 15 10 9 8 7 6 5 4 3 2 1

Teaching
Adolescents
With
Autism

Contents

**Instructional Assistant Inclusion Support Guide:
Online at www.corwin.com/adolescentautism**

The complete Instructional Assistant Inclusion
Support Guide may be found online at
www.corwin.com/adolescentautism

Foreword

Supporting students with disabilities of all kinds to access the core curriculum and take part as full members of school and classroom communities requires information, collaboration, and a shared vision among team members. At the heart of this book is a desire to share from real school experiences—the ups and downs of teaming, providing supports, teaching together, and addressing learning and social challenges with creativity and consistency.

The author brings his experiences as an inclusion support teacher, and as a parent, to life, through practical and easy-to-follow strategies that he has utilized in his quest to successfully support individuals with autism spectrum disorders (ASD) in the general education core curriculum, classrooms, and all aspects of school life. He is primarily speaking to general education teachers; however, parents, paraprofessionals, and other school faculty and staff will also benefit from these easy-to-read chapters and easy-to-follow suggestions. Written in a friendly, yet informative, style, the book brings to life many of the day-to-day experiences that teachers with heterogeneous classrooms, including students with disabilities, will have.

Chapters 1 and 2 give the reader background information in ASD and the history of inclusive schools. The remaining chapters provide practical strategies for social supports, modifications and adaptations to the core curriculum, classroom organization, instructional strategies, positive behavioral supports, and communication. Each chapter also includes resources for further information.

Schools are learning communities. This means that teachers have to be lifelong learners if we are to expect our students to be lifelong learners. The author has clearly taken this to heart as he has diligently gone to conferences, read books and journals, and gathered information to be more successful at serving his students. I know this, because he is a graduate from the program I coordinate at California State University, Sacramento. Now, in this book, he has taken time to share with the reader the strategies that he has found to be most successful. I think you will enjoy this book, and, more important, find practical and easy-to-use suggestions.

—Kathy Gee

Preface

This book is born from the experience of raising a son diagnosed with autism and informed through research and 34 years of experience teaching in public schools. In other words, it is written from the heart of a father combined with the expertise of a veteran educator.

Allow me to share a personal story. Back in 1991, when our 4-year-old son Steven started preschool, we did not know much about developmental disabilities and just assumed Steven was "different." The differences, we would later learn, were symptoms of autism, but back then, we did not or could not see the signs—not until our next-door neighbor Ken, an Air Force doctor, called out from next door to my wife, Laura, "There's something wrong with Steven! He's not normal!" This unfortunate comment across our conjoined yards served as a wake-up call that led us to a pediatric psychiatrist and the diagnosis of Asperger syndrome. At first, we struggled to understand and accept this label. Our initial sense of concern for our beautiful boy brought tears and heartache.

Over the years, Laura and I researched autism, attended conferences, and welcomed a parade of therapeutic specialists into our home. The initial feelings of uninformed dread were gradually reshaped by countless positive and joyful experiences with Steven. Our perceptions evolved, replaced with optimism. We learned, as we hope you will learn, that a person is far more than the diagnosis he or she carries.

One highlight from Steven's early years will illustrate what I mean. We enrolled Steven in Suzuki violin lessons and over the next three years watched him develop into an amazing violinist who performed violin pieces by Bach and Mozart. Some of our proudest moments came while watching Steven perform in front of his classmates at school assemblies. I learned from these early experiences the power of guided practice.

Steven, as of this writing, just celebrated his 23rd birthday and is a sensitive and caring young man. He graduated from high school, attends college, and is in search of a girlfriend. He is everything a parent wants in a grown son. He is loving, integrity centered, affectionate, and very reliable. When Steven gives you his word, you can be sure he will keep his promise. His future truly looks bright.

Why this book? Despite research studies that continue to warn of the detrimental effects of uninformed support for students with developmental disabilities, teachers who have little experience with autism are held responsible for supporting students with complex needs in general education settings.

Traditional methods of instruction may not work for students with autism. Many of these students benefit from informed academic, social, and behavior support. Without support, many will risk failure and rejection.

Too often, when things go wrong, the student, rather than the support system, is blamed. Considering these consequences, training and support for the general education teacher is urgently needed. The National Research Council (2001) indicates that "personnel preparation remains one of the weakest elements of effective programming for children with autistic spectrum disorder" (p. 225).

Despite increasing awareness of autism, surprisingly few evidence-based resources exist to help teachers understand and support adolescents with autism in middle and high school general education settings. Most available literature focuses on younger students or is generalized to reach all disability categories. Clearly, this book is a welcome resource that addresses the needs of this large and diverse population of adolescents and young adults.

ABOUT THE BOOK

Teaching Adolescents With Autism is written for general education teachers, support specialists, administrators, parents, and others interested in learning research-based interventions for adolescents with autism and other developmental disabilities. The reader will gain a thorough understanding of the social, sensory, cognitive, and behavioral challenges students with autism experience. The book is well grounded theoretically, featuring a generous collection of practical strategies designed to help the teacher successfully support a diverse group of students across a variety of settings. The intervention strategies presented will benefit nondisabled students as well.

We present a book that is organized and visually interesting. Each chapter offers numerous research-based strategies, insights, and resources to support chapter objectives. Important concepts are reinforced with bulleted lists, tables, figures, and photographs. Personal examples support important concepts in a tangible way. Quotes and anecdotes are sprinkled in to impart bits of wisdom and brevity.

The substance of the book contains an abundance of information that will increase understanding and improve support practices in several overlapping areas of concern. The "how" is supported throughout with the "why." We believe that every introduced support strategy needs to be tied to the relevance of the practice.

The teacher will learn how the combination of environmental, psychological, physiological, and social stressors characteristic of middle and high school can impact the student and what can be accomplished to improve conditions for the student. Strategies are introduced that promote a welcoming and comfortable classroom setting with an emphasis placed on meaningful participation, peer support, and friendship development. Emerging research in the field of social development for students with autism continues to stress the importance of nondisabled peer engagement as a critical component in reducing autistic symptoms. The book's emphasis on natural peer support is woven throughout the text.

An entire chapter is devoted to adaptations. The teacher will learn how to utilize a variety of support strategies to improve access to instructional content across settings and subjects. Specific adaptations are included for every major subject area, as well as general adaptations that apply across all content areas. The author introduces the teacher to the acronym "SPECIAL" translated to reinforce the idea that good adaptations should be Simple, Practical, Explicit, Community building, Independence promoting, Age appropriate, and Logical and meaningful.

Attitude is everything. The teacher must believe in the capacity of students with autism to achieve . . . not easy in a society that unfairly characterizes persons with disabilities as tragic or lesser human beings "suffering" from their diagnosis. The book dispels misperceptions about these students by discrediting inaccurate descriptors like "less fortunate," "needy," and "challenged" that continue to perpetuate this view. By doing so, unfair stereotypes about the nature of disability are cast aside in favor of increased expectations for the person behind the label.

Each chapter concludes with a summary followed by suggested readings for further study. The reader is directed to the book's extensive resource section for further information and support. Also, an Instructional Assistant Inclusion Support Guide is available online at www.corwin .com/adolescentautism.

The knowledge base that supports the book's content is extensive. The author draws from current and emerging research in the fields of autism, inclusive education, instructional methodology, learning theory, behavior, communication, and peer intervention strategies.

The authors, educators, and researchers most frequently cited are leading experts in the field, including Simon Baron-Cohen, Kathy Doering, Mary Beth Doyle, Nancy French, Uta Frith, Kathy Gee, Michael Giangreco, Jean Gonsier-Gerdin, Temple Grandin, Ann Halverson, Norman Kunc, Robert and Lynn Koegel, Philip Strange, Emma Van der Klift, and Brenda Smith Myles.

The book also includes heartfelt insights based on the author's extensive experience as an autism specialist, inclusion coordinator, and father of a 23-year-old son diagnosed with Asperger syndrome. Featured throughout the book are personal stories of students the author and his staff have supported over the years. These stories add a personal dimension to the values and practices consistently reinforced throughout the book.

From his dual perspective of educator and father, the author places a high value on the importance of understanding each student as a unique individual beyond the diagnostic label. It is a capacity-based perspective that strives to challenge students with ASD to reach their full potential. These values are reinforced with a generous array of pictures and vignettes that convey powerful messages about each person's potential to grow and develop.

Acknowledgments

I wish to express my heartfelt gratitude to Dr. Kathy Gee and Dr. Jean Gonsier-Gerdin, professors of special education at Sacramento State University, for their steadfast support and guidance over the years. Their extraordinary dedication to inclusive education, along with their vast expertise in research-based practices, has served as the guiding force behind my efforts to develop an inclusive program for students with autism spectrum disorders. I am honored to associate with these distinguished experts.

Thank you, Dr. Kathy Doering, San Francisco State University, for allowing us to include your brilliant "Reflection Tools for Facilitating Positive Student Outcomes, 2010" in the resource section of this book. This set of valuable resources will guide inclusion programs toward best practices. I appreciate your support for this project! Your ideas and explicit vision for inclusion are enormously helpful.

Thank you, Dr. Mary Beth Doyle, for your encouragement and enthusiastic support for this project. Your suggestions have helped guide the book's development and gave me needed encouragement along the way.

A special thank-you to Lisa Herstrom-Smith, principal, John Barrett Middle School, for her support and leadership in the development of a full inclusion program. Her consistent advocacy in pursuit of inclusive opportunities for students with disabilities makes a significant difference in our whole-school program growth and development. Public education needs more administrators like Lisa.

Many thanks to Dayle Cantrall for her support during times of challenge. Dayle provided district-level support that helped improve our support strategies without impeding our efforts. When help was needed, she offered advice and good-natured humor. Thank you, Ted Darrow, for helping us through the initial stages of our program. Your encouragement made challenges easier to overcome. Vice-principal Valerie Lott demonstrated great wisdom on many occasions. Her impressive insight and patience helped countless students during times of crisis.

There are not enough superlatives to accurately describe the contributions of Speech Pathologist Laura Enos Grover, Autism Specialist Mike Prentiss, and School Counselor Laurie Faniani. They are the "gold standard" in their chosen specialties. Their steadfast devotion to students with disabilities, coupled with their immense expertise, has made a huge difference in the lives of many children in our area.

Thank you to my instructional assistants, who helped our inclusion program develop and thrive. Thank you, Sarah Delrio, Shelly Russ, Trish Esquer, and Jillian Netzley. In my view, you are among the most devoted professionals in the field.

I am grateful to my teacher colleagues Anne Anderson, Brenda Danzinger, Anne Billington, Glen Bisquera, Kathryn Blodgett, Cynthia Book, Wendy Carlson, Amy Conti, Jennifer Daniels, Debra Ethington, Brian Gayek, Geoffrey Gill, Vicki Hallberg, John Higgins, Colleen Honegger, Tom Hunt, Tami Irvine, Jean Keller, Beverly Lockhart, Tim Mccandless, Rebecca McEnroe, Angela Nodolf, Jean Osterkamp, Karen Patterson, Jennifer Smiley, Tom Strobel, Terri Thacker, Dave Thompson, Anne Varanelli, Normajean Viramontes, Grace Wahl, and Don Wright, for nurturing all students while helping to build a welcoming inclusive learning community. We worked together to overcome challenges inherent in the development of a viable whole-school inclusion program. Your enthusiasm for new ideas and willingness to take risks opened the doors to valuable experiences and friendship for many students.

Thank you, Carol Kimpson. You are more than a school nurse and health consultant to our district. You are my wise friend who has the extraordinary ability to keep complicated issues in perspective. I appreciate the times you reminded me to view all issues from the needs of the family and to view obstacles in the best light regardless of how challenging and complicated some issues get.

Teaching Adolescents With Autism would not have been possible without the guidance and support of the Corwin editorial staff. I would first like to thank acquisition editors Jessica Allan and David Cho for believing in this project and going forward. David provided the initial ideas to improve the manuscript, and Jessica carried the project forward through the peer review process and then presented her findings and recommendations to the Corwin/Sage Publications Editorial Board for acceptance. In essence, Jessica and David made possible all the steps that followed. I would also like to thank Lisa Whitney, the editorial assistant who was especially helpful in managing numerous details related to permissions and photo releases, along with helping answer my questions as the publication process moved forward. My sincere appreciation and gratitude to the production editor, Amy Schroller, and copy editor, Brenda Weight, for their expert assistance in preparing the manuscript for publication. Amy helped me understand the production process and coordinated responsibilities among departments while overseeing the production process as a whole. I am especially grateful to copy editor Brenda Weight. She is a first-rate copyediting professional who attended to the meticulous details that need to be addressed during the manuscript preparation process. Finally, thank you to the Corwin Art Department, and especially Michael Dubowe for his beautiful cover design.

I wish to express deep love and affection to my sons, Wayne and Steven, and my beautiful daughter-in-law, Eowyn, for expressing support and encouragement along the way.

Last but not least, a huge thank-you to my wife, Laura, for her enormous help with this project. There is not enough space to list all the good deeds you have provided me along the way! Everything from proofing to typing and, most of all, your immense patience and understanding for the time spent in completing this manuscript is most appreciated. I can't thank you enough, Dear!

I love you!

About the Author

**Walt Kaweski, MA,** is a teacher, autism specialist, and inclusion coordinator in the San Juan Unified School District of suburban Sacramento, California. With 35 years of experience in public education, he has taught a wide variety of subjects and grade levels, including high school English, intervention reading and math, history, and instrumental music. Mr. Kaweski was awarded the 2007 Teacher of the Year Award by his school district for his work developing a successful inclusion program for students with autism. In partnership with Sacramento State University, Mr. Kaweski trains teacher candidates pursuing the special education credential. He has presented at local, state, and national conferences on topics concerning inclusion support and friendship development for students with autism.

Mr. Kaweski earned his Master of Arts in Special Education from Sacramento State University. He is a certified Moderate-Severe Special Education Specialist and Cross-cultural, Language and Academic Development Specialist.

ABOUT THE CONTRIBUTOR

Jean Gonsier-Gerdin, PhD, is Associate Professor in the Department of Special Education, Rehabilitation, School Psychology and Deaf Studies at California State University, Sacramento. She received a master's degree in social sciences in education from Stanford University, School of Education, and a doctorate in special education from the University of California, Berkeley, with San Francisco State University. Dr. Gonsier-Gerdin's teaching and research interests include inclusive education practices; instructional strategies for students with autism spectrum disorders; peer supports and social relationships; positive behavioral support; interprofessional collaboration; family support; and special education teacher preparation to promote advocacy, leadership, and systems change.

ABOUT THE ILLUSTRATOR

 **Devon Smith** is an eighth-grade student formerly enrolled at Barrett Middle School in Carmichael, California. Devon is a remarkable self-taught cartoonist who demonstrated an early talent for drawing. Devon was awarded the "Fine Arts Department Award" for his talents. He is respected throughout his school community for his humor and wit as displayed in his hilarious drawings.

Dedication

*To my beloved wife, Laura,
for the love, encouragement, and thoughtful advice you provided throughout
the process of developing this book. You are the best, Dear!*

SPECIAL THANKS

*Thank you, Dr. Jean Gonsier-Gerdin, for your incredible insight
and advice during the preparation of this manuscript. I will forever be grateful to
you for your helpful support during the final weeks prior to the production stage of this book.*

Introduction

> *"No one likes me! I'm a complete failure!" cried 13-year-old Adrianna, a pretty seventh-grade girl diagnosed with autism. She had just spent another lunch period wandering around the schoolyard alone while her peers engaged in laughter and conversation, played games, and enjoyed each other's company. Adrianna spent many lunch periods this way, without friends, wanting to fit in but not knowing how. (Author)*

Students like Adrianna are not unusual. She represents thousands of school-age students who are diagnosed with an autism spectrum disorder (ASD) and need special education services. Despite this label, Adrianna's disability does not define who she is as a person. So who is Adrianna? She is Joseph and Sarah's daughter and Aaron's sister. She loves to dance and bubbles over with enthusiasm when the date of the school dance is announced. Adrianna is an excellent student who conscientiously completes each assignment to the best of her ability. She is the proud recipient of the "Excellence in Math Award" given each school year to the top-achieving math student in the school. Because Adrianna struggles to understand abstract concepts, she receives support in reading comprehension. She wants to get married someday and have a family. In many respects, Adrianna is a typical teenager with hopes and dreams very similar to her typically developing peers.

Let's face it . . . the adolescent years are a challenging transitional time when all students undergo significant physical and emotional changes. Academic demands and social expectations increase. Course content involves more abstract concepts and there is a lot more homework. Peer relationships become more nuanced and complex. Because students move through a daily schedule of several classes, it is not easy to organize, meet academic responsibilities, satisfy teacher expectations, and make friends. For students with ASD, these challenges can be especially difficult (Farrugia & Hudson, 2006).

There are countless kids like Adrianna who struggle to cope with academic and social demands on their own. Many have potential on a par with their nondisabled peers, but too many of these students experience social isolation, ridicule, self-doubt, lowered self-esteem, and academic failure. It doesn't have to be this way!

Here is the issue: Research studies show that the general education setting can be an optimal learning environment when informed support strategies are practiced. However, research also demonstrates that careless, uninformed support can stigmatize the student with ASD in the eyes of his peers and lead to overreliance on adults and reluctance to engage in learning activities and independent task completion (Giangreco, Edelman, Luiselli, & MacFarland, 1997). Without informed support, many of these students could develop clinically significant levels of behavioral or emotional challenges during their adolescent years. To avoid these detrimental effects and effectively include these unique students in the general education setting requires training, thoughtful planning, and support for the teachers assigned to assist them.

How do we make it work? Including students with autism is best accomplished when teachers understand autism as it applies to the individual. They practice person-centered strategies to promote academic achievement, emotional growth, independence, self-determination, and friendship. Effective teachers deliver instruction appropriate to the student's learning style. They deliver the kind of participatory learning experiences that inclusion was intended to provide. Not easily discouraged, they dwell on possibilities and are excellent problem solvers. They are by nature optimistic, energetic, and integrity centered.

This book is written in support of teachers who seek to understand and improve intervention strategies for students with ASD across a variety of middle and high school settings. As an educational partner with parents, special education teachers, administration, and instructional support staff, general education teachers are important members of educational teams specializing in making school experiences work for these wonderful and sometimes complex students.

There is a lot to learn. You will need to understand the social, sensory, cognitive, and behavioral challenges that characterize the diagnosis of ASD and acquire the skills necessary to successfully support the student's full participation and membership in the school community. This book will help you understand these students as unique individuals beyond the autism label. The knowledge and skills presented in the chapters to follow will help overcome many of the obstacles to learning and friendship these students face.

Keep in mind just how important your role is to these students. Successful school experiences during adolescence increase the likelihood for better adult outcomes and are therefore critical to healthy adolescent development. No one wants to see Adrianna and students like her struggle through their teenage years. We want her to learn and prosper, develop her talents, and reach her potential. We want her to enjoy school, make friends, and *belong*—just like everyone else. The content of this book will help.

The author draws on multiple sources of information with a high priority placed on proven research-based practices, also known as "evidence-based practices," in the fields of autism intervention and special education. The author's personal experiences as a father of a son diagnosed with autism in addition to his work as a special educator and inclusion coordinator make this book especially valuable.

Thank you for your interest! You deserve respect and appreciation for the central role you play in directing instruction and encouraging understanding and acceptance among students. Thank you for your commitment and dedication! Thank you for your willingness to learn more. We hope you find the ideas contained in this book illuminating.

While they were saying among themselves it cannot be done, it was done.

—Helen Keller

1

Understanding Autism

Autism is a way of being. It is pervasive; it colors every experience, every sensation, perception, thought, emotion, and encounter, every aspect of existence. It is not possible to separate the autism from the person.

Jim Sinclair (1993)

Our first chapter will focus on understanding autism spectrum disorder (ASD) for one simple reason: Informed support leads to better outcomes. Although topics related to autism are frequently in the news, the disorder is not widely understood. Many people still perceive individuals with autism based on movie depictions like *Rain Man, Forrest Gump, Mozart and the Whale,* and *Adam.* Although there is some truth to these depictions, each is really just a portrayal of one individual. To complicate matters, a student with autism may show little evidence of a disability. The student is not using a brace or walking with a guide dog. He appears typical, with no physical evidence of a challenge. Despite outward appearances, the diagnosis leaves the student disconnected from others while distorting his perceptions of the world in which he lives.

There is less tolerance in schools and society in general for disabilities that are hidden. It's much harder for students and adults to understand differences they can't see. The student with ASD senses things differently than his typical peers and may respond in unusual ways.

As a result, the student is frequently misunderstood. Misunderstandings can lead to mistreatment, exclusion, and perhaps even abuse. Understanding the range of potential characteristics of this disorder will empower you to be an effective advocate and teacher.

In addition to supporting students' academic needs in the classroom, you will also need to bridge the gap of understanding between students with autism and their peers without disabilities—not always an easy task when you consider the sometimes baffling behaviors of the student with autism that at times seem far from typical. Nevertheless, with knowledge and training you can reduce misunderstandings, while increasing acceptance and even friendship.

Relationship building is the key to reaching the potential of students with ASD. Strive to establish a connection with the person. Your time and effort will be rewarded.

INTRODUCTION TO AUTISM

Autism is a neurological developmental disorder, believed to have a genetic basis, affecting the brain's ability to process and interpret varying types of information. Deficits can occur in a constellation of behaviors, but generally fall into three broad areas:

1. Social interaction

2. Verbal and nonverbal communication

3. Restrictive patterns of interest and behavior

Autism is considered a developmental disability because symptoms of autism typically manifest before age 3 and continue throughout the life span. In fact, autism has a profound impact on a child's development. Students with autism have significant challenges with communication development. They lack appropriate expressive language starting in early childhood. They may not engage in eye gaze when a parent approaches their crib or smile and interact as typical babies do. Later, the varieties of typical play behaviors like spontaneous make-believe play and sharing of interests with others is noticeably reduced or absent. They struggle to understand and relate to the thoughts of others. Nuanced forms of nonverbal and spoken communication, like body language, gestures, tone of voice, sarcasm, and the use of idioms, are misinterpreted or go unnoticed. Some students display "stereotypical behavior," meaning they are drawn to narrow, atypical interests and behaviors that identify them with the disorder.

The term "autism" was first described in the 1940s by Leo Kanner, an American psychiatrist, when writing about a group of children who displayed similar patterns of behavior (Kanner, 1943). Today, more than 60 years later, autism is referred to as a pervasive developmental disorder or an autism spectrum disorder (ASD) because the range (spectrum) of potential differences varies widely from very moderate to significant and affects each person differently and to varying degrees. In fact, The *Diagnostic and Statistical Manual of Mental Disorders, Fourth Edition, Text Revision (DSM-IV-TR)*, published by the American Psychiatric Association (2000) to assist in the diagnosis of mental disorders in both children and adults, has actually identified five subgroups under the umbrella of pervasive developmental disorders: autistic disorder, Asperger syndrome, pervasive developmental disorder not otherwise specified (PDD-NOS), childhood disintegrative disorder, and Rett's syndrome.

To gain a better understanding of autism/autistic disorder, look over the following *DSM-IV-TR* diagnostic criteria:

DSM-IV-TR DEFINITION OF AUTISM/AUTISTIC DISORDER[1]

(A) A total of six (or more) items from (1), (2), and (3), with at least two from (1), and one each from (2) and (3):

(1) qualitative impairment in social interaction, as manifested by at least two of the following:

(a) marked impairments in the use of multiple nonverbal behaviors such as eye-to-eye gaze, facial expression, body posture, and gestures to regulate social interaction

(b) failure to develop peer relationships appropriate to developmental level

(c) a lack of spontaneous seeking to share enjoyment, interests, or achievements with other people (e.g., by a lack of showing, bringing, or pointing out objects of interest to other people)

(d) lack of social or emotional reciprocity

(2) qualitative impairments in communication as manifested by at least one of the following:

(a) delay in, or total lack of, the development of spoken language (not accompanied by an attempt to compensate through alternative modes of communication such as gesture or mime)

(b) in individuals with adequate speech, marked impairment in the ability to initiate or sustain a conversation with others

(c) stereotyped and repetitive use of language or idiosyncratic language

(d) lack of varied, spontaneous make-believe play or social imitative play appropriate to developmental level

---

[1]Reprinted with permission from the *Diagnostic and Statistical Manual of Mental Disorders* (Fourth Edition, Text Revision), Copyright 2000. American Psychiatric Association.

(3) restricted repetitive and stereotyped patterns of behavior, interests and activities, as manifested by at least one of the following:

    (a) encompassing preoccupation with one or more stereotyped and restricted patterns of interest that is abnormal either in intensity or focus

    (b) apparently inflexible adherence to specific, nonfunctional routines or rituals

    (c) stereotyped and repetitive motor mannerisms (e.g., hand or finger flapping or twisting, or complex whole-body movements)

    (d) persistent preoccupation with parts of objects

(B) Delays or abnormal functioning in at least one of the following areas, with onset prior to age 3 years: (1) social interaction, (2) language as used in social communication, (3) symbolic or imaginative play.

(C) The disturbance is not better accounted for by Rett's disorder or childhood disintegrative disorder.

ASPERGER SYNDROME

Complicating the autism spectrum further is a group of individuals who do not fit the "classic" autism profile. Students diagnosed with Asperger syndrome (AS) share many of the same challenges as students with ASD; however, their cognitive and linguistic profile is closer to typically developing students.

In 1944, Hans Asperger, an Austrian physician, described children seen in his Vienna pediatric clinic who tended to have average to above-average intellectual functioning with less apparent communication and social interaction challenges than children with more classic autism. In four boys, Asperger identified a pattern of behavior and abilities that he called "autistic psychopathy," meaning autism (self) and psychopathy (personality disease). The pattern included "a lack of empathy, little ability to form friendships, one-sided conversation, intense absorption in a special interest, and clumsy movements" (Asperger, 1944). Asperger noticed that these children could talk about their favorite subject in great detail. While they talked in a more typical manner compared with children with classic autism, they appeared very eccentric and socially awkward.

Students with Asperger syndrome tend to appear more typical in early childhood (i.e., more typical parental attachment patterns and the seeking of adult and peer social interaction). Because they seem to interact like typically developing babies and toddlers and to have no evident cognitive delay, they may remain undiagnosed longer than children with autistic disorder. From the perspective of many diagnosticians, typical early language development and social and adaptive behavior coupled with the age of onset disqualify these children from the diagnostic label of autism (Attwood, 2008; Volkmar & Lord, 2007).

Confounding their profile further, as these children with Asperger syndrome mature, they tend to speak with grammatical form and content in a more mature manner than children without disabilities. As they enter the highly social world of elementary school, their communication challenges become more apparent. Conversational topics center on their narrow, unusual interests without regard for or apparent awareness of the listener's level of interest or engagement. Although their speech *seems* mature, in actuality these students are simply displaying more nuanced forms of a social-communication challenge. Not surprisingly, children with Asperger syndrome may not be diagnosed until they start elementary school, with mean age of diagnosis being 11 years (Howlin & Asgharian, 1999).

There is some controversy over the diagnostic criteria for Asperger syndrome. The validity of Asperger syndrome as a diagnosis separate and distinct from autism is currently under review (Tryon, Mayes, Rhodes, & Waldo, 2006). It is anticipated that Asperger syndrome will be eliminated as a distinct disability subcategory of autism when the American Psychiatric Association (APA) publishes the *Diagnostic and Statistical Manual of Mental Disorders, 5th Edition (DSM-V)* in 2012 (Swedo, 2009). Despite the anticipated official elimination of this diagnostic label, you will most likely encounter students and parents who identify with Asperger syndrome. It therefore seems appropriate to include the diagnosis as a subcategory of autism until the change occurs and for you to familiarize yourself with the following *DSM-IV-TR* diagnostic criteria:

DSM-IV DEFINITION OF ASPERGER SYNDROME

A. Qualitative impairment in social interaction, as manifested by at least two of the following:
   1. marked impairment in the use of multiple nonverbal behaviors such as eye-to-eye gaze, facial expression, body postures, and gestures to regulate social interaction
   2. failure to develop peer relationships appropriate to developmental level
   3. a lack of spontaneous seeking to share enjoyment, interests or achievements with other people (e.g., by a lack of showing, bringing, or pointing out objects of interest to other people)
   4. lack of social or emotional reciprocity

B. Restricted repetitive and stereotyped patterns of behavior, interests and activities, as manifested by at least one of the following:
   1. encompassing preoccupation with one or more stereotyped and restricted patterns of interest that is abnormal either in intensity or focus
   2. apparently inflexible adherence to specific, nonfunctional routines or rituals

3. stereotyped and repetitive motor mannerisms (e.g., hand or finger flapping or twisting, or complex whole-body movements)

4. persistent preoccupation with parts of objects

C. The disturbance causes clinically significant impairment in social, occupational, or other important areas of functioning.

D. There is no clinically significant general delay in language (e.g., single words used by age 2 years, communicative phrases used by age 3 years).

E. There is no clinically significant delay in cognitive development or in the development of age-appropriate self-help skills, adaptive behavior (other than in social interaction) and curiosity about the environment in childhood.

F. Criteria are not met for another specific Pervasive Developmental Disorder or Schizophrenia.

As previously mentioned, along with autism and Asperger syndrome, there are three other diagnostic labels that fall under the umbrella of pervasive developmental disorders: pervasive developmental disorder not otherwise specified (PDD-NOS), childhood disintegrative disorder, and Rett's syndrome. Each will be described in brief. PDD-NOS is a condition in which there is marked impairment of social interaction and communication and/or stereotyped behavior patterns or interest, but when full features for autism or another explicitly defined autism spectrum disorder are not met (Volkmar & Lord, 2007). Rett's syndrome is an X chromosome–linked dominant disorder that primarily affects girls. It is characterized by normal early growth and development followed by a progressive slowing of development, loss of purposeful use of the hands, distinctive hand movements, slowed brain and head growth, problems with walking, seizures, and intellectual disability (Ellaway & Christodoulou, 1999; Volkmar & Lord, 2007). Childhood disintegrative disorder is considered a rare condition and occurs more frequently with boys than girls. A child with this disorder shows typical development of verbal and nonverbal communication; social relationships; and motor, play, and self-care skills until about 2 to 5 years of age. Then, over several months, the child will dramatically deteriorate or regress in the areas of intellectual, social, language, play, and self-care (e.g., bladder and bowel control) abilities and may resemble a child with a severe form of autistic disorder (Attwood, 2008; Volkmar & Lord, 2007).

FUNCTIONING ALONG THE SPECTRUM

No two individuals on the autism spectrum share exactly the same characteristics, strengths, and challenges. Each individual experiences autism uniquely, in both form and degree of symptoms. Unfortunately, the diagnosis of autism is often divided along an arbitrary continuum based on how nearly the person "functions" to typically developing individuals. In general, individuals who have the most severe forms of autism with intellectual challenges are referred to as "low functioning." Individuals who possess characteristics closer to typical development and intellectual functioning are referred to as "high functioning."

Be aware of preconceived notions. A one-dimensional, low- or high-functioning label is too imprecise and most often misleading. Understand that these labels are controversial and not that useful in fully understanding the student's learning and behavioral profile. There are students who appear low functioning with minimal verbal language, are very eccentric, and display atypical behavior, but who are quite intelligent. They don't show their intelligence in ways that we understand given the level of autistic-like behaviors and social challenges they present.

Figure 1.1   A Person—Not a Label

Some students with ASD have a mixed profile of traits showing both "high" and "low functioning" characteristics. Autism can exist with or without intellectual challenges. Some students with ASD have excellent written language skills but atypical verbal language. Others may be highly intelligent but need attendant care.

The point is this: Don't jump to conclusions about the student's level of functioning based on outward appearances or even a single formal test score. Tapping into the potential of a student with autism takes time, multiple observations in a variety of settings, and a thorough understanding of the student's expressive and receptive communication styles and abilities.

Assume competence. The student who is nonverbal can expand his expressive vocabulary through alternative and augmentative communication systems. The student who is intellectually challenged can perform modified academic tasks with support and encouragement. Students who struggle to interact with peers can make friends if a support system is in place that encourages acceptance and respect. Get to know the student and develop a relationship. You will most likely be pleasantly surprised at what you learn.

Also, remember that individual outcomes vary widely and are highly dependent on the quality of support the student receives. One of the most fascinating aspects of autism and Asperger syndrome is how highly individualistic students tend to be. Each person is a unique individual with his own set of characteristics, talents, strengths, and challenges. Take this into account when working with the student. Avoid the temptation of relating to the diagnosis at the expense of the person behind the label. View each student as a unique individual.

PREVALENCE OF AUTISM

Autism is one of the most common developmental disorders, affecting approximately 1 in 110 births (Centers for Disease Control and Prevention,

2010). Roughly translated, this means more than 1.5 million Americans today are believed to have some form of autism, and this number is on the rise. Considering statistics from the U.S. Department of Education and other governmental agencies, autism is growing at a startling rate of 10% to 17% per year. At this rate, the Autism Society of America (ASA) estimates, the prevalence of autism could reach 4 million Americans in the next decade. The diagnosis of autism occurs with equal frequency across diverse racial, ethnic, social, and economic lines. Family lifestyle and educational level do not influence the disorder's prevalence. Although the overall incidence of autism is consistent around the globe, the ratio of boys to girls with autism is approximately 2 to 1, while for Asperger syndrome it is 5 to 1 (Fombonne, 2005).

CAUSES AND RISK FACTORS

We do not know all of the causes of autism. However, we have learned that there are likely many causes for multiple types of autism. There may be several risk factors before and after birth that make a child more likely to have autism, including environmental, biologic, and genetic factors (Centers for Disease Control and Prevention, 2010). Furthermore, we do know that the once common belief that poor parenting practices could cause autism is not true.

To understand why genetics play a role, researchers have studied the rate of autism in identical twins. Identical twins share 100% of their genes because they are conceived from a single egg cell that splits in two. Fraternal twins are genetically different. They are conceived from two separate egg cells. In studies of identical twins, it has been found that in 60% to 96% of births where autism was diagnosed, both twins were found to have autism (Centers for Disease Control and Prevention, 2010). By comparison, in fraternal twins, the likelihood that both will have autism ranges from 0% to 3%. This rate matches the number found in non-twin siblings.

Researchers are now attempting to locate the exact genes that cause autism. It is currently suspected that as many as 15 different genes could be involved. The pattern of how these genes interact to cause autism is complex. Each may play a small role, or mutations among these genes may interact in some way to cause autism. Adding to the research challenge is the fact that how autism is diagnosed really involves a subjective description of behaviors and characteristics, which may actually hide the fact that several different causes could have an outwardly similar presentation. In other words, what looks like autism may be a different disorder or combination of factors.

There is no consensus in the research community about what specific environmental factors contribute to the likelihood a child will acquire autism. Scientific evidence does exist that exposure to toxins, chemicals, pesticides, flame-retardants, and pre- and postnatal viruses may be linked

Table 1.1   What Causes Autism?

Possible Cause	Likelihood	Comment
Vaccines	Low	CDC and the NIH say that there is no relationship between vaccines and autism.
Genetics	High	Parents from families with autism tend to have children with autism at a higher rate.
Immune Deficiency	Low	National Institutes of Health studies say evidence is weak.
Food Allergies	Low	Some connection has been found but the evidence is weak.
Atypical Brain Development	High	Researchers have found differences between the autistic and typical brain, particularly the frontal cortex region.
Bad Parenting	Unfounded	There is no causal relationship between autism and the parenting style of the child's parents.

Source: Centers for Disease Control and Prevention. Autism Information Center (2010).

to autism (Roberts et al., 2007), but conclusive proof is lacking. Exposure to excessive amounts of mercury, particularly in the preservative thimerosal, once found in childhood vaccines, was suspected to be a causal agent. However, scientists have not discovered a definite link (Sears, 2007) and the substance is no longer used.

Some parents worry that the increasing number of vaccines given to children may compromise their child's immune system—especially the measles, mumps, and rubella (MMR) vaccine—and lead to the child developing autism. Extensive investigation by researchers (Dales, Hammer, & Smith, 2001; Taylor et al., 1999) have failed to find evidence that the MMR vaccine causes autism (Sears, 2007).

More research will be needed before researchers conclusively identify the genetic and environmental causes for autism. We may not know the cause of autism with 100% certainty for many years.

As complex as studying autism is, solid research is taking place across the globe, and newly acquired knowledge influences the direction of future inquiry. Funding for autism research has increased dramatically in the past 10 years and continues to increase as nonprofit and government sources focus more resources on the disorder. Today, autism as a research area involves many different types of science, from medical and biological to behavioral, communication, and educational.

FROM DIAGNOSIS TO THE CLASSROOM

As previously mentioned, there continues to be misunderstanding about the diagnosis of autism in schools that adds to the challenges of educating students with ASD in general education settings. Dealing with the unknown leads to discomfort and even fear by teachers and students. Some teachers worry that the student's presence in the classroom will disrupt the learning process. Evidence is lacking to support this concern. Research suggests that the majority of high school students diagnosed with ASD function in general education settings with minimal to moderate academic support. The National Center for Special Education Research reports that overall 33% of students with ASD receive the same instruction in general education classes as their neurotypical peers, while approximately 47% need "some modifications" to the general education curriculum (Newman, 2007). These statistics call into question the notion that students with ASD need separate educational placements.

It can be argued that the presence of students with autism can actually enhance the learning experience for typical students and increase awareness (Chandler-Olcott & Kluth, 2009).

It is encouraging to know that instructional interventions designed to support learning for students with ASD actually help students without disabilities as well. We will explore these strategies in detail in later chapters.

The student's ability to participate and learn depends on informed support. Once teachers understand the diagnosis of autism, they are less apprehensive and more willing to accept the student as their own. Please keep in mind: It is not enough simply to be aware of the student's diagnosis. Teachers also need to understand how autism affects the individual student's experiences. Parents report that teachers who understand ASD are typically more tolerant of the student's personality profile (Jackson-Brewin, Renwick, & Schormans, 2008).

An understanding of ASD also allows teachers to perceive potential challenges and to help the student cope by creating a supportive classroom environment.

The following sections will assist you in understanding the range of potential social, communicative, sensory, motor, and behavioral characteristics unique to this disorder and to develop the knowledge and skills necessary to advocate for and support the student's full participation in the classroom.

SOCIAL SKILLS AND COMMUNICATION

For the adolescent and teenage person with AS, deciphering other kids'
meanings is harder than deciphering hieroglyphics.

(Jackson, 2002, p. 100)

Communication as a means of sharing information and experience is an important social activity that forms the basis for relationship building.

It is essential for making sense of experiences and connecting with others. Students who know how to listen well and convey their message to others are almost always more confident than students who haven't learned these skills.

There is a common myth that individuals with ASD are antisocial or apathetic toward others. This is untrue. They are perfectly capable of forming connections with friends and family. The disconnect lies in fully expressing their emotions in a manner easily understood by friends and loved ones. They struggle to express internal thoughts and feelings and are frustrated and anxious when others misunderstand their communicative intent.

The unusual interests of children and adolescents with ASD complicate friendship making. Conversational topics are usually of their own choosing with little awareness of the listener's level of interest. They tend to miss nonverbal cues and have difficulty understanding that other people have their own thoughts, feelings, and perspectives. If the person doesn't share the same interest as the student, there's little compromise in finding common ground to form the basis for friendship. When they attempt to join in conversation, they miss the point while asking off-topic, irrelevant questions; digress to an unrelated topic; or switch the focus to their special interest with no transition to inform the listener of a change in conversational direction. This personality profile is referred to as "unskilled social activeness" (Myles, 2005).

> ### Autism Myth
>
> "Bad parenting causes autism."
>
> **Fact**
>
> Bad parenting does not cause autism. If bad parenting causes autism, why would one child in a family be affected but not an other?

Social skills training sessions do not always improve social awareness. The student may be very successful during social skills training at choosing the meaning of facial expressions on picture cards or practicing the appropriate response to a social encounter in isolation. Despite this clinical practice, students with ASD struggle to generalize these skills to real-life spontaneous meetings with people outside the clinic setting (Koning & McGill-Evans, 2001; Myles, 2005). The range of human expression is much too nuanced and complex to quantify into simple categories to then retrieve and use in meaningful ways to fit the hundreds of social situations that occur spontaneously each day. If role-playing sessions are conducted, it is essential that skills be generalized through repeated practice embedded across settings with neurotypical peers.

Many students with ASD appear to lack common sense and misapply social rules in real-life settings. Social rules are often applied too literally. It is not unusual for students with ASD to extend a greeting and ask a classmate his or her name. The problem is that the greeting looks rehearsed and unnatural. For example, when Sam approaches someone to speak, he extends his arm to measure his distance from the person and adjusts himself back and forth until he's sure the distance rule has been properly applied. His greeting comes off as robotic and rigid. Instead of gaining a connection with the person, an impression is conveyed: "This guy is strange!"

Annie, after being trained to greet people when entering a room, states "Good morning!" to all 28 students by name when she enters the classroom. Needless to say, her literal interpretation of "greet people when you enter a room" causes much annoyance among her peers. After hearing "Good Morning Susan, Good Morning Lawrence, Good Morning Jay, Good Morning Michelle, Good Morning Chris, Good Morning Kori, Good Morning Steve, Good Morning Ina," Annie's classmates call out, "Stop the greeting thing!" (Author)

Although students with ASD lack social awareness, many are painfully aware that they are different from their peers. This awareness increases when students reach middle school and self-esteem is challenged. Without informed support, these students can spiral into depression leading to anxiety, emotional episodes, and withdrawal (Adreon & Stella, 2001).

Embedding social skills training in natural, age-appropriate settings and learning in context with the support of typical peer role models has gained favor in the research literature (Koegel & Koegel, 2006; Odom & Strain, 1984; Strain & Schwartz, 2001). The generalization of age-appropriate communication is naturally embedded into regularly occurring classroom experiences. We see impressive reductions in "autistic-like" behaviors when students are exposed to repeated and prolonged interactions with typically developing peers. We will discuss intervention strategies in depth in later chapters.

THE NAIVETÉ FACTOR

Compared with nondisabled students, children with autism are four times more likely to be bullied and twice as likely to be abused by adults, peers, and siblings (Little, 2002). Students with expressive communication challenges may lack the tools to communicate the abuse to an adult.

Some adolescents with autism wear clothes more appropriate for younger students. Instead of moving into adolescent interests like Facebook and Twitter, they remain preoccupied with their atypical interest, making it challenging to connect with peers.

Many students have poor motor coordination. This leaves them out of school sports, typically an important area of status and friendship. A 14-year-old adolescent with ASD may have a fully developed male or female body, but lack understanding of flirtation and nonverbal sexual cues, making him or her susceptible to harassment, inappropriate advances, and exploitation. Clearly, much education, guidance, and support are needed in this area.

We arranged a field trip for our students with ASD and their neurotypical peer partners to visit the train museum downtown. Instead of driving by car, we traveled by light rail train for the experience. Our group of 12 students, accompanied by four adults, is randomly seated in the passenger car while happily moving down the track looking forward to a fun day at the museum. At one of the stops, a disheveled man in his 50s enters our car. He is dirty, smells bad, and is clothed in rags. To my surprise, he sits on the same bench next to my female student, 14-year-old Melissa, a pretty girl diagnosed with autism. As luck would have it, I am sitting in the seat in front of her. The moment the man sits down, Melissa turns to him and says, "Hi, I'm Melissa! Would you like a kiss?" Before the man can respond, I calmly take Melissa to another seat where we have a chat about talking to strangers. (Author)

BEHAVIOR AND EMOTIONS

The behavioral and emotional challenges students with ASD experience are largely connected to social and environmental factors that they perceive as beyond their understanding and control. They sense that "unpredictable things happen, and I don't understand them." Wanting to interact with a peer and not knowing how; trying to follow teacher directions, but not understanding what is being said; hearing peers laugh around you and not getting the joke—these are all stressful situations that students with ASD experience daily (Myles & Southwick, 2005).

Behavior challenges occur for many reasons. Although knowing the why behind the behavior is not always easy, one thing is certain. Challenging behavior signals that something very important is missing from the student's life. During class, Jim blurts out angry words similar in content to the argument he heard between his parents last night. He looks traumatized. When the teacher hands out a worksheet for Jim to complete, he gets agitated and pushes the paper aside. Jim's response to the arrival of a math worksheet on his desk is to get angry. Is it the math or is it something else?

Challenging behaviors may be a reaction to disliked tasks, the setting, people, sensory needs, confusing or mixed social signals, changes in routine, problems at home, and many other external and internal stimuli. The child may have an underlying mental health issue (e.g., depression, anxiety disorder, etc.). Students with ASD are more vulnerable to anxiety-producing situations. It takes a relationship with the student to begin to understand the reasons behind the behavior.

Figure 1.2 Accentuate the Positives

For adolescents with ASD, attending school can be enormously stressful. Compared with elementary school, the school size is larger. Expectations are higher. Social expectations increase and peer relationships are more complex (Mullins & Irvin, 2000). Students experience a larger and more diverse student population where conformity and social competence are stressed. Alongside these demands, students must handle difficult situations with the physiological changes associated with puberty. Students who lack the skills necessary to cope with these demands often experience significant problems in adjustment, achievement, and feelings of self-worth (Shoffner & Williamson, 2000). As Temple Grandin reflects,

> At puberty, fear became my main emotion. When the hormones hit, my life revolved around trying to avoid a fear-inducing panic attack. Teasing from other kids was very painful, and I responded with anger. I eventually learned to control my temper, but the teasing persisted, and I would cry. Just the threat of teasing made me fearful; I was afraid to walk across the parking lot because I was afraid somebody would call me a name. (Grandin, 1995, p. 88)

There is enormous pressure to conform during adolescence. Students with ASD may be excluded, teased, and bullied, leading to conflicts and emotional outbursts. They are especially vulnerable in less structured settings where misunderstandings with peers lead to rejection and social isolation. Depression, anxiety, and aggression can follow (Barnhill, 2001; Bauer, 1999).

The anxiety experienced by Dr. Grandin in adolescence forced her to withdraw to avoid painful experiences. Many students with autism respond this way. Because their ability to understand the environment and the actions of others is limited, they overcompensate by withdrawing into a protective shell to relieve the extreme anxiety caused by their sense of helplessness (Bellini, 2006).

Other students may lash out in response to confusing social signals. Research suggests that students with ASD frequently misinterpret the actions of others as aggressive (Carothers & Taylor, 2004; Kaland et al., 2002).

> *Dean, a student with ASD, is standing in line for lunch. Suddenly, the line surges forward, causing the student behind Dean to press against Dean's back. In response, Dean spins around and swings his lunch pail, smacking the boy behind him in the side of the head. Dean misinterpreted the boy's actions as aggression. In reality, the boy was nudged forward in line, causing him to unwittingly move into Dean's space. Instead of stating, "Hey back, up!" or adjusting by moving slightly forward, Dean's agitation escalated. His inability to verbalize his discomfort coupled with his tactile sensitivity caused Dean to lash out and smack the boy. (Author)*

Emotions can rise when the student's routine is interrupted. School assemblies, fire drills, and unfamiliar people can cause emotional outbursts. Avoid upset. Prepare students with and without disabilities in advance. In addition, bullying and teasing by insensitive and uninformed peers can cause considerable upset, leading to emotional outbursts.

> *I am reminded of an incident where a child was in crisis. Fourteen-year-old Brittany, an 8th-grade girl diagnosed with ASD and bipolar disorder, was cycling into a depressive period that rendered her especially vulnerable to criticism. While seated in the cafeteria eating lunch, a boy called her fat. The insult*

was more than Brittany could take. She screamed out, "Leave me alone!" and then hurled a cup of yogurt across the floor. When we intervened, Brittany was in tears and unable to speak. Streaks of yogurt covered the floor from the cup she had slung across the room. We attempted to comfort her. Later in the day, we arranged a meeting between Brittany and the student who teased her. She expressed to the boy how his teasing upset her and he apologized. This intervention helped the boy see Brittany as a person with feelings. We later learned that the boy became a friend who helped her in times of crisis. (Author)

Would the above challenges be present across all environments and situations? Are they unique to particular settings, unforeseen changes of routine, people, and environmental challenges? Being teased, bullied, pressured to conform, and coping with loud noises and crowded rooms are situations that occur in context and under specific circumstances. They influence behavior and emotions. All of us act differently according to the time, place, and situation we're experiencing at the moment. Our behaviors are influenced by the presence or absence of certain people.

Considering the circumstances that lead to emotional incidents is the first step when a student with autism lashes out. When the student can't sort out a difficult or painful situation, we need to help. Think through all the potential reasons for the outburst. Every reason you consider is a possibility that might unlock the origins of challenging behaviors and emotions and lead to improved outcomes.

COGNITION AND LEARNING

The cognitive abilities of students with ASD are sometimes hard to measure and often misunderstood. It is widely believed, for example, that all persons diagnosed with autism possess extraordinary skills or talents in a specific area of knowledge or ability. The term "autistic savant" is the label used when referring to individuals matching these characteristics. Many people diagnosed with autism have special interests and talents. However, less than 10% are considered autistic savants. In reality, the learning capacity of students with ASD varies widely—from gifted to intellectually challenged.

Figure 1.3 Connecting Through Shared Experiences

Accurate measures of intelligence for students with ASD are difficult to obtain because the symptoms of autism affect the assessment process (Edelson, 2005). A valid measurement of cognitive abilities requires student motivation, social interaction, communication, and compliant/cooperative behavior. The adolescent is required to interact and cooperate with the examiner, often a stranger. As we have learned, this is extremely difficult for students with ASD. They are extremely sensitive to novelty and uncomfortable around strangers. They follow rigid routines; are less flexible to change; and have repetitive and stereotypic patterns of behavior, interests, and activities, which are often at odds with the examiner's test protocols. It takes just a few stubborn refusals, off-topic irrelevant responses, or a test booklet thrown across the room to prompt the examiner to nervously write "untestable."

> *If you judge a fish by its ability to climb a tree, it will live its whole life believing that it is stupid.*
>
> (Albert Einstein)

If you run across low IQ scores or excessive, negative reporting when examining a student's school records, be mindful of the information learned here and de-emphasize their significance. Encourage others to look beyond negative input as well. School records that focus on deficits far more than capacities may not be objective or accurate. If you work with students long enough, sooner or later talents and capacities will emerge that challenge the validity of IQ testing and deficit-based perspectives. Look for and share the students' abilities and advocate for their talents and strengths.

Big idea to remember: Make sure IQ scores and other standardized measurements of intellect and ability do not limit opportunities for students. As mentioned, standardized assessment practices follow strict protocols that may not allow for the idiosyncrasies of some students with special needs, especially students with ASD. The true potential of the human intellect defies measurement. De-emphasize test results, while providing opportunities for the student to show competence in other ways. In so doing, perceptions are formed that more accurately reflect the person's potential.

Students diagnosed with autism spectrum disorders vary widely in their learning capabilities and needs, just like their nondisabled peers. A few of the common challenges to learning that students with ASD experience include, but are not limited to, (1) fine motor control—many find handwriting very difficult; (2) difficulty understanding abstract concepts; (3) challenges maintaining attention and concentration; and (4) difficulty following lengthy verbal directions. No single method for addressing these learning challenges and teaching students with ASD is successful for all students. Also, a student's needs change over time, making it necessary for teachers to be flexible in their approach.

Supporters of inclusive education reject the notion that placement decisions should be determined based on the "readiness model" where students *earn* the right to belong in general education classes based on academic skill. As you will learn in later chapters, subject content and time lines can be modified to meet the student's unique learning needs. Learning challenges can be overcome with the classroom teacher's support in cooperation with the student's family, the special education teacher, support staff, and the student's peers.

SENSORY CHARACTERISTICS

Sensory integration refers to our natural ability to absorb information through the senses of touch, movement, smell, taste, vision, and hearing, and then combine, organize, and interpret the information in meaningful ways. For most people, this process is automatic. We can selectively listen to a single person in a crowded, noisy room while our minds automatically filter out the extraneous sounds around us. We gain pleasure from the sensory input of music, a massage, smelling the aroma of fresh-cut flowers, and viewing a beautiful landscape. Students with ASD frequently experience unusual responses to their sense perceptions. They may struggle to "modulate" (alter the intensity) of incoming sounds, smells, light, and touch. Some students struggle to filter out unwanted stimuli. They might not tolerate one or more sensory stimuli and become agitated from the interference the incoming stimuli bring.

Like other challenges for students with autism, sensory issues are highly individualistic. Some students struggle with filtering out the sounds of a leaf blower but have no issues with lighting. What bothers one student may have no effect on another.

Many students struggle with the same sounds typical people find annoying: car alarms, loud intercoms, and passing bells. Yet, certain students may react negatively to sounds we find pleasing. As Temple Grandin explains,

> My hearing is like having a sound amplifier set on maximum loudness. My ears are like a microphone that picks up and amplifies sound. (Grandin, 2000)

Some students with ASD have the opposite challenge. They are underresponsive to incoming sensory input and have an almost insatiable desire to seek more. They may seek out constant stimulation by pressing and squeezing sand between their fingers, rubbing a small object between their thumb and index finger, seeking pressure from tight squeezing, bouncing on a trampoline, or listening to music. These sensory seekers sometimes have a high tolerance for pain or objects that are too hot or cold. They may need high-intensity input to relax and concentrate.

REPETITIVE MOVEMENTS

Repetitive movements are commonly found in students with autism and often serve to help the student regulate incoming sensory stimuli. The behavior may include hand flapping, object spinning, and rocking. Temple Grandin (1995) describes how repetitive rocking and spinning helped shut out the world when noise became overwhelming:

> Rocking made me feel calm. It was like taking an addictive drug. The more I did it, the more I wanted to do it. My mother and my teachers would stop me so I would get back in touch with the rest of the world. I also loved to spin, and I seldom got dizzy. When I stopped spinning, I enjoyed the sensation of watching the room spin. (p. 45)

Repetitive movements help the student cope with stress, fatigue, and sensory overload. When the senses are bombarded by competing incoming stimuli impossible to filter, the student may use repetitive movements to center attention on one sense. Vigorously shaking the hands draws the mind away from the sensations that can't be sorted. The student is unconsciously thinking, "I can't deal with all this noise and light, so I'll just rock in my chair." Other examples of repetitive movement and sensory-seeking behaviors include the following:

- Visual: staring at lights, blinking, gazing at fingers, lining up objects
- Auditory: humming, mumbling under one's breath or making noises
- Smell: smelling objects, sniffing food
- Taste: licking objects, placing objects in mouth
- Tactile: scratching, clapping, feeling objects, hair twisting, toe-walking, rubbing parts of the body
- Vestibular: wiggling legs, tapping fingers, flapping, rocking, spinning, jumping
- Proprioception: repetitive pacing, bumping into people and things

Let's face it: Most people engage in repetitive behaviors when stressed or excited. During a typical day, we notice people tapping fingers, twiddling locks of hair, and rhythmically chewing gum. It becomes a problem when excessive movement stigmatizes the student and interferes with learning. Liane Holliday Willey, a woman diagnosed with Asperger syndrome, describes how her behaviors seemed unique to her peers:

> I came to notice that everyone had some odd little habit they used in times of distress and absent-mindedness. I noticed the nail biting, the lip biting, the hair chewing, and the tiny muscle twitches. I heard friends humming to themselves, sucking their teeth, and tapping their feet. I knew there were all kinds of rules that people followed in order to calm themselves or occupy their time, but I think my favored habit was unique, at least among my friends. (Willey, 1999)

What should the teacher do when a student engages in these behaviors? If possible, leave the student alone. Allow him or her to self-regulate incoming sensory stimuli through one of the above-mentioned behaviors. If the behavior becomes a distraction to the student or others, interferes with learning, or is self-injurious, like hair pulling or repeated rubbing of skin, then express your concerns to the parent, special education teacher, or therapeutic specialist.

Occupational therapists (OTs) specialize in helping students with autism manage sensory input challenges. The OT may involve the student in exercises and activities that improve performance and reduce repetitive movements. Sensory activities, when used on a regular basis, can help with focus, alertness, and organization. Sometimes the OT will develop a sensory diet—a set of scheduled activities designed to meet the student's specific sensory needs.

For some students, deep pressure to parts of the body can promote relaxation. Things like elastic tight-fitting vests that wrap around the student's trunk and midsection may work for reducing stress. Weighted tube collars that rest on the shoulders and neck can also help. Headphones are extremely comforting to students who find auditory stimuli aversive. Simply turning off the lights and using incandescent lamps instead can comfort students who are ultra-sensitive to fluorescent light.

Although students diagnosed with Asperger syndrome have similar sensory issues to those of students diagnosed with autism, students with Asperger are more likely to have an emotional reaction when they experience sensory overload (Myles et al., 2004). The important point to remember is this: Be aware of the student's environmental stressors and work to avoid these stressors, or at least minimize their effect on the student.

MOTOR ABILITIES

Children with ASD often have gross and fine motor challenges. Motor development may be delayed in early childhood. More often, the delays involve the more complex motor skills that come later in a child's development, like riding a bike, catching a ball, and using small tools.

Students with autism sometimes display asymmetrical or uneven gait, poor manipulative skills, and deficits in visual-motor coordination. The areas of challenge we most frequently encounter include holding a pencil; fastening buttons, snaps, clasps, and zippers; and tying shoes. Competitive sports can be challenging for students with ASD but should not be avoided due to the student's physical coordination challenges. Encourage coaches and PE teachers to de-emphasize competition or at least brainstorm ways the student can participate successfully in the game.

Figure 1.4 De-emphasize Difference by Showcasing Talent

Therapeutic interventions can help students with fine and gross motor challenges reasonably participate. Solutions may include targeted physical exercise and adaptive equipment to improve fine and gross motor functions.

SUMMARY

The challenges and capacities of students diagnosed with ASD are many and varied. Autism is a complex neurological disorder that can occur in a large constellation of behaviors but generally falls into three broad areas: social interaction, verbal and nonverbal communication, and restrictive patterns of interest or behavior. Students with all forms of autism have difficulty understanding and relating to the thoughts of others. They struggle to understand subtle or nuanced forms of nonverbal and spoken communication. As a result, they struggle to make friends. Without some form of intervention, misunderstandings and social isolation follow.

Autism is a developmental disability in which characteristics of the condition are present before age 3 and continue throughout adulthood. To date, there is no known cure. There is disagreement in the medical and research communities as to the causes of autism; however, there is substantial evidence that autism is genetically derived with an environmental agent acting as the triggering mechanism. The exact environmental agents that trigger autism have not been discovered to date. The rates of autism have increased substantially over the past 20 years, causing alarm in the medical community and general public. The current rate of autism is estimated at 1 in 110 births. Roughly translated, as many as 1.5 million Americans today are believed to have some form of autism, and this number is on the rise. This increase may be due to improved diagnostic practices. Increased awareness by the medical community is, in part, responsible for the increase in the number of identified cases.

Among the most critical factors contributing to school success are communication support, academic and environmental modifications, peer support, and positive behavior support. Inclusive education with informed support in cooperation with the student's family is key to improving outcomes.

RESOURCES

Autism Information Center
http://www.cdc.gov/ncbddd/autism/

Autism Research Institute
http://www.autism.com/index.asp

Autism Society
http://www.autism-society.org

Centers for Disease Control and Prevention
http://www.cdc.gov/ncbddd/autism/index.html

FURTHER READING

Grandin, T. (1995). *Thinking in pictures: And other reports from my life with autism.* New York, NY: Vintage Press.
Grandin, T., & Barron, S. (2005). *Unwritten rules of social relationships: Decoding social mysteries through the unique perspectives of autism.* Arlington, TX: Future Horizons.
Offit, P. (2008). *Autism's false prophets: Bad science, risky medicine, and the search for a cure.* New York, NY: Columbia University Press.
Simpson, R. L. (2005). *Autism spectrum disorders: Interventions and treatments for children and youth.* Thousand Oaks, CA: Corwin.
Myles, B. S. (2005). *Children and youth with Asperger's syndrome: Strategies for success in inclusive settings.* Thousand Oaks, CA: Corwin.

2

Understanding Inclusive Education

In a completely rational society, the best of us would be teachers and the rest of us would have to settle for something else.

Lee Iacocca (1989)

Inclusive education is, first, *an attitude*, a value system validated from years of research that strives to include students with disabilities in all aspects of the school experience, regardless of disability label. Inclusive education is an *educational practice* that, when implemented through research-based methods and techniques, provides students traditionally excluded from regular educational experiences with rich, standards-based content and meaningful participation. Inclusive education is based on the assumption that *all students can learn*, given the appropriate support and instructional content. Inclusive education recognizes the *importance of belonging* and friendship as an integral part of adolescent development. Inclusive education calls for *a more complete merger* of regular and special education (Hines & Johnston, 1996).

Inclusive education is not mainstreaming. While mainstreaming was viewed as a benchmark where students "earn" their right to belong in the regular classroom, inclusion establishes the student's "right" to be there in the first place. Services and supports are brought to the regular classroom as needed. With respect to social skills development, pull-out services are

25

discouraged in favor of systematically developed support strategies embedded in regular classroom settings. Inclusion challenges teachers to look beyond mainstreaming and use student-centered support to meet individual needs (Robertson & Valentine, 1998).

Researchers have documented that students with disabilities, including students with autism, who are fully included in general education settings,

- display higher levels of engagement and social interaction,
- give and receive higher levels of social support,
- have larger friendship networks, and
- have developmentally more advanced individualized education plan goals than their counterparts in segregated placements (Fryxell & Kennedy, 1995; Harrower & Dunlap, 2001; Hunt, Farron-Davis, Beckstead, Curtis, & Goetz, 1994; Lewis, 1994).

Teachers' working together with special education colleagues and support staff to include students with autism raises the awareness that these students have *similar talents and interests* as their nondisabled peers. We come to the realization that *all students have talents and abilities.* When students with autism are placed in a properly supported and welcoming environment, many participate and learn beyond predictions. This realization raises expectations and leads to *increased achievement and acceptance.* Nondisabled students develop positive attitudes toward their peers with autism and other disabilities (Copeland et al., 2004). From this understanding, true friendships can develop. Studies show that general education teachers, administrators, and support staff come to recognize the substantial benefits of inclusive education for the entire school community (Carter & Hughes, 2006). The general student population is more understanding and accepting of differences when they are taught alongside students with disabilities (McGregor, 1993; Staub & Peck, 1994–1995).

It is important for you, as a teacher responsible for educating students with autism, to understand the benefits of inclusive education. It's important because including students with complex support needs is not always easy. You will experience challenges, leading to questions that may test your commitment to this educational practice. Easy or difficult, what is most important is the teacher's level of understanding and commitment to the principles of inclusive education. It is these principles that drive our efforts toward meaningful participation and friendship making.

BRIEF HISTORY

No less than other social struggles, education reform was born from the struggle for human rights. Along with other factors, the civil rights movement inspired education policy in the United States. Constitutional principles ultimately decided the landmark 1954 school desegregation case,

Brown v. Board of Education. In speaking for the majority, Chief Justice Earl Warren wrote,

> In these days, it is doubtful that any child may reasonably be expected to succeed in life if he is denied the opportunity of an education. Such an opportunity, where the state has undertaken to provide it, is a right, which must be made available to all on equal terms.

Brown v. Board of Education overturned earlier rulings that maintained separate public schools for black and white students. "Separate educational facilities are inherently unequal," the court ruled. As a result, racial segregation was ruled a violation of the Equal Protection Clause of the Fourteenth Amendment of the United States Constitution.

Despite this landmark civil rights ruling, students with disabilities, if they were educated at all, continued to receive their education in state-run institutions, separate schools, and segregated classrooms. Studies would later show that segregated classroom experiences hampered student emotional and social development, increasing the likelihood that significant challenges would persist into adulthood (Cole & Meyer, 1991).

> **Autism Myth**
>
> "Children with autism cannot show affection."
>
> **Fact**
>
> Children with autism show a wide range of affection depending on the individual. Some children are very affectionate while others are less so.

The statistics were alarming. Students attending segregated programs dropped out of school at twice the rate of their nondisabled peers (Blackorby & Wagner, 1996). Many who did graduate struggled to adjust to the demands of adulthood. They were frequently unemployed, lacked satisfying relationships, and were unable to live independently (Affleck, Edgar, Levine, & Kortering, 1990; DeStefano & Wagner, 1991). Instead of participating in society as viable contributing members, they remained dependent on federal, state, and local financial assistance (Bellamy, Rhodes, Bourbeau, & Mank, 1986).

Continued unsatisfactory outcomes would cause much debate about the validity of segregated placement practices and the need to restructure special education. Education professionals, parents, and advocates for persons with disabilities took their concerns to court.

In a 1986 article, Madeleine C. Will, then Assistant Secretary of the Office of Special Education and Rehabilitative Services, U.S. Department of Education, stated that

> there is the stigmatization of students who have been placed in special programs which segregate them from their peers and from general school activities. Often the results are lowered academic and social expectations on the part of students . . . which can lead to poor performance and an inability to learn effectively. (Will, 1986)

FOUR PRINCIPAL CRITICISMS OF SEGREGATED PLACEMENTS

1. The dual system it creates (general and special education) also creates dual levels of expectation from teachers. Students who are known to be in special education are marginalized by stereotypic attitudes about the nature of disability. They are often viewed as incapable, less intelligent, and deficient. These attitudes lead to educational practices that lower expectations and limit opportunity.

2. General education classroom teachers without the skills and training needed to accommodate diverse learning styles are more willing to refer students to special education (and out of their classrooms). This practice is called overidentification.

3. Students who are placed in special education settings are unfairly stigmatized by their peers and the school community in general. Undesirable in itself, this social stigma damages the student's self-esteem and interferes with learning.

4. Dividing a student body leaves students with disabilities and students who are not disabled unexposed to each other, perpetuating each group's ignorance and insensitivity about the other. A divided school experience makes each group more ready to accept discrimination against individuals with differences in the future (Sands, Kozleski, & French, 2000).

INTRODUCTION TO THE IDEA

The Individuals with Disabilities Education Act (IDEA) is the federal law that governs how states and public agencies provide early intervention, special education, and other related services to children, adolescents, and young adults with disabilities from birth to age 22.

In addition to establishing the importance of a free and appropriate education and least restrictive environment provisions, the IDEA also provides procedural safeguards.

Free and Appropriate Public Education (FAPE)

Under the IDEA, "free" means that special education and related services are provided at public expense, under the direction and supervision of the public school without charging families for the costs incurred. "Appropriate" means that students are provided educational services that meet their individual needs stemming from the disability.

Least Restrictive Environment (LRE)

The IDEA requires public schools to provide students with disabilities an education in the "least restrictive environment" (LRE) possible. The term *least restrictive environment* stresses the importance of educating students in the most natural, integrated setting possible, usually considered to be the regular classroom where the student learns enriched, standards-based content alongside typically developing peers (Pardini, 2002).

Individualized Education Plan (IEP)

The IEP is the educational plan that details how the school team addresses the unique educational needs of the individual student. The document describes how the student learns and best demonstrates knowledge, and what teachers need to do to help the student learn more effectively. The IEP document is a contract between the student's family and the school district that includes measurable annual goals, special education and related services, and needed supports.

Protection of Student and Parent Rights

Under the IDEA, students with disabilities and their parents have the following protections:

- to refer the child for special education services and be informed of all appropriate program options both public and private;
- to receive prior written notice in the parents' native language when the district seeks to assess the child, initiate or discontinue a service, or change disability designation or special education placement;
- to participate in the development of the IEP and attend all meetings;
- to examine all educational records and obtain copies at no expense;
- to obtain an independent educational evaluation of their child;
- to "stay put" in the current program and/or setting if the child's placement is disputed between district and parents until the matter is resolved; and
- to present a complaint related to FAPE including the right to have an attorney, advocate, and/or student present. The law includes several ways to resolve disputes.

Parents feel a strong sense of propriety toward their children. Some parents are distrusting of school officials due to negative experiences with the education system in the past. They may be sensitive to criticism and vigilant in protecting their child's right to a quality program. Seek their input and respect parent concerns while avoiding misunderstandings and conflicts. Use capacity-based language that emphasizes the student's strengths. Express your commitment in a positive manner. Advocate on behalf of the best interests of the child regardless of how the parent expresses concern.

Confidentiality

The handling and disclosure of confidential information about students and their families is an important consideration. During a typical school year, the teacher is privy to sensitive information about students and their families. Information like test scores, behavior, attendance, family issues, living conditions, and parent employment status are the kinds of personal information that arise in confidential meetings and discussions. Avoid inadvertent and careless exposure of this information. Teachers are required by law to keep this information confidential. Exchange information on a need-to-know basis only out of the earshot of students and adults.

Confidentiality Guidelines

- When in doubt if information is confidential, say, "I'm not sure I can discuss that with you," and then refer your concerns to the special education teacher responsible for the student's IEP or administration.
- Never discuss students in a public place. It is easy to be overheard, and students are naturally curious. If you need to communicate an immediate concern, then "talk in code" with the need-to-know team member by referring to the student using mutually understood letters or initials. In such cases, you are providing a reference point to the other professional for a future discussion in private.
- When you must share information, inform the other team member of the need and arrange a time and a private place to meet to discuss the issue.
- Do not leave personal records, observation sheets, evaluation reports, notes, lists, and so forth, lying around in view of others. When taking data, or reviewing information about the student, avoid exposing the student's name and other sensitive information. Position yourself in a location where students cannot look over your shoulder and see the information.
- Do not discuss confidential information about the student's classmates with parents.

Be sensitive to the need for privacy. Remember your responsibilities. No matter how cordial the conversation, you are a school official bound by confidentiality laws. Confidentiality rules do not expire when teachers leave the school parking lot. Remember the ethical and legal responsibilities you are entrusted to uphold beyond the school boundaries.

TEAMWORK AND COLLABORATION

Inclusive education is based on the premise that "no one teacher can or ought to be expected to have all the expertise required to meet the educational needs of all students in the classroom" (Lipsky, 1994, p. 5). Uncertainty is inherent in teaching. Although we can seldom guarantee the results of our decisions, we can minimize misjudgments through teamwork and collaboration with colleagues and parents who share responsibility for the student's development.

Teamwork refers to the process of working together in a cooperative, purposeful manner in pursuit of strategies that support successful learning experiences. *Collaboration* occurs when team members share expertise in an atmosphere of mutual respect and cooperation. Communication is coordinated and direct. Shared goals, good communication, role clarification, and clear direction are important for team success (Picket, Gerlach, Morgan, Likins, & Wallace, 2007). When teachers plan together, they benefit from each person's unique skills and expertise (Friend & Cook, 1998).

The general education teacher has a broad perspective on standards-based content and curriculum. The special education teacher has unique skills in modifying and adapting instructional content that benefits students with diverse learning styles (Thousand, Villa, & Nevin, 2002). Because general education teachers work with large groups of students, they can apply their management and organizational strategies to counterbalance individualized approaches the special education teacher recommends.

When working together in pursuit of ideas, think outside the box. Be willing to explore unconventional strategies that may challenge the status quo. Be mindful of the importance of thoughtful, person-centered planning. In so doing, consider the student's perspective. What works for him and why? What doesn't work? What does the school experience *feel* like to him? Consider why the student is experiencing challenges, and then sort out how to approach the problem in a way that considers the individual's needs.

Figure 2.1 IEP Team Participants

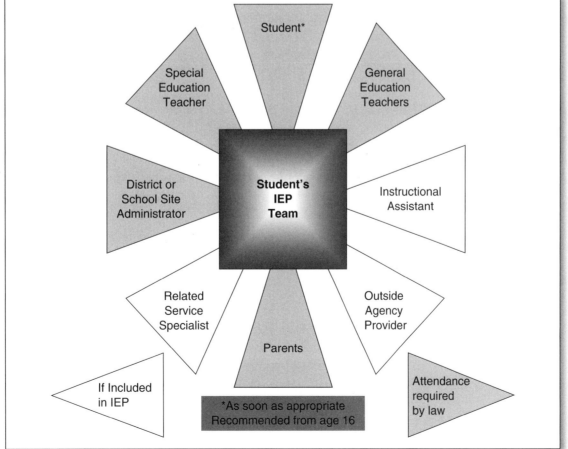

CHARACTERISTICS OF EFFECTIVE TEAM MEMBERS

The general education teacher is an integral part of the IEP team responsible for implementing the student's individualized program. Depending on the types of services written into the IEP, potential members include related service specialists, representatives of outside agencies, student advocates, and instructional assistants. In cases where there are disputes, an attorney may be present to represent the family or serve as an independent arbitrator.

Teams that demonstrate the following characteristics are most effective in accomplishing student-centered planning. Effective team members

- understand the roles and responsibilities of each member. They demonstrate integrity-centered enthusiasm for the team process by working cooperatively to further the educational and social goals of students with disabilities.
- are good communicators. They actively work to build positive relationships with their colleagues. They understand how to constructively respond to concerns. They accept and respect each team member's area of expertise and demonstrate respect for his or her ideas.
- are keen observers of student behavior and academic performance. They understand how to communicate their perceptions to the team and are open to ideas for improving outcomes.
- are flexible, analytical thinkers, capable of considering several possible solutions to a problem.
- are mindful of the debilitating effects of misinformed perceptions about the nature of disability. They are sensitive to bias and prejudice and work to eliminate inaccurate stereotypes and the lowered expectations that follow.

How Effective Is Your Team?

- Are meetings scheduled for a specific time that does not conflict with other commitments?
- Do all team members regularly attend meetings when needed?
- Do all members of the team understand the roles and responsibilities of each team member?
- Do team members respect the expertise of fellow team members, openly share information, and seek their advice?
- Do all team members feel comfortable sharing ideas and offer possible solutions?
- Do all team members acknowledge and address conflict openly in an atmosphere of respect?
- Is constructive feedback built into the meeting agenda to improve communication, team processes, and decision making?
- Is there an atmosphere of collegiality and friendship among team members?
- Is there a group facilitator or leader?

PROFESSIONAL RELATIONSHIPS

This section introduces you to the variety of individuals who support the needs of students with ASD. Chances are good you will encounter these dedicated professionals many times during the school year.

Related service specialists provide specialized interventions that help reduce challenges stemming from the student's disability. The related service specialist may provide services outside the classroom setting or work with teachers to embed services within the classroom.

Figure 2.2   Positive Relationships Matter

Consider the following suggestions in your work with these dedicated professionals:

- Respect the role of the support professional in the student's education.
- Discuss intervention strategies with the provider or case manager.
- Carry out therapeutic interventions as directed and follow observation and data collection guidelines.
- Share results, ask questions, and discuss concerns with the provider or special education teacher.

Speech Pathologist

Speech pathologists, sometimes called speech therapists, assess, diagnose, treat, and help to correct problems related to speech, language, communication, voice, and speech fluency. They work with students who struggle with speech production or are challenged with speech clarity. For students diagnosed with ASD and other communicative disorders, speech pathologists help improve everyday language and social skills.

Occupational Therapist

Occupational therapists (OTs) help students improve academic and physical performance in school, home, and community settings through the use of specialized therapeutic exercises and equipment that develop, improve, and maintain basic fine motor functions and motor planning abilities.

Physical Therapist

Physical therapists (PTs) provide services to improve functional mobility with the goal of increasing freedom of movement for students with physical challenges.

Adapted Physical Education Teacher

Adapted physical education (APE) is physical education modified for the individualized needs of students with gross motor challenges. Services include (a) assessment and physical education instruction based on IEP goals, (b) instruction in regular physical education (PE) classes with appropriate modification of the physical education curriculum, and (c) individualized instruction designed to address the physical challenges of each student. APE is not required for every special education student. APE services should provide developmentally appropriate physical education in regular PE classes to the greatest extent possible.

School Psychologist

The school psychologist helps teachers, parents, and students understand, prevent, and solve psychological, behavioral, emotional, and academic problems impacting school performance. School psychologists administer and interpret standardized tests to determine eligibility for special education services. They design, implement, and evaluate positive behavior support plans. They provide individual and group counseling for students as well as parents and families. They also serve as IEP team members while providing advice, strategies, and training to teachers and other educational professionals.

School Nurse

School nurses are responsible for appropriate health assessment, planning, intervention, evaluation, management, and referral services for students with and without disabilities.

School nurses screen students for various health-related conditions such as scoliosis, vision and hearing impairments, and poor hygiene. They report results to parents and school personnel. School nurses work to remove health-related barriers to learning while promoting optimal health for students and staff. The nurse is responsible for developing and monitoring student individual health plans.

Special Education Teacher

The special education teacher can serve many functions, depending on the needs of the students and the characteristics of the school program. Special education teachers are trained to perform a broad range of support functions in several overlapping areas of need. In a full-inclusion model, the special education teacher may teach specific intervention classes, run learning centers, or coteach with the regular classroom teacher while taking primary responsibility for IEP planning and implementation.

The special educator may serve as a facilitator and consultant while supporting the classroom teacher's role as instructional leader. In this model, the classroom teacher determines the details of classroom organization, discipline, and general education curriculum while the special educator adapts and modifies curriculum to meet the needs of students within the class. In a coteaching arrangement, the special education teacher may assume major responsibility for instruction, curriculum development, adaptations, and the selection and use of materials.

Instructional Assistant

Instructional assistant, paraeducator, paraprofessional, and teacher's aide are just a few titles that school districts use when referring to instructional support personnel delivering support services to students with disabilities. We will use the term "instructional assistant" when referring to adult support staff.

Under the direction of the classroom and special education teacher, instructional assistants deliver instructional support services and other duties to students with and without disabilities across school settings. These duties vary widely but generally include the following:

- Delivering teacher-designed instruction and support to individuals and small groups of students in the classroom
- Helping to facilitate the inclusion of students with disabilities in general education settings
- Making on-the-spot adaptations to tests, assignments, and class projects as needed
- Collecting data and documenting student performance information that helps the teacher plan and modify instruction in support of students with learning challenges
- Supervising students during passing times, during lunch, and in class
- Completing teacher-assigned record keeping, clerical duties, and classroom organization needs

Instructional assistants can play an important role in reinforcing learning and enhancing friendship for students with disabilities. A well-trained instructional assistant can be a valuable partner. However, studies show that uninformed instructional assistant support can interfere with natural peer interactions, reduce teacher engagement in the student's learning, and compromise typical classroom experiences and the learning opportunities that full inclusion was intended to provide (Giangreco & Broer, 2007).

A word of caution when assigning duties to instructional assistants: Be careful not to place yourself in the position of relying on the least trained individuals to provide primary support for the most complex students. School districts across the country face criticism for hiring instructional assistants without prior training and experience. Despite congressional legislation placing a high priority on highly qualified staff, far too many instructional assistants remain inadequately trained and supervised in the duties they assume (Giangreco & Broer, 2005; Giangreco, Smith, & Pinckney, 2006).

Careless and uninformed support can lead to unintended consequences. To help prepare instructional assistants for the duties and responsibilities they assume in the classroom, the Instructional Assistant Inclusion Support Guide can be accessed at the *Teaching Adolescents With Autism* companion website at www.corwin.com/adolescentautism.

Finally, consider the following guidelines for supporting the duties of instructional assistants:

- Recognize the contributions that support staff make in the daily delivery of instructional supports.
- In cooperation with the special education/inclusion support teacher, clearly define the roles and responsibilities of support staff.
- Make clear the differences between the teacher's roles and responsibilities and those of the instructional assistant.
- Direct and monitor the day-to-day work of support staff and provide regular feedback.
- Schedule times to meet with support staff to discuss class and individual goals, and plans for achieving lesson goals and objectives.
- Ensure that support staff follow district and school procedures for ensuring the health, safety, and well-being of all students.

Students and Parents

Parents vary greatly in response to the challenges of raising a child with a disability. Some parents place their complete trust in the school and cooperate with the IEP team in the decision-making process. Other parents distrust school authorities and are adversarial. They feel this way for a variety of reasons, both legitimate and unwarranted. Regardless of how the parent responds to the school, recognize that parents have the ultimate responsibility for the child and respect their wishes, opinions, attitudes, and desires.

- Take seriously concerns expressed by parents, students, and others and seek advice when needed.
- Be positive when discussing the child's progress, challenges, and educational program.
- Be encouraging. Demonstrate to the parents your confidence in their child's ability to learn.
- Be mindful of the effects of medication on the student's ability to concentrate at night. If medication is an issue, be open-minded and flexible with course requirements and homework.
- Ask parents for additional information that will help you effectively support the student to maximize success. Seek to understand challenges that may not be obvious: stress signs, stress triggers, or suggestions to reduce anxiety. Learn the student's strengths and interests while building a trusting relationship.

- Return phone calls and e-mails promptly (within 24 hours). Respect the privacy and individuality of the student and his parents. Treat students in a manner consistent with their age and be cautious not to overstep physical and verbal boundaries.

VALUING THE PERSON

Every individual is a complex collection of components. Each of us has a variety of interests, skills, and capacities, as well as a unique background. We all have our different physical characteristics and our own idiosyncratic personalities. In our interactions with others, we want to be understood and seen for who we are, and we hope that we will not be judged simply at face value. (Van der Klift & Kunc, 1994)

Figure 2.3   Understanding Leads to Friendship

We conclude this chapter with a set of important concepts regarding "person-first language" and the nature of disability. Reading through these guiding principles will help you gain a deeper appreciation for the person behind the label.

Person-First Language

Language is powerful. The words we use reveal our beliefs about the person behind the label. One can argue that the student with ASD actually has two disabilities: first, the actual diagnosis, and second, limiting attitudes that view the student as the disability. The diagnosis of autism does not cause teasing, bullying, and demeaning treatment. It is the misinformed attitudes and perceptions of others that lead to mistreatment.

Students with autism are people first. Promote the perception of the whole person while lessening the debilitating effect of labeling. The student may have autism, but she is *not* autism. Person-first language puts the person before the disability label and describes what the student *has,* not what the person *is.* Students with ASD are *people first* (Snow, 2003).

Descriptors like "handicapped" and "retarded" are no longer considered acceptable terms when referring to persons with disabilities. These terms create limiting perceptions. Avoid terms like "autistic student" to identify the person. The single adjective "autistic" creates inaccurate assumptions that lead to lowered expectations and inaccurate conclusions. These descriptors preempt the real person behind the label and reduce the chance the student will be identified for his strengths and talents.

Disability Is Not the "Problem"

Today's conventional wisdom regarding disability is based on the medical model: Identify the problem, and provide a cure. This paradigm places the "problem" of disability within the person, so that treatments and services attempt to "fix" the person. People with disabilities are not broken. They do not need to be fixed (Snow, 2003). Think of disability as part of the human condition, another form of diversity no less than any other form of diversity in the human experience.

"I am not defective. I am different . . ."

(Liane Holliday Willey)

Use words that accurately describe the whole person, beyond just the disability label. For example, Alex is a 16-year-old boy who loves to build things, is interested in girls, is Bob and Roberta's son, and is diagnosed with autism. Language is powerful. By using person-first language, we offer a more just and accurate description of the whole person, while setting up possibilities for more opportunity. We start to dwell on possibilities instead of limitations.

SUMMARY

Inclusive education is a belief in the values inherent in the individual's right to a life filled with relationships, opportunity, and promise, a life not limited by a disability label and the bias that follows in all forms. The overriding goal of inclusive education is to provide the conditions necessary to prepare young people for independent, self-determining adult lives. School activities and classroom experiences should naturally lead to meaningful employment and leisure-time activities after the student leaves the education system.

Special education is a service designed to support the needs of children and young adults with disabilities in public and private schools and in community, work, and leisure environments. Special education in the United States is the product of years of legislative and court action in response to unequal treatment of children with disabilities. Disability rights laws like PL 94-142 and the IDEA were born from the efforts of parents and disability rights advocates in response to substandard and restricted opportunities in education for children with disabilities.

The civil rights movement in the 1950s and 1960s served as the inspiration and catalyst for change. Specifically, the Supreme Court decision in *Brown v. Board of Education* led to the abolition of the separate-but-equal doctrine that before 1955 gave tacit approval to school segregation. Judicial rulings and congressional legislation continue to shape public policy, resulting in a significant shift away from segregated school placements and toward more inclusion.

When we state that special education is a service, we mean that students receive specially designed instruction and supports that address their learning challenges stemming from their disabilities. Being "placed" in special education does not automatically mean the child vacates the general education classroom to a separate setting. Studies repeatedly suggest that with appropriate supports and services, most students with disabilities succeed in regular education settings and thrive where daily interactions with nondisabled peers promote age-appropriate behavior and friendship.

The Individuals with Disabilities Education Act (IDEA) governs special education policies and practices in the United States. The law covers children from birth to age 22.

Four main principles drive IDEA practices. These include the principle that students with disabilities receive a free and appropriate education—preferably in the student's neighborhood school—in the least restrictive environment, which generally means the general education classroom where students with disabilities receive standards-based enriched content alongside their typical nondisabled peers. The IDEA also provides additional special education services and procedural safeguards. Services are individualized to meet the unique needs of the student stemming from the disability.

The Individualized Educational Program, or IEP, is the key planning component for students qualified for special education. The IEP is designed to meet the unique educational needs of the qualified student. The IEP describes how the student learns and demonstrates understanding and what teachers, instructional assistants, and other service providers need to do to help the student participate and learn more effectively.

Your duties and responsibilities as the child's teacher are determined by the student's unique needs described in the IEP and from what you come to learn about the student, being mindful of the person behind the label. Each teacher in the student's life brings his or her unique contribution to the school experience. Your relationship with the student is an important determiner of success. As much as possible, view the student as a typically developing child and modify circumstances and standards only when necessary. Let your knowledge and student-centered experience be your guide above any label or preconceived notion.

Whenever possible, promote natural peer supports over adult supports. Studies show that overreliance on adults is potentially counterproductive to the student's full participation in the classroom setting and the development of independence (Malmgren & Causton-Theoharis, 2006).

Educating students diagnosed with autism spectrum disorder most likely will not be boring! Each student is a unique individual with his or her own set of strengths, interests, and challenges. That applies to all students in your class, with disabilities or not. Challenges are really opportunities to make a positive difference in the student's life.

RESOURCES

Appendix 1: Glossary of Frequently Used Terms

The special education field is full of specialized words that make one feel as though he or she is hearing a foreign language! Learn the meaning behind commonly used terms in special education to better understand the program you support.

Appendix 2: Special Education Acronyms
Find out what many common acronyms mean in order to understand special education procedures and services.

Broad Reach Training and Resources
http://www.normemma.com/nkevbio.htm

Council for Exceptional Children (CEC)
http://www.cec.sped.org/

Disability is Natural
Brave Heart Press, PO Box 7245, Woodland Park, CO, USA 80863-7245
www.disabilityisnatural.com

TASH: Equity, Opportunity, and Inclusion for people with Disabilities since 1975
http://www.tash.org/index.html

FURTHER READING

Giangreco, M. F., & Doyle, M. B. (2007). *Quick-guides to inclusion: Ideas for educating students with disabilities* (2nd ed.). Baltimore, MD: Paul H. Brookes.

Gore, M. C. (2010). *Inclusion strategies for secondary classrooms: Keys for struggling learners* (2nd ed.). Thousand Oaks, CA: Corwin.

Jorgensen, C. M., McSheehan, M., & Sonnenmeier, R. M. (2009). *The beyond access model: Promoting membership, participation, and learning for students with disabilities in the general education classroom.* Baltimore, MD: Paul H. Brookes.

Kochar, A. C., & Heishman, A. (2010). *Effective collaboration for educating the whole child.* Thousand Oaks, CA: Corwin.

Maanum, J. L. (2009). *The general educator's guide to special education.* Thousand Oaks, CA: Corwin.

Thousand, J., Villa, R. A., & Nevin, A. I. (Eds.). (2002). *Creativity and collaborative learning: The practical guide to empowering students, teachers, and families.* Baltimore, MD: Paul H. Brookes.

3

Promoting Positive Behavior

Punishment and reward proceed from basically the same psychological model, one that conceives of motivation as nothing more than the manipulation of behavior.

Alfie Kohn

In this chapter, we will explore factors that contribute to understanding students with ASD and why knowing the person behind the label is the key to supporting his or her needs. We will learn how behavior challenges can be reduced when we consider the person's needs through the lens of his or her life experience. Behavior support is not about blaming the student and forcing compliance through threats and promises of reward. Instead, we will examine behavior from a person-centered perspective while challenging the notion that all behavior is functional—used by the student to either gain something he or she wants or to avoid something undesirable.

We discuss behavior early in the book for a reason. The atypical and sometimes baffling behaviors of the student with ASD can potentially stop teachers and peers from building a relationship with the person. Outward appearances obscure the communicative intent behind the behavior and prevent understanding and acceptance.

For students with ASD, the issue is not about the need to manipulate, get attention, or avoid work; instead, many students lack the skills necessary to manage classroom and interpersonal dynamics. Once the student's behavior is understood from the context of his or her life experience, we can begin to understand and appreciate the person. Support strategies, as a result, accurately reflect the person's needs.

Many contributing factors may be involved when students experience behavior challenges. Behavior can be interpreted in many different ways, depending on the situation, the setting, the needs of the student, and the person doing the interpreting. Just like "Beauty is in the eye of the beholder," likewise, each teacher's interpretation and response to student behavior is unique. The right response can improve behavior significantly. The wrong response can make matters worse. We will examine our own perceptions about behavior and learn ways to prevent ill-informed conclusions that lead to the wrong decisions. Ultimately, the action taken in response to the behavior must be based on the correct assumptions.

Building a relationship with the student and his or her family is critical to understanding the person behind the label. The student's parents can help us understand stressors that trigger behavior challenges and how to avoid or at least reduce their effects. Parents know their son or daughter best and can bring nuanced insight to situations involving variations in behavior. Knowing this critical information, ask yourself, "What kind of life is this person living?" How would it feel to live this person's life? How would *you* behave? How would you communicate your needs? To help guide your thoughts toward a deepening understanding of the person, we invite you to examine "Nine Respectful Notions" and Table 3.1, "Effective Behavior Support," later in this chapter.

Finally, when a student with ASD loses control of his emotions, we need to understand what can happen as a result. We will examine the stages of an emotional episode and strategies that can help stabilize and calm the student.

INTRODUCTION TO BEHAVIOR

Behavior is defined as the actions or reactions of a person, in relation to his or her environment, experiences, or needs. Behavior can be conscious or unconscious, overt or covert, voluntary or involuntary.

Behavior is often perceived as totally within the student's control. When a student is "acting out," he needs a consequence, the thinking goes. Punishment is threatened as a deterrent in the belief that the consequence will force compliance. The student's behavior is defined as the problem. And once the student is seen as the problem, the question is, "How do we fix the problem?" We assume the student is capable of controlling the behavior or is motivated to change in order to avoid the threatened consequence.

We must be careful with our assumptions. What if the environment is the problem? What if the student is frustrated with an unmet need and does not know how to express his thoughts? What if the challenging behavior satisfies the student more than the desired behavior? What if the punishment given seems small in comparison with the reward the challenging behavior brings?

Human nature is complex. Challenging behavior is an expression of an unmet need or an intolerable situation coupled with the student's inability to skillfully solve the issue in a more acceptable manner. How we respond to the behavior is determined by what we believe, and what we believe reflects our actions.

BEHAVIOR CHALLENGES

Behavior challenges are "messages" that can tell important things about the student and the quality of her life (Pitonyak, 2005).

Challenging behavior is a signal that something very important is missing from the child's life. It is easy to make the mistake of misunderstanding a person's behavior because of her label, past reports, or the misinformed impressions of others. This is a tragic mistake. Supporting a person with challenging behaviors begins when we assume nothing until we invest the time necessary to really know the person.

When students present behavior and compliance issues, school authorities will impose systematic and progressive consequences (rewards and punishments) to force compliance without considering why the behavior occurred in the first place. Do they work? Yes and no. For some students, threats can buy a short-term change in behavior, but they can never help students who act out for reasons they cannot explain or control. In a consequence-based classroom, students wonder, "What does she want me to do, and what happens to me if I don't do it?" In a reward-based classroom, the student is led to ask, "What does she want me to do, and what do I *get* for doing it?" Rewards and punishments are really two sides of the same premise. And notice how different either one is from what we'd like children to be thinking about: "What kind of person do I want to be?" (Kohn, 1995).

In the most basic terms, challenging behavior is an expression of an unmet need. The student may be reacting to an intolerable situation, struggling with a physiological condition, or avoiding something aversive (Crone & Horner, 2003). When the student's behavior achieves the intended need or purpose, the behavior is reinforced. Reinforcers strongly contribute to the likelihood the behavior will repeat.

It is sometimes possible to determine the cause of challenging behavior by thinking about what happened before the behavior occurred. Antecedents are incidents, situations, and experiences that happen just before the behavior that increase the likelihood challenging behavior will occur. Setting events are situations the student experienced at an earlier time of the day or week that set the stage for challenges later. Antecedents and setting events cause stress and can lead to behavior challenges (Ghaziuddin & Butler, 1998).

Consider these contributing factors when attempting to determine the student's stressors:

- Environmental stressors (odors, touch, loud noises, bright lights, crowded rooms)
- Social stressors (confusing social situations, annoying people, abusive treatment)
- Internal stressors (student is lonely and unhappy, fearful, anxious, stuck on one thought, overly stimulated, tired, hungry, sick, too warm or cold)

There are countless external and internal reasons why challenging behaviors occur. It is not possible to list every potential reason; however, here are a few examples to consider:

- Unmet needs that are hard for the student to communicate
- Feeling misunderstood or devalued
- Undesirable tasks, boredom, lack of meaningful activity
- Unplanned events, sudden changes
- Being teased or bullied, feeling unsafe
- Encroaching into the student's personal space
- Taking away a preferred item or privilege
- Crowded hallways and unruly classroom behavior
- Sensory challenges, illness, physiological condition and discomfort
- Mental health challenges
- Difficulties stemming from a dysfunctional chaotic family situation

Setting events are real situations in the student's life that affect the person's mental state. Mom and Dad had a fight. The baby cried all night, keeping the student awake. The student's brother was involved in an accident. The first period class bully picked on the student. As a result, the student arrives to class irritated, exhausted, or upset and some minor situation that would normally not be a problem sets off a challenging behavior. When the student lacks a reliable means to communicate anxiety and stress, emotional episodes may follow (Myles & Simpson, 2001).

It is important to understand that not all students with ASD respond to anxiety-producing situations with challenging behavior. Some students withdraw or display emotions inappropriate for the situation, for example, laughing out of context, turning inward, hyperfocusing on a special interest, and daydreaming. Some students may engage in repetitive hand flapping, rocking, rubbing fingers on objects, scratching skin, or fixating on patterns in an effort to focus away from the anxiety-producing situation or person.

PERSON-CENTERED SUPPORT

Teachers and support specialists are most effective when they understand the individual student and are mindful of the person's needs beyond the autism label. They go beyond common notions of behavior like "attention seeking" and "task avoidance" to advocate for the student in a manner that improves the person's situation.

Student behavior challenges are sometimes typical of a school culture that frustrates students' needs for relationships, choice-making, and meaningful contribution (Pitonyak & O'Brien, 2009). Helping students find their voice, and then listening to their concerns, can build understanding leading to improved outcomes.

Reducing behavior challenges takes time. Observe the student across multiple settings and during different times of the day. When a student is disrupting classroom instruction, not complying with directions, refusing to participate, or any number of other behaviors that interfere with learning, ask yourself: Is she uncomfortable in the setting? Is the subject or activity at the student's instructional level? Does the teacher's instructional delivery match the student's learning style? Do specific individuals in the room contribute to the student's anxiety? Were there unexpected changes to the routine? Did the student forget to take his medication? Do challenges occur at a specific time and/or day of the week? Is there a pattern? Determining the reason behind the behavior is the first step to improving the behavior.

Two similar behaviors can result for entirely different reasons. "Being consistent" does not mean we address every challenging behavior with the same consequence. Teachers sometimes remove students from class for misbehavior. "Go stand outside!" the teacher sternly commands. Out goes Johnny, who leaves the classroom to sit outside. The teacher has temporarily freed himself from the student's misbehavior. The question is, what if Johnny's quality of life actually improved by being sent outside? Has the teacher solved the behavior challenge or reinforced it?

Some students behave especially well in an attempt to gain favor or praise. Problems occur when adults ignore positive behavior because "that's what is expected." If the desirable behavior goes unrecognized, the student may revert to challenging behavior to obtain the attention she desires. Unfortunately, students sometimes learn that challenging behavior can be more efficient than positive behavior in producing desired results.

Determining the reason behind the behavior can be challenging. It takes a knowing relationship with the student where the teacher understands what the student is seeking. Helping the student satisfy his needs requires brainstorming how the student can gain what he needs without resorting to challenging behavior. For example, if a student needs recognition, consider ways the student can gain respect and recognition by demonstrating competence. Encourage the student to share her special interest with the class, show family vacation pictures, or read the morning announcements. The following is a real example worth sharing:

> *Throughout this book, the reader will find cartoons created by a former student in the author's inclusion program. Devon is a gifted artist with a great sense of humor. He is included in general education classes and is respected by typical peers for his talents in art. His art teacher, Mr. Wright, is inspired by Devon's work and uses Devon as a mentor for art students seeking to learn cartooning. Devon is an example of how a gifted student can transcend labels to become a respected member of the school community. (Author)*

Through these experiences, the student gains respect and is reinforced for his talents and strengths. The key is to ensure that positive behavior results in "more bang for the buck" in fulfilling the student's needs. If there is an underlying emotional issue, positive support from a trusted adult can help the student avoid problems. The following examples illustrate potential causes for challenging behavior and how a few simple modifications can potentially improve the student's situation:

- Sam is a student who has temper tantrums during math class. The teacher sends him out of the room where he sits against the wall, watching people walk by while his classmates work on their math assignment.

  o *Math is very challenging for Sam. The content is too difficult and the pace is too fast. The instruction does not fit his learning style. Provide Sam with age-appropriate content that aligns with his instructional style and level. Slow down the pace. Allow for more practice. Provide math manipulatives and visual graphics to aid understanding.*

- Fourteen-year-old Austin reads at the second-grade level. During whole-class round-robin reading, Austin covers his head with his sweatshirt hood and closes his eyes when asked to read in front of the class.

  o *To Austin, appearing incompetent in the eyes of his peers is worse than any punishment the teacher can impose. Instead of round-robin reading, use choral readings, echo readings, or teacher reading to provide some modeling. If it is necessary for students to read aloud, let Austin pass.*

- Alexis, an eighth-grade student with Asperger syndrome, is fascinated with heating and air conditioning systems. She finds the reading assignment on medieval life unmotivating. She will not read the book or complete workbook assignments. The teacher is frustrated with her lack of interest.

  o *Use Alexis's interest in heating and air conditioning systems to increase her class participation. Have Alexis develop a report outlining how people in the Middle Ages heated and cooled their homes.*

- Amy, a 13-year-old girl with tactile sensitivity, hates it when people touch her. Substitute teacher "Mr. B" unwittingly pats Amy on the back and is shocked when Amy shouts out, "Don't touch me!"

  o *Include information about Amy's condition in the lesson plan so the substitute teacher can avoid upsetting Amy.*

- Alberto likes his teacher and will perform good deeds to gain approval. Unfortunately, in an effort to gain praise, he will tattle on students for minor acts of misconduct. "Mr. Turner, Lupita just looked at me funny and made a face!"

  o *Alberto needs support to understand how to gain recognition in class without resorting to tattling. Perhaps Alberto could serve as class messenger and assignment collector. He might be enlisted to read the daily bulletin or help the teacher prepare the holiday bulletin board.*

Student actions can look similar from one student to the next. However, depending on the student, the reason behind the behavior may be very different. Jumping to conclusions based on outward appearances and unsupported assumptions may lead to a misguided response.

- Cole shares his sandwich with a peer who often comes to school without food or money to buy lunch. Cole advertises his good deed to the teacher in an effort to gain favor and privilege. After his "good deed" is rewarded with a free movie pass, he stops helping.
- Josh shares his sandwich with a peer who often comes to school without food or money to buy lunch. Josh seeks no recognition from adults. He just sees a need and wants to help. No one notices but it does not matter to Josh. He just wants to do what is right.

In the example above, Cole's good deed is strictly self-serving to gain a reward. Josh acts out of concern for someone in need. When the school culture is built around rewards and punishments, we tend to see more kids acting like Cole and fewer acting like Josh.

Figure 3.1   Evaluating Challenging Behavior

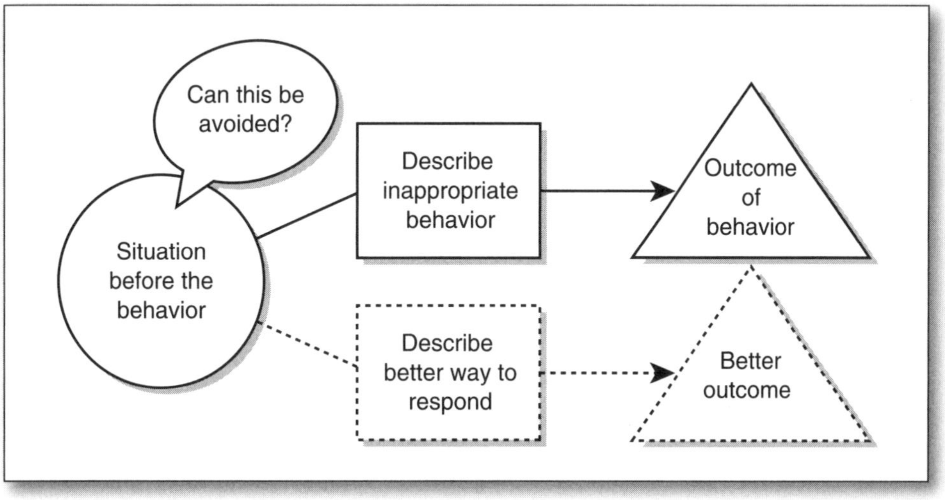

BEHAVIOR IS INTERPRETIVE

Challenging behavior can be explained in many different ways, depending on the observer. Two different people can view the same behavior and come away with entirely different interpretations of what happened and why. Understanding what triggers challenging behavior requires careful thought and analysis based on your understanding of the individual student in question.

"Be still for a moment and consider the complexity of the situation."

(Van der Klift & Kunc, 1995)

It is very easy to misinterpret behavior when students do not or cannot interpret their own actions. We tend to jump to conclusions without thoroughly understanding the numerous factors that would help us arrive at a more valid conclusion.

Be aware that last year's reports represent the student's behavior at an earlier age and in a different setting. Teenagers change over short periods, especially related to behavior issues. Rather than leaping to a conclusion based solely on information gleaned from past reports, allow time to really consider the child's life story and the circumstances this person is experiencing in the present that may contribute to the puzzling behavior. Starting out the year with a collaborative parent-professional partnership and maintaining that connection will help the teacher avoid pitfalls and move forward exponentially with the right interventions.

When student behavior begins to escalate, our job is to use our knowledge of the student to avoid further escalation. Our reaction to the student's behavior can either reduce tension or escalate emotions toward an emotional episode. The situation can get worse if we become angry and confrontational. Our job is to remain calm and dispassionate while working toward a positive outcome. We will explore emotional episodes later in this chapter.

RELATIONSHIP DEVELOPMENT

The three most important factors in behavior support are

1. Relationship

2. Relationship

3. Relationship

Spend time getting to know the students in your class. Learn about their interests and develop a caring relationship. Every kind gesture and act of goodwill is like depositing cash in the "relationship bank." When students misbehave, or when they are irritable or challenging, instead of saying, "You need to be quiet!" or worse, "Stop or else!" say, "Are you OK?" "Is there anything I can help you with?" "Can I get you some water?" or "Why are you acting this way?" Expressing concern can de-escalate the situation and increase the chance for a positive outcome.

Figure 3.2 Patience, Patience, Patience

We get in trouble when we are the wrong person at the wrong time. Before we can solve behavior challenges, we must first think about ways to allow the student to get her needs met and save face. If a student is very upset or angry, she is vulnerable. At times like these, we need to be the lifeguard, not a swim coach. You cannot teach people to swim when they are drowning.

Avoid saying, "I told you so!" Remember the person's life story, family situation, and the nature of her disability before making a judgment. In the words of David Pitonyak, PhD, positive behavioral support lecturer and teacher,

"Trying to understand someone's behavior outside the context of the person's life is fundamentally disrespectful to the person."

STANDARDS OF FAIRNESS

When considering what to do about challenging behavior, and before reaching a conclusion, ask yourself, Is it true? Is it right? Does it work? Consider the following "Nine Respectful Notions" before determining the action to take.

NINE RESPECTFUL NOTIONS

Understanding: Have the desirable behaviors been explained to the student in specific terms he or she understands?

Communication: What is the person trying to communicate with this behavior? If you were this person, what would this situation mean to you?

Unmet Needs: How does the student learn? Does the student have friends? Is the student safe at home? Hungry? Tired? Does the student need a bathroom break?

Self-Determination: Has the student had a "say" or input into the decisions affecting him? Has the student's dignity been preserved?

Hidden Benefit: Did the student want anything before the behavior occurred? Does the student have other ways of getting what he wants or needs? What happened to the student immediately after the behavior occurred?

Survival Strategies: Did the student seem anxious or afraid before the behavior occurred? Did the student see herself as being in danger or threatened in any way? Could the situation have reminded the student of another situation in which there was a threat of danger?

Family and Cultural Factors: Is the behavior considered acceptable to the student's family? Does the behavior conform to the student's cultural norms?

Roles: Are there people with whom the behavior does not occur? What is different about how those people interact with the person?

Medication: Is the student on medication? If so, are there any side effects? When is the last time the student had his medication reviewed by the supervising physician?

Source: Adapted from Van der Klift, E. & Kunc, N. Session: *Non-coercive Responses to Puzzling Behavior* (2005) Annual TASH Conference, Milwaukee, WI. Used with permission.

REDUCING BEHAVIOR CHALLENGES

A comfortable and welcoming classroom can reduce and even eliminate the potential for challenging behaviors before they occur. Students with ASD like structure and predictability. Rules and procedures need to be clearly displayed in a manner the student understands. A comfortable and welcoming classroom is also organized and free of clutter. The old adage "There is a place for everything and everything is in its place" applies. The optimal classroom setting includes the following:

1. Schedules and procedures are prominently displayed.

2. Room arrangement is designed to eliminate distractions, enhance instruction, and manage materials.

3. Student seating arrangements place a high value on peer support. Students with ASD sit next to nondisabled peers who are good role models, not other students with ASD.

4. Plans for transitions between activities are carefully developed and consistently applied. Students are forewarned of change ahead of time and, through practice, know how to transition with minimal disruption and delay.

Class Schedules and Rules

Teach and reteach classroom rules and procedures in a positive manner. Post a classroom schedule of activities on the front board or wall. Give advance notice when changes will occur to avoid unexpected last-minute changes. If the class is attending a school performance assembly, discuss proper etiquette for audience behavior.

> *Everyone look at our schedule for today. Instead of going to 2nd period, we will attend a dance assembly in the multipurpose room. The assembly will last all period. Be ready to sit on the floor and quietly enjoy the dance performance. Be sure to applaud politely and be careful not to distract others who are enjoying the performance.*

Classroom rules should be explicit and concrete. Five or fewer positively worded rules are more effective than a long list of "Do nots." When teaching the rules, focus on the positive behaviors you want from the students. Be sure to define, model, and demonstrate the desired behavior. Avoid threats of punishment and promises of reward. Instead, focus on why the rules and procedures are important.

Room Arrangement

Avoid cluttered tables, desks, closets, and walls. Teach students to be organized by setting a good example. Make sure students know where to find the materials they need and where to turn in completed assignments and homework. Arrange the room so traffic patterns to and from materials and instructional areas are least disruptive to students with ASD. The classroom should be arranged to

- increase student engagement,
- decrease confusion and unnecessary distractions,
- maximize your ability to work with and monitor students,
- encourage students to interact with each other and the teacher, and
- allow students easy access to materials.

Transitions

Time is a challenging, abstract concept for some students with ASD. Students who are unable to gauge how much time is left to finish an activity need advance warning prior to the transition. If the student is disorganized, more time may be required. Problems arise when the student is rushed to complete preferred academic tasks at the last minute.

Middle and high school passing periods are short. If the student needs to cross campus for his next class, allow enough time for him to pack up and get going. Some of these problems can be avoided if the following apply:

- The routine for making transitions is consistent. When changes must occur, they should be reviewed with the student at the beginning of the day.
- Students are given 5 to 10 minutes notice before the transition must be made.
- A daily schedule is posted and reviewed throughout the class period.
- Students' individual schedules are posted or kept on or near their desks. Individual schedules are reviewed with students after each activity or period.
- Changes are made on the posted classroom schedule and students' individual schedules to reflect any changes in the routine (assemblies, shortened-day schedules, field trips). Involve the student in noting the change whenever possible. For example, the student with ASD helps change the schedule by pulling off the Velcro-backed card with the word "Math" and replaces it with "School Assembly" to denote that math class has been cancelled in favor of a school assembly for today.

Consider the Student

Your knowledge and understanding of the student will increase the likelihood he or she will succeed in the setting. Consider the following student-centered adaptations proven effective in reducing behavior challenges:

- Strategically seat students with ASD in close proximity to nondisabled peers, not other students with ASD. Students with ASD respond especially well to nurturing, supportive peers. The presence of this type of student reduces the likelihood of a behavior challenge.

- Seat students with behavior challenges away from the student with ASD, especially if the misbehaving student is likely to tease or harass others.
- Create seating arrangements that promote positive peer-to-peer interactions.
- Schedule calming-down times or exercise breaks before challenging situations.
- Alternate more difficult and demanding work with easier and more enjoyable activities and tasks.
- Provide choices.
- Provide access to preferred activities and peers.
- Have a place where the student with ASD can go to relax when stress is building. Send along meaningful work for the student to complete. Do not overutilize this strategy. We want the student to view this option as a place to complete work, not a place to escape from work.

Proximity to Distractions

Many students with ASD fixate on objects and materials at the expense of their attention to task. Seat students who are distractible away from high traffic areas and the presence of desirable objects that distract. For example, avoid placing students near

- assignment pickup or turn-in area;
- the teacher's work area;
- classroom doors and windows;
- classroom sink, pencil sharpeners, water fountain, fish tanks, pet cages, computers, DVDs, and TVs; and
- sensory challenges.

Difficulties with concentration and classroom performance may occur when the student is overresponsive to sensation and feels he is being bombarded with sensory input. The student may try to minimize sensory overload by covering his ears, avoiding touch, or placing his head down with eyes closed. Helping the student overcome sensory challenges may involve an occupational therapist. The range of possible interventions depends on the nature of the sensory challenge. For more information, see Chapter 1, Sensory Characteristics.

EMOTIONAL EPISODES

Temper tantrums, meltdowns, and angry outbursts are a few of the terms used for emotional episodes. Not all students with autism have emotional episodes, but chances are you will encounter students who do. Understanding the stages of emotional episodes and the triggering factors causing them will help to avoid an emotional episode or at least reduce its effects. Knowing what to expect in advance will help keep the student safe during the emotional episode and promote a quicker recovery. Emotional episodes typically occur in three stages (Myles, 2005). These stages are (1) agitation, (2) rage, and (3) recovery.

STABILIZATION STRATEGIES

Resume instruction when the student has calmed and is ready to learn. Be patient! If you have just been pulled to shore after almost drowning, chances are you are not ready to work on your math word problems! Aid the child's return to stability. Give calm reassurance, go for a quiet walk without talk, relax in a quite area, change environmental stimuli (turn off lights, provide quiet area, listen to music through headphones, provide alternative activities). It's counterproductive to hold the emotional episode

Figure 3.3 Student Behavior During an Emotional Episode

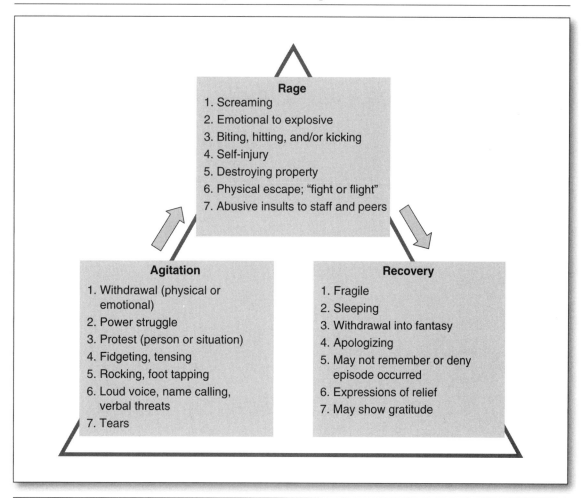

Rage
1. Screaming
2. Emotional to explosive
3. Biting, hitting, and/or kicking
4. Self-injury
5. Destroying property
6. Physical escape; "fight or flight"
7. Abusive insults to staff and peers

Agitation
1. Withdrawal (physical or emotional)
2. Power struggle
3. Protest (person or situation)
4. Fidgeting, tensing
5. Rocking, foot tapping
6. Loud voice, name calling, verbal threats
7. Tears

Recovery
1. Fragile
2. Sleeping
3. Withdrawal into fantasy
4. Apologizing
5. May not remember or deny episode occurred
6. Expressions of relief
7. May show gratitude

Source: Adapted from Myles, B. S. (2005). *Children and Youth With Asperger Syndrome: Strategies for Success in Inclusive Settings.* Thousand Oaks, CA: Corwin.

against the student or take it personally. Remember, students with ASD are vulnerable to emotional episodes. Determine what the stressors are and work to decrease their effect.

Figure 3.4 Adult Behavior During Student's Emotional Episode

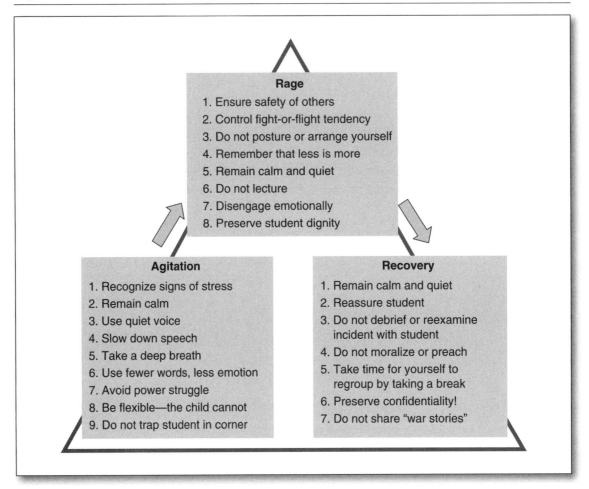

Source: Adapted from Myles, B. S. (2005). *Children and Youth With Asperger Syndrome: Strategies for Success in Inclusive Settings.* Thousand Oaks, CA: Corwin.

LEARN ABOUT THE STUDENT

Gather Information

Learn the factors causing stress from the student's parents, special education teacher, and other reliable sources of information. Students with ASD may not be capable of recognizing what causes their anxiety, frustration, anger, and depression. Many students with ASD perseverate over one thought and get locked into inflexible thinking that can spiral out of control. Even if they can explain the reasons, it does not mean they have the ability to control their thoughts and emotions.

Determine the Environmental Stressors

When considering why the student is beginning to escalate into an emotional episode, consider the following:

- Has the regular schedule been interrupted (assemblies, fire drill, testing, minimum day)?
- Has the student been teased or bullied, or is she just not coping well with another student?
- Is the room too bright? Too loud? Too active? Too crowded? Too disorganized?
- Is the assignment too long? Too confusing? Too aversive?
- Is the current class activity intense, and was it preceded by another activity equally as intense?
- Are you or another adult projecting impatience and frustration?
- Is the student struggling with an illness or lack of sleep? Is she menstruating?

Decrease Environmental Stressors

Modify requirements for disliked tasks and activities and temporarily stop teaching new skills. Increase supports immediately and reduce stressors if you see signs of agitation starting. Be mindful of situations that induce meltdowns and provide alternative activities to satisfy the same class requirement. For example, if filling out a science worksheet on plant biology is anxiety producing for the student yet he loves to draw, let him demonstrate understanding by drawing a picture of the plant and labeling all the parts instead.

Provide a Predictable Environment

Avoid changes in routine and unannounced events unless the student has sufficiently recovered. If an assembly is scheduled, make certain the student has recovered to the extent she is prepared to participate. However, don't automatically leave the student out of the event because of the emotional episode. Check to see if the student is calm enough to attend. Let her participate in the decision. Sometimes a change of routine can serve as a much-needed distraction from the original upsetting situation. Other times, the event may cause an increase in anxiety.

Increase Regular Demands

As the student returns to normal functioning, monitor closely her reaction to stress and ability to perform tasks. Be careful to not overhelp the student. Overzealous hyperenergetic help can cause stress, too. Special pull-out activities like social skills groups can cause stress if the student dislikes missing class.

Andrew's teacher created a pull-out social skills group for him. After a couple of weeks, his teacher noticed an increase in Andrew's anxiety behaviors (humming, pulling his hair, covering his ears) the day of the group meeting. Mindful of this rise in stress, Andrew's parents and teacher decided he would benefit more from embedded social skills in his general education classroom than from participating in the pull-out social skills group. (Author)

Have a Plan B

Make certain a plan is in place when all else fails and the student's anxiety is rising to a level where an emotional episode is imminent. Many times, all the student needs is a short walk to relax. Try giving the student an errand to run, a library book to return, or paper to deliver to the class across campus. This type of strategy is far less stigmatizing than removal from class. Students frequently deliver messages or return books to the library for the teacher. Taking books back to the library or materials to another class serves two purposes: It gets the student out of a stressful situation and builds independence while promoting community. The student wins and a damaging emotional episode is avoided.

Amanda struggled with an intense need to be perfect. If the teacher marked her answer wrong, she would quickly cycle into an emotional episode. Despite efforts to redirect her, she would scream her answer was not wrong and attempt to grab the paper to erase the mark. We learned the best way to reduce Amanda's fixation with perfection was to problem-solve with her when she was relaxed and open to new ideas. We managed to get Amanda to agree to using calming strategies the next time a missed question was marked wrong. The next day, just before marking her answer wrong, we said, "Remember how we talked about you accepting having a wrong answer checked on your paper?" Amanda: "But I want to be perfect!" Teacher: "What did we say about that, Amanda?" "That I can't be perfect." Teacher: "Good! OK, take a deep breath, relax . . . here I go." (Teacher marks answer wrong.) Amanda breathes deeply and her eyes blink but she holds her emotions in check. Teacher: "Good girl! You did not get upset. Very impressive, Amanda!" (Author)

EFFECTIVE BEHAVIOR SUPPORT

Students with ASD often rely on the skilled help of teachers and therapeutic specialists in finding solutions to their challenges. The roles of various adults who may be called in to support the student include school psychologist, autism specialist, behavior specialist, and behavior therapist. The effectiveness of adult specialists depends on their training, values and beliefs, capacity to form and maintain good relationships, and ability to identify and assist support staff and peers in the use of best practices that will improve the student's situation. Reflect on the practices for facilitating person-centered behavior support listed in Table 3.1 and consider incorporating areas of need into your strategies:

Table 3.1   Effective Behavior Support

Effective Behavior Support			
Relationship Building			**The teacher/specialist . . .**
Always	With many people	Seldom or never	. . . asks the person for permission to offer help.
Always	With many people	Seldom or never	. . . asks the student's permission to talk with others about him or her.
Always	With many people	Seldom or never	. . . takes time to develop a relationship with the student by doing things with him or her they enjoy.
Always	With many people	Seldom or never	. . . takes time to learn the student's story and conveys the story in a way that is respectful and worthy of the person's confidence.
Always	With many people	Seldom or never	. . . takes time to get to know the student's supporters.
Always	With many people	Seldom or never	. . . strives to respect the student's cultural values and viewpoints so that the student feels safe and encouraged to express himself or herself.
Always	With many people	Seldom or never	. . . makes time to celebrate successes with the person and supporters.
Always	With many people	Seldom or never	. . . actively involves the student and his or her supporters in developing support plans.
Always	With many people	Seldom or never	. . . bases support plans on the knowledge and information that grows in gathering the person's story and thoughtfully defining the behavior in question.
Understanding Behavior			**The teacher/specialist . . .**
Always	With many people	Seldom or never	. . . develops clear definitions of the behavior in question.
Always	With many people	Seldom or never	. . . accounts for the history of the behavior in question.
Always	With many people	Seldom or never	. . . identifies strategies and interventions that have helped and those that have not helped.
Always	With many people	Seldom or never	. . . identifies conditions associated with high and low levels of the behavior in question— daily, weekly, and monthly.

(Continued)

Table 3.1 (Continued)

Always	With many people	Seldom or never	. . . systematically collects useful information and summarizes it in a form that improves decision making.
Always	With many people	Seldom or never	. . . considers and addresses the physiological issues that may influence behavior, particularly self-injurious behavior.
Always	With many people	Seldom or never	. . . considers and addresses the effects of medications and their interactions on the behavior.
Advocacy			**The teacher/specialist . . .**
Always	With many people	Seldom or never	. . . can see the big picture and identifies system and organizational structures, policies, and practices that contribute to the behavior in question or compromise the effectiveness of support.
Always	With many people	Seldom or never	. . . uses the big picture view for organizational and system change.
Always	With many people	Seldom or never	. . . effectively provides concrete, practical information that educates peers about autism and follows up with an active plan for developing and maintaining friendships, tools for maintaining focus on the person, and school conditions that respect and promote peer-to-peer relationships.

Source: Pitonyak, D., & O'Brien, J. (2009). *Effective Behavior Support Version 2.* www.dimagine.com. Used with permission.

Note: Thanks to Dr. David Pitonyak for this adapted table.

IT'S NOT REALISTIC

Behavior challenges are usually the excuse teachers and administrators use when they struggle to understand how to successfully include students with ASD in general education settings.

In trying to decide whether to include the student, the discussion inevitably focuses on evaluating the student's behavior and suitability for the classroom setting. In some cases, the student's emotional episodes are so severe it seems impossible for the student to participate in classroom activities without seriously disrupting the education of his or her classmates. The tendency, therefore, is to not include the student, for what seem to be valid reasons. Yet, although the decision may appear appropriate, often these very sensible conclusions deny the student, his peers, and his teacher the opportunity to discover ways in which they could successfully include the student in the classroom setting. The question of what is realistic isn't as clear-cut as it may seem. Kunc (1984) states, "How many times have we prevented individuals with disabilities from figuring out ways of overcoming problems simply by saying, "It is not realistic" (p. 2).

The reasons for this attitude stem from honest ignorance about students with autism coupled with a lack of knowledge regarding the positive behavior support strategies mentioned in this chapter. Teachers and other support providers are often unaware of the possible minor adaptations that could be made in the classroom to support students diagnosed with ASD. As Kunc (1984) so beautifully illustrates,

> The statement, "not realistic," is often a reflection of honest ignorance. However, in deciding that a certain placement is "not realistic," the speaker immediately minimizes the opportunity to brainstorm about the possible ways of overcoming a specific problem. Moreover, in committing oneself to the view that integrating a certain student is "not realistic," one immediately makes a judgment about that situation and now has a vested interest in maintaining the validity of that judgment. (p. 3)

The issue then becomes, how can we remove obstacles preventing the student with ASD from fully participating? What modifications can we make to the environment to reduce the student's challenges? What strategies can we use to inform the student's typically developing peers about the student's disability in a way that they become empowered to support the student's full participation? What factors contribute to the student's challenges, and how can they be removed?

The "problem" most often does not rest with the student with autism. The problem is usually the situation and the circumstances present in the classroom environment that cause anxiety and lead to inappropriate behavior. By analyzing the situation and making adjustments, we can nearly always turn a challenging situation into a nonissue and transform the classroom setting into a familiar, comfortable, and welcoming place for all students.

SUMMARY

Behavior is defined as the actions or reactions of a person, in relation to the environment, his or her experiences, or an unmet need. Challenging behaviors are really messages that signal the student is in distress and unable to fulfill his or her needs. Behavior can be conscious or unconscious, overt or covert, voluntary or involuntary. When the student's behavior achieves the desired results, the behavior is reinforced. Reinforcers strongly contribute to the likelihood the behavior will be repeated.

Challenging behavior is best understood from the context of the person's life. Supporting a person with difficult behaviors begins when we make a commitment to *know* the person. Sadly, it is often the case that the specialist who develops an intervention to stop someone from engaging in challenging behaviors does not know the person in any meaningful sense. Instead, he or she sees the person as someone (or some*thing*) that needs to be fixed, or modified. However, attempting to "fix" a person's behavior outside the context of the person's life is usually ineffective and always disrespectful (Pitonyak, 2005).

What constitutes a behavior challenge can be interpreted in different ways depending on the observer. Two different people can view the same behavior and come away with two entirely different interpretations of what happened and why.

Behavior challenges are situational as well. Student behavior changes from setting to setting depending on many environmental, social, and personal factors. Student behavior fluctuates based on the presence or absence of certain people, class expectations, and structure, how the student feels, and the comfort level of the classroom setting. The student may act entirely differently based on these factors. Sometimes behavior issues can be reduced by altering factors in the setting.

Building a positive, caring relationship with the student can go a long way toward reducing behavior challenges. We get in trouble when we are the wrong person at the wrong time. Before we can reduce challenging behaviors, we must first consider the child's needs and work with the student from the context of his or her life experience.

> ### Autism Myth
>
> "Children with autism are antisocial."
>
> ### Fact
>
> False: Children with autism struggle to understand the complexities of communication. They want to communicate but need help to learn how.

Emotional episodes follow a predictable cycle. When you understand what to expect in advance, the chances for a more positive outcome increase. Know the student you are supporting and work to reduce environmental stressors that raise the student's anxiety level. Some behavior challenges can be avoided if the teacher alters the factors he or she can control that contribute to inappropriate behavior. Sometimes the student is struggling with issues outside the classroom and these factors impact the student's sense of well-being. Understanding the underlying factors contributing to the student's challenges takes time. A trusting, supportive teacher-student relationship can make an enormous difference in reducing student challenges. By analyzing the situation and making adjustments, most challenging behavior can be reduced or eliminated.

RESOURCES

Resource L: Instruction and Group Management Goals and Desired Outcomes

This excellent form explicitly lists effective class and student management strategies and desired goals for systematic instruction and tracking student performance.

Resource S: Behavior Support Tools Introduction
A concise guide to using the positive behavior support tools included in this resource section.

Resource R: Situational Analysis Form
This useful chart is designed to compare the relationship between factors affecting behavior and the student's response.

Resource S.1: Scatter Plot Analysis—Sample. S.2: Scatter Plot Analysis—Form
Sometimes behavior challenges can be solved by plotting behavior within small increments of time to see if there is a pattern of behavior during certain times of the day. This form is useful for analyzing potential problems based on time of day.

Resource T: Positive Behavior Support Analysis
This form will help you analyze and reduce challenging behavior by analyzing what occurred before the challenging behavior and the outcome or consequence that occurred as a result.

FURTHER READING

Algozzine, B., Daunic, A. P., & Smith, S. W. (2010). *Preventing problem behaviors: Schoolwide programs and classroom practices* (2nd ed.). Thousand Oaks, CA: Corwin.

Belvel, P. S. (2010). *Rethinking classroom management: Strategies for prevention, intervention, and problem solving* (2nd ed.). Thousand Oaks, CA: Corwin.

Koegel, L. K., Koegel, R. L., & Dunlap, G. (Eds.). (1996). *Positive behavioral support: Including people with difficult behavior in the community.* Baltimore, MD: Paul H. Brookes.

O'Neill, R. E., Horner, R. H., Albin, R. W., Sprague, J. R., Storey, K., & Newton, J. S. (1997). *Functional assessment for problem behavior: A practical handbook* (2nd ed.). Pacific Grove, CA: Brooks/Cole.

Queen, J. A., & Algozzine, B. (2010). *Responsible classroom management, Grades 6–12: A schoolwide plan.* Thousand Oaks, CA: Corwin.

Sugai, G., Horner, R. H., Dunlap, G., Hieneman, M., Lewis, T. J., Nelson, C. M., et al. (2000). Applying positive behavioral support and functional behavioral assessment in schools. *Journal of Positive Behavioral Interventions, 2,* 131–143.

4

Communication

Building Competence

Viewed individually, human beings are exceedingly vulnerable and powerless. We have no fangs, claws, poison, armor, horns, wings, or even fur. Our senses are laughably feeble in comparison to many so-called "lesser creatures." Sure, opposable thumbs are cool and useful—but ask any raccoon how far that famed appendage really elevates you in the evolutionary pecking order. As a species, our most valuable characteristic probably is our ability to connect through communication. This gift literally saves us by allowing us to cooperate and share experiences, impressions, skills, and knowledge. It empowers us to transcend our considerable physical limitations, to form a "group mind" of sorts. As much as we trumpet individualism, our true strength is our deep interdependence.

Gahran (2005)

Communication is a complex process of sending and receiving information, terms we refer to as expressive and receptive communication. The information sent and received comes in a variety of forms, including words, gestures, tone of voice, inflection, and body language, that we interpret based on our unique thoughts and feelings. How and what we communicate is influenced by our background, age, culture, nationality, beliefs, socioeconomic status, race, ethnicity, education, prior experience, gender, and point of view.

It's safe to say that most people have experienced the discomfort of misinterpreting someone's message: "That's not what I meant!" "I beg your pardon!" We wonder if we were misunderstood: "I hope he didn't take that the wrong way!" Sometimes we worry about what the meaning of the message was: "Ah, what did you mean by that comment?" "Could you explain?"

There are many forms of communication beyond sending and receiving messages between people. We also engage in a dialogue inside our heads called "self-talk." This form of communication is our day-to-day thoughts, affirmations, and concerns. Self-talk helps us sort out feelings, make plans, and determine how to respond to someone's message. It's the personal consultation we have with our most trusted confidant—our inner voice—before deciding what to say or do. "Think before you speak." Sometimes we bypass thinking before speaking and things go terribly wrong. "Wow, I wish I hadn't said that!" The point is, communication is central to the human experience. It allows us to connect with others and overcome the challenges life brings.

FORMS OF COMMUNICATION

Communication takes many different forms, each serving a particular purpose. Two primary methods of communication convey information. One form is language-based or linguistic communication, and the other is symbolic communication based on physical gestures.

Linguistic Communication

- Spoken and written language
- Sign language

Symbolic Communication

- Body language
- Facial expressions
- Symbols and gestures

Figure 4.1   Create the Need to Communicate

Although students with ASD possess a common set of core challenges (i.e., difficulty with the "give and take" of typical conversation and the inability to connect with the interests of others), the range and degree of challenges varies enormously from individual to individual. Some students with ASD have limited spoken language. They communicate using images, visual clues, or typing on a keyboard. Others use language in atypical ways, retaining features of earlier stages of development, while others repeat a learned phrase repeatedly. Some students repeat what they hear from other sources. Students with Asperger syndrome may show only slight delays in language or even have mature, adultlike language with unusually large vocabularies, but have great difficulty in sustaining typical conversations (Church, Alisanski, & Amanullah, 2000).

The student may share his special interest using typical speech; however, after listening to the student's one-sided monologue about her special topic and apparent lack of concern for the listener's interest level, it's clear there is something different about the student.

Students with ASD frequently struggle in social interactions with peers and may be bullied at school due to their inability to perceive and respond appropriately to nonverbal cues. They may interpret what is said too literally and have difficulty interpreting and responding to sarcasm and tone of voice. The following range of language characteristics may be found in students with ASD.

Echolalia

Echolalia is the immediate or delayed literal repetition of the speech of others. There are two forms of echolalia: immediate and delayed. With immediate echolalia, the student repeats the conversation partner's words immediately after the words are expressed. For example, Teacher: "How was your weekend, Ryan?" Student: "How was your weekend, Ryan?" Delayed echolalia refers to words or phrases repeated hours, days, or even weeks after they were first heard. When echolalia serves a function, in other words, is used in context, it is called *functional echolalia.* Sometimes delayed echolalia is nonfunctional—meaning the listener cannot determine the function of the comments.

There are several reasons why echolalia occurs. Because the student lacks the ability to create spontaneous responses to situations, he resorts to using phrases heard before to communicate what he wants to say in the present. For example, an angry student with ASD could struggle to express his anger appropriate to the situation. The frustrating situation triggers a memory of a different time when the student was angry. Lacking the ability to speak in context, he uses the echoed phrase from that previous situation to communicate how he is feeling now. In this way, echolalia can be a useful way for the student to communicate when he lacks the ability to customize his response specific to the situation.

It is also believed that students with ASD express themselves using preassembled whole phrases retrieved from memory instead of choosing words "in the moment" to construct a more relevant phrase (Baltaxe & Simmons, 1977). This explains why the student's language seems contrived and unnatural. The student misses the immense variety of nuanced expression available to customize his response to the situation. There is a lack of coupling to the communicative partner's intent. Instead, the student's response seems out of context and disconnected.

Special Interests

Students with ASD tend to focus intensely on their special area of interest at the expense of other activities. This strong interest can dominate the students' free time and interfere with relationship building. In pursuit of their interest, they will accumulate a large number of objects, facts, and information. Their extreme motivation and attention to the interest can lead to them becoming experts in the focus area. For example, a student will develop a large vocabulary centering on his strong interest in shipwrecks. He will pull from his vast shipwreck vocabulary to extend his conversation on the sinking of the Titanic. Many students have good memories for information they find interesting.

In some cases, the student's special interest can lead to friendship with peers who enjoy the same interest. Make sure to tap into the student's special interest as a means to display competence. The special interest can serve as a trigger or lead-in to other areas of study. For example, a deep interest in airplanes can be used as a bridge to mathematics, social studies, and other areas of study. For those living in earthquake-prone areas, an interest in earthquakes can be employed for having the student research and develop a report, and possibly class materials, on safety when an earthquake strikes.

Be mindful of the potential for the special interest morphing into an obsession. If the student is consumed with his interest, consider setting limits. "Okay, Jeff, you can ask a maximum of two questions about medieval-era drainpipes; then you need to discuss something else."

From age 14 to 18, our son Steven was consumed with building a car from small pieces of Knex. He literally devoted hundreds of hours to building his specially designed car from thousands of 3-inch and 4-inch Knex pieces paid for with money earned mowing lawns, cleaning house, and working at a nearby roller rink. The pieces were carefully connected together in an intricate design Steven formed as the car grew in size. The only non-Knex components were 18-inch metal rods used for the car's axels and wheelbarrow wheels for tires. When completed, the car's dimensions were approximately 4 feet long and 2 feet wide. What eventually happened to his creation? When Steven lost interest in Knex, he disassembled the car and took all the thousands of pieces to the Goodwill! That was the end of that! (Author)

Nonverbal Communication and Eye Contact

Students with ASD seldom use gestures like facial expression, hand movement, eye contact, and body posturing to give meaning to their speech. The absence of gesturing adds to the impression that the student is rude, uninterested, or inattentive. The student's affect is flat, lacking the variety of physical gesturing and facial expressions found in typically developing students.

Eye contact can be especially discomforting for students with ASD. The face is a complex map of confusing signals that can cause discomfort and anxiety. Some students purposely avoid eye contact to enhance communication. By looking away, the face is removed from the visual equation, making communication easier. Luke Jackson (2002) offers this insight into his challenges with eye contact:

Sometimes it is too hard to concentrate on listening and looking at the same time. People are hard enough to understand as their words are often very cryptic, but when their faces are moving around, their eyebrows rising and falling and their eyes getting wider then squinting, I cannot fathom all that out in one go, so to be honest I don't even try. (p. 71)

Problems develop when authority figures take the student's avoidance of eye contact as a sign of disrespect. "Look at me when I'm talking to you!" the teacher states with furrowed brow and raised voice. Unknowingly, the teacher is setting the student up for an emotional episode due to this lack of understanding.

Researchers have recently discovered that distractibility and discomfort issues may be extended to the fear mechanism in the brain. Brain tests at the University of Wisconsin–Madison suggest that students with ASD avoid eye contact because they perceive even the most familiar face as an uncomfortable threat. Tracking the correlation between eye movements and brain activity, the researchers found that in subjects with autism, the amygdala, an emotion center in the brain associated with negative feelings, lights up to an abnormal extent during a direct gaze upon a non-threatening face (University of Wisconsin–Madison, 2005).

Perspective Taking and Empathy

Figure 4.2 Explore Feelings

Perspective taking and empathy enable us to understand, internalize, and respond to another person's thoughts and emotions (Premack & Woodruff, 1978). A typical teenager may think, "My best friend is upset because her boyfriend broke up with her. She's crying. I feel bad for her." Typical students have the ability to dwell on their friend's thoughts and feelings and express empathy in a manner that validates the friend's emotions. They can "walk in the other person's shoes." The innate ability to understand the other person's feelings and emotions forms the basis for friendship development. It is the seed that connects people to each other.

Students with ASD do not connect as typical students do to the thoughts and feelings of their peers (Baron-Cohen, 2009). They are puzzled by how to respond to another person's emotions (Grandin, 1995). They notice that someone is crying and figure out he or she is upset, but they do not know why or how to comfort the other person.

Driven by Rules and Systems

"Be less curious about people and more curious about things."

—Marie Curie (Curie, 1939)

Individuals with ASD thrive on predictability. They are driven to construct a world based on rule-bound structures and feel an ultimate sense of pleasure when the outcome is the same every time. This explains why empathy and perspective taking are so challenging for students with ASD. Emotions do not follow rules. Emotions are not predictable across individuals. Emotions are abstract and extremely variable.

Simon Baron-Cohen, a leading autism researcher, explains that individuals with ASD are predisposed to organize their world into systems. *Systematizing* is the drive to analyze or construct systems. What defines a system is that it follows rules. Identify the rules that govern the system and you can predict how the system will behave (Baron-Cohen, 2009). Examples of systems include numerical systems (e.g., a train timetable), technological systems (e.g., computer programming), natural systems (e.g., tidal wave patterns), collectible systems (e.g., sorting coins), and moral systems (e.g., codes of conduct). Students with ASD know that telling the truth is a rule and assume everyone is telling the truth. They are shocked by the idea that other people do not always say what they mean (Baron-Cohen, 1992, 2007). According to Baron-Cohen (2009),

> Systematizing is a way of explaining the narrow interests, repetitive behavior, and resistance to change/need for sameness in individuals with ASD. This is because when you systemize, it is easiest to keep everything constant, and only vary one thing at a time. That way, you can see what might be causing what, rendering the world predictable. (p. 72)

It is hard to take someone's perspective if his or her ideas do not conform to the student's rigid, rule-bound sense of order. The potential friend has little in common that connects with the student. The inability to see a different point of view poses many challenges when attempting to make friends. A lack of perspective taking can cause students with ASD to appear insensitive to the needs of their classmates. This disconnect can cause frustration and anger in the student with ASD (Frith, 2001). In the words of Grandin and Barron (2005),

> Neurotypicals refer to it as being "clueless" or laugh it off as people who "put their foot in their mouth." Neurotypical people recognize the nonverbal clues that something has gone amiss in the social interaction. Body language, a shift in the other's tone of voice or dead silence tell them they've done something wrong and better repair the situation—and quickly. The student with ASD who functions with low perspective taking ability and rigid thinking patterns misses this entire world of nonverbal communication. (p. 288)

In your work supporting students with ASD, make sure to avoid jumping to conclusions that assume students with ASD are insensitive and uncaring. They may simply be unaware! Remember, just like other autistic traits, empathy and perspective taking vary along the autism spectrum.

COMMUNICATION CHALLENGES

Although their language and communication styles vary, all students with ASD display communication challenges, especially in the context of social interaction. The following characteristics contribute to the student's challenges with communication:

- Has tendency to make irrelevant, off-topic comments and interrupt.
- May talk over the speech of others and use volume, tone, and speed inappropriately.
- Engages in one-sided monologues around special topic of interest without any apparent concern for the other person's interest level.
- Has difficulty understanding complex language, following directions, and deciphering intent of words with multiple meanings.
- Loses focus when listening to long strings of verbal instructions and multistep directions.
- Opening comments can sound contrived or out of context.
- Has challenges with turn-taking during conversation and knowing when and how to reply, interrupt, or change the topic.
- Doesn't get the meaning of metaphors, figures of speech, and double meanings.
- Does not usually understand jokes and other forms of humor.
- Naive: does what is suggested without thinking about the consequences.
- Interprets literally what is said . . . doesn't "read between the lines."
- Misreads the emotions of others.
- Lacks tact. Says what is on his or her mind without regard for the impact on the listener.
- Has problems judging social distance and appropriate physical contact. Stands too close or too far from listener. Inappropriate hugging.
- Is unaware of the difference between public behavior and private behavior. May touch or scratch private parts in the presence of others.
- Has difficulty understanding "unwritten rules" of conversation. When the individual does learn a rule, he or she will apply it too rigidly.

COMMUNICATION INTERVENTIONS

Understand the Student's Unique Voice

Supporting students with ASD must start with an understanding of each person's mode (method) of communication. For some students, the appropriate goal is to expand *verbal communication* through pragmatic language training coupled with opportunities to interact in natural settings. For others, the development of *gestured communication* like *sign language* is the best goal. Augmentative and alternative communication (AAC) technology can provide students with limited speech a means to effectively communicate. AAC technology helps students express themselves through picture and symbol communication boards and electronic devices. Preprogrammed buttons, when pressed, generate common phrases unique to the student's needs. AAC can increase social interaction, school performance, and feelings of self-worth.

Create Communication Opportunities

Providing opportunities for students with ASD to communicate with teachers and peers is critical to improving communication and social skills. Including students with ASD in general education settings provides continuous opportunities to observe, interact with, and learn from typical peer role models. Studies conclusively demonstrate that students with ASD who are included with their typical peers in natural, age-appropriate settings (general education classrooms) comment and respond appropriately at a higher rate compared with students receiving language instruction in a clinic or segregated setting (Koegel & Koegel, 2006). In addition, studies note a decrease in disruptive behaviors (Koegel, Koegel, & Surratt, 1992), improvements in academic learning (Dunlap & Kern, 1993), and decreases in autistic-like behaviors (Baker, 2003; Baker, Koegel, & Koegel, 1998).

Figure 4.3 The Need to Be Understood

In this section, strategies are introduced that increase the student's communication skills in a manner that simply cannot be reproduced in a clinic setting alone. A conversation between two people usually begins spontaneously, unplanned, "in the moment," and is highly dependent on the situation. Teachers can help create connections between students with ASD and their peers by encouraging active talk across settings such as the classroom, hallways, cafeteria, and library.

Advocating for the student with ASD requires an understanding of the student's voice, his communication style. Anxiety occurs when the student cannot express his thoughts and needs. Imagine how frustrating it would be if you lacked the ability to express yourself using typical speech. Think for a moment about the number of situations we encounter each day that require complex language and what it would be like if we could not communicate our thoughts. It is frustrating to not be understood!

Students who lack a reliable method of communication may resort to challenging behavior to communicate their needs. Instead of protesting an intolerable situation by explaining why he is upset, the student may lose emotional control and act inappropriately (Laurent & Rubin, 2004).

The speech pathologist, in consultation with the student's family and teachers, searches for alternatives to assist the student in developing a more acceptable and reliable communication system.

Practical Help Strategies

- Provide clear expectations and model appropriate responses when communication errors occur. Have the student repeat the response.

- Explicitly teach rules of social conduct "in the moment" as they occur.
- Coach peers about how to respond to the student during social interactions.
- Use other students to model how to talk and what to do. Coach peers on ways to explain why the model was correct.
- Encourage cooperative games.
- Provide supervision and support for the student during lunch and breaks. Monitor from a distance, sensitive to the negative effects of adult proximity.
- Use peer support to assist the student during nonstructured times.
- Show the student how to start, maintain, and end conversations.
- Encourage flexibility, cooperation, and sharing among students.
- Teach students how to monitor their own communication.
- Directly model specific skills and practice during actual events.
- Preplan encounters with peers and decide in advance what outcomes to target.
- Teach the student how to use Internet Instant Messaging (IM) "and cell phone texting.
- If necessary, find out what the student wants to tell others and help her find the words she is most comfortable using. Practice what she will say in advance.
- Answer questions of peers, being careful not to breech confidentiality.

SUPPORTING STUDENTS WHO HAVE LIMITED VERBAL LANGUAGE

Typical students are skilled communicators who use their advanced verbal skills to get their needs met. They speak out when they don't like something. They have the ability to protest verbally and explain why they're upset. If you've ever debated with a teenager, you understand this point!

Students with ASD who have limited verbal language frequently communicate through behavior rather than through speech. In the absence of a reliable form of communication, the student may express frustration physically. He may start rocking, hand flapping, humming, or using echolalia. If the student finds a situation or person intolerable and doesn't have a means to communicate his frustration in a way people understand, anger can build to the point where the student lashes out by screaming or throwing objects. Be mindful for the reason behind this behavior. As stated in Chapter 3, behavior is an expression of an unmet need coupled with the inability to use communication to resolve problems.

Interact with the student and observe her forms of expression. Notice how she responds to her peers, how she

> **Autism Myth**
>
> "Autism can be cured."
>
> **Fact**
>
> False: While there are treatments created to improve a person's abilities, there is no known cure for autism.

gains what she needs or protests something aversive. Recognize behaviors that foreshadow an emotional episode and take the necessary steps to prevent escalation. Know the signs that signal frustration and anger. Emotional episodes can be avoided by anticipating potentially frustrating situations. In this way, the student's dignity can be preserved. Friendships develop when opportunities for communication are actively sought and promoted. The student who is nonverbal or limited verbal will miss these opportunities unless someone takes the initiative to promote peer-to-peer interactions. Encourage and assist typically developing peers to interpret and engage the student in conversation. Doing so will improve the student's communication over time.

Typical kids will join in the conversation of their peer group by listening, then adding their own voice to an ongoing conversation. A student who is nonverbal cannot do this without support. The teacher can act as an interpreter in an ongoing conversation or activity with the student. Support could be as simple as having a friend walk with Ben to lunch. While passing students in the hallway, mention how Ben wants to say "Hi. I think the girl next to you is really cute!" When students with ASD are paired with typical peers, opportunities to learn and practice communication skills increase dramatically. Typical peers come to learn and appreciate the person behind the autistic label.

Understanding the feelings of others is crucial for communication and developing friendships. If the peer cannot understand the student who has limited verbal communication, the teacher will need to interpret for the peer. For example, when a student asks why Ben can't talk, a whole discussion develops around how he "talks" without words. His teacher encourages Ben's peers to think about other ways a person might express anger, sadness, or happiness. Teach kids how to recognize the student's attempts to communicate and help bridge understanding.

Questions about students with ASD can be viewed as opportunities to provide typical peers with information about autism. It is essential that similarities between students be shared beyond the diagnosis. For example, you might explain that Ben doesn't talk much, but he likes to swim and is good at computer games, just like the student asking the questions. Alternatively, you may volunteer that Ben's brother just had a birthday, and then initiate a discussion about the peer's siblings.

Augmentative and Alternative Communication (AAC)

Some students benefit from augmentative and alternative communication (AAC) technology. AAC technology helps students express themselves through a variety of modes, including picture and symbol communication, boards, and electronic devices. The two primary forms of AAC used with individuals with ASD include *unaided communication*, for which no equipment is required and which is external to the body (use of symbols such as manual signs, pantomimes, and gestures), and *aided communication*, or "low-tech" picture-based systems (e.g., Picture Exchange Communication

System: PECS), communication books, and speech-generating devices. Pre-programmed buttons, when pressed, generate common phrases unique to the student's needs. In addition, a variety of other assistive technology, such as portable word processors, can support effective written expression. AAC can increase social interaction, school performance, and feelings of self-worth while reducing challenging behaviors (Mirenda, 2001).

Cell Phones and Texting

Most adolescents use cell phones to communicate with their friends and families. Text messaging has become the primary mode that teens use to reach their friends, surpassing face-to-face contact, e-mail, instant messaging, and voice calling as the go-to daily communication tool for teenagers (Lenhart, Ling, Campbell, & Purcell, 2010).

Cell phones with text messaging are age-appropriate, socially acceptable, and very portable devices that are easy to use in a wide variety of school and community settings. They offer an excellent way for students with ASD to communicate with their family and peers. Cell phones carry no social stigma and can enhance the ability of adolescents with autism to connect in an age-appropriate manner. Hoch, Taylor, and Rodriguez (2009) demonstrated that cell phone technology provided students with ASD a means to seek assistance when needed in public places.

Emerging Technologies

The Apple iPad™ and iPhone™, along with similar touch-screen portable devices, promise to expand the possibilities for students with ASD to more effectively communicate. Developers are working diligently to create applications for this technology. For example, the application iMean™ turns the entire iPad screen into a large-button keyboard, with text display and word prediction. It allows students with limited speech to communicate their needs and ideas directly, distinctly, and independently.

Planned Encounters Using Communication Books

The use of picture albums to jump-start conversation is a useful method for getting students with limited verbal ability to talk with peers. The student brings a small photo album from home with a variety of pictures of family vacations, the family pet, or family events like birthdays. The pictures serve as a starting point for conversation with typical peers. Many times, peers discover through these exchanges that they share a lot in common with the student with ASD. This realization forms the basis for friendship development.

Here's a possible scenario: The student with ASD carries the picture book to lunch. On the way, two typical peers (who have been briefed on the planned encounter) stop the student and say, "Hey, Ben, what are you carrying? Can I see?" Ben shows the first picture. The peer points to the picture and says, "Where was this picture taken?" Ben replies, "Disneyland."

Peers: "Oh, you went to Disneyland!? So did my family! How cool!" " . . . Who's in the picture with you?" Ben: "My brother, Adam, my mom, Susan, my dad, Armando." And so it goes . . . continuing through the set of pictures. Communication books are inexpensive and easy to use. New sets of pictures can replace the old, and new conversations can be generated.

Figure 4.4 Handheld Picture Albums

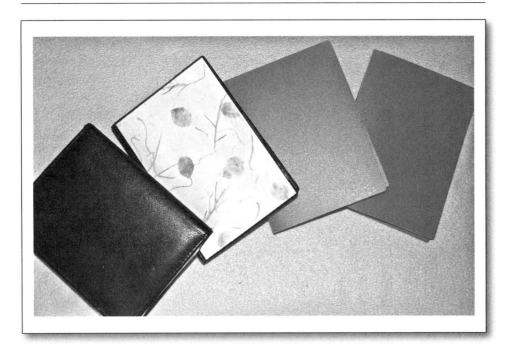

Figure 4.5 Conversation Support

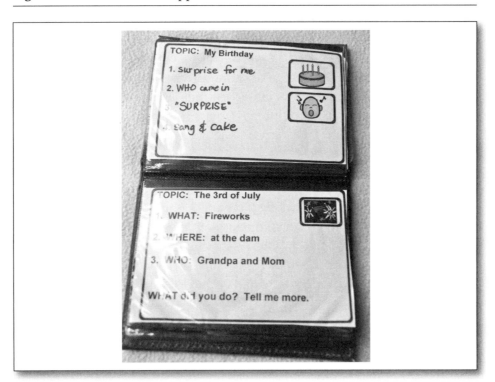

Figure 4.6   Sharing a Topic of Interest

Help Peers to Interact With the Student

Interpersonal communication is challenging for the student with ASD and his neurotypical peers. Help peers to understand the student's mode of communication, but don't interfere with the natural flow of their interactions. Here are some concepts to consider:

- Help peers learn to interpret the student's linguistic and symbolic forms of communication. Offer clear information about what his facial expressions and body language mean. Sometimes, just the fact that the student with ASD stayed in close proximity to his peers without running away is a sign he wants to interact. Look for the signs, help peers interpret, and then fade out of the way. For example, if Juan expresses happiness by making vocalizations and rocking his upper body, share the message with his peers so they can correctly interpret his actions.
- Remind peers to speak directly to the student instead of talking through an adult. Help peers interpret the answers the student provides. This requires explaining and physical modeling to get the idea across. For example, Jessica might come up and say, "Do you think Amy wants to go outside now?" You might say something like, "I don't know. Why don't you ask her?" Then interpret Amy's response if needed.
- Help students to include their classmate with ASD in decision and choice making. Students with ASD are frequently misunderstood. Their preferences are not always clear. We need to promote independent decision making. Encourage peers to notice both the verbal and nonverbal messages expressed by students and help them use the information to guide their actions.

- Encourage typical peers to respond to the student with ASD as they would a typical peer. They can't learn what not to say if their peers don't tell them! When students with ASD learn for themselves through natural encounters with peers, they are expanding their ability to function independently.

Communication Temptations

Communicative temptations involve creating a situation that compels the student to communicate. A response is required by the student in order to solve a problem or to obtain something. Each of the following situations should be considered on an individual basis, understanding the student's potential for anxiety. The goal is to compel the student to communicate by creating the need without causing undue stress. When applied in a sensible manner with full knowledge of the student, communication temptations can increase communication.

- Engage the student in a familiar routine, like using the computer. Interrupt the activity (e.g., turn the computer off) and wait for the student to protest.
- Eat a desired food item in front of the student without offering to share.
- Pass out materials to each student in the class. Walk past the student without giving him the materials. Make sure the student's peers understand the plan so they do not intervene.
- Begin a favorite video, play for 5 minutes, and then turn off without an explanation.
- Engage the student in an activity with a substance that can be easily spilled (or dropped, broken, or torn); suddenly spill some of the substance on the student's desk or table in front of the student and walk away. Observe and wait.
- Offer the student a food item or object that he or she dislikes.
- Place a required item in a clear container that the student cannot open; then put the container in front of the student and wait.
- Engage the student in a group project that requires materials. After the student begins to work, offer her an item that is not related to the project without explanation.
- Give the student materials for an activity of interest that requires the use of an object for completion (e.g., pair of scissors, thermometer, lab scale); keep the object out of the student's reach and wait.
- Involve the student in an activity that requires the use of an object for completion (e.g., pen, scissors, stapler, calculator); have a peer come over and take the object and then leave for the other side of the classroom while holding the object within the student's sight, and wait.

Encourage Independence

Self-determining behavior improves the student's self-esteem. The student is exercising control over his behavior when he learns through experience. It also helps improve the student's image in the eyes of his peers. He is seen as competent and capable of learning from mistakes.

Many learning opportunities naturally occur when students are allowed to just hang out, make some mistakes, find their own solutions, and choose how to respond to their peers on their own terms. Isn't that the way we played with our friends growing up? We didn't have our mothers or teachers by our side prompting us on how to act or what to say when we played with our friends. We just played, told silly jokes, and talked about the girl next door who liked to tattle on us all the time. Support is important; however, allow students with ASD to decide whom they wish to connect with as well.

Opportunities for students to communicate and learn from one another are likely missed if adults continuously hover around them. Student interactions increase as peers become more comfortable and skilled at interacting with the student with ASD. The presence of an adult in close proximity acts as a symbolic barrier to communication and friendship (Malmgren & Causton-Theoharis, 2006). If possible, stay out of the way to allow natural interactions to develop.

Royce's Story

"Royce" hardly spoke the first week of school and our staff was cautious. Reports from elementary school detailed a pattern of violence and aggressive behavior toward staff and other students, including throwing objects across the room, biting, kicking, and high-pitched screaming. To prevent Royce from throwing his chair across the room, his previous teacher placed weights on the chair's legs.

How could we end this pattern of behavior? We brainstormed possible reasons for his aggressive acts. Thoughts centered on his former classroom setting, a segregated classroom for students with autism. Opportunities to engage in activities with typical peers were extremely limited. His primary contacts were other students with ASD and instructional assistants who disliked Royce. It became clear that Royce needed opportunities to communicate and interact with typical peers. He needed to be out of a segregated placement.

We started including Royce in general education settings with staff and peer support. We set up planned encounters using a communication book his parents prepared. Royce responded positively to these interactions. He communicated details about the pictures in his book. He enjoyed sharing with typical kids. We could see he especially liked girls. We used communication temptations and learned that Royce had a sense of humor! Because Royce felt very uncomfortable with face-to-face communication, we used a laptop computer to convey and share information. Sitting side-by-side, Royce and a peer typed messages back and forth. From these experiences, we learned a lot about his interests and hobbies. The information gained provided more topics for conversation. We learned he loved to fish, and on one family vacation, Royce caught seven trout while his brother caught one. We called his mother to verify what Royce shared with us and she was astounded that we were able to learn so much about Royce through shared keyboarding. (Author)

Knowing Royce needed a means to reduce tactile sensitivity, we included him in regular physical education class. During the square dance unit, we trained female peers on least intrusive prompting strategies to help Royce find his way through the square dance maneuvers. This strategy was highly successful in reducing his aggressive behaviors and tactile sensitivity.

We learned a lot from Royce. Opportunities to interact with typical peers coupled with a change to a less restrictive setting provided Royce with what he needed: opportunities to interact and enjoy the same kinds of experiences as his typical peers. We did not experience a single chair-throwing incident after the first month of school. His mother informed us in February that for the first time in his life, Royce wanted to have a birthday party. Every past birthday, his Mom would ask and Royce would say no. On Royce's 13th birthday, we all gathered at the local bowling alley and enjoyed cake, bowling, and laughs. In addition to his mother and father, his entire family attended—both sets of grandparents, his brother and aunts and uncles—along with several of his classmates. Since that first party, we have celebrated each year. The number of people attending keeps getting bigger, too!

SUMMARY

Communication is the defining challenge for many students with ASD. Communication challenges vary greatly in scope and intensity from individual to individual. Some students possess the ability to use spoken language but struggle with the "give and take" of typical conversations. Others remain unspeaking throughout their lives. Lacking a reliable means of communication causes some individuals to resort to inappropriate behavior to express what they need. When frustration builds, they may act out physically. The words needed to express what they need are missing. Compounding this frustration is the real possibility they will be misunderstood and, worse, mistreated by the adults and peers in their lives.

It's important to realize that the inability to communicate influences everything else. Therefore, when we help the student develop his communication system, we help make school a less threatening and frustrating place. Teachers must constantly seek opportunities for students to communicate. This includes learning the diverse ways the student expresses himself and watching and listening for opportunities for the student to connect with his neurotypical peers.

Communication is a complex process involving multiple levels of incoming information in the form of words, gestures, tone of voice, and body language. The more we do to bridge the communication gap, the less likely it is that the student will resort to inappropriate behavior.

An important part of bridge building is educating and informing typically developing peers and staff about autism as a diagnosis coupled with an understanding of the person's interests, talents, and capacities. This two-pronged approach—person-centered information mixed with ASD-specific information—will help demystify the diagnosis and open the doors to a better and more understanding relationship with peers and adults. Studies show that when peers learn that the student with ASD shares similar interests and qualities with themselves, they are more likely to accept the student (Campbell, 2007).

Finally, understand the challenges students with ASD experience with perspective taking and empathy. When you can "relate" to others, and understand their thoughts and feelings, you establish a connection that can lead to satisfying interpersonal communication and friendship. Individuals diagnosed with ASD need support in learning to relate to the thoughts and feelings of others. As a result, communication and social awareness can be developed. Keep this important concept in mind and work with the student to understand others.

RESOURCES

Resources A–J: Inclusion Support Resources

These assessment blueprints help evaluate inclusive practices across school settings (i.e., general education classroom, physical education class, recess, and lunch period). In addition, the roles and responsibilities of teachers, instructional assistants, and inclusion support personnel are defined.

Resource L: Social Engagement Observation Charting

This useful form allows you to measure social interactions across settings. The easy-to-understand coding system ensures accurate recording of observations over time.

Resources M and N: Assessment of Student Participation in General Education Settings are forms that track several areas of classroom behavior and social skills. Use these helpful tools when pondering under what circumstances student challenges may occur.

FURTHER READING

Farrell, S. C. T. (2009). *Talking, listening, and teaching: A guide to classroom communication.* Thousand Oaks, CA: Corwin.

Gangwer, T. (2009). *Visual impact, visual teaching: Using images to strengthen learning* (2nd ed.). Thousand Oaks, CA: Corwin.

Goldstein, H., Kaczmarek, L. A., & English, K. M. (2002). *Promoting social communication: Children with developmental disabilities from birth to adolescence.* Baltimore, MD: Paul H. Brookes.

Koegel, R. L., & Koegel, L. (2006). *Pivotal response treatments for autism: Communication, social & academic development.* Baltimore, MD: Paul H. Brookes.

Young, S. B. (2010). *Teaching with the tools kids really use: Learning with web and mobile technologies.* Thousand Oaks, CA: Corwin.

5

Friendship and Belonging

High school was torture for me. I was the weirdo all the "cool" kids teased. When I crossed the parking lot, they would yell "Bones!" because I was skinny, and "Tape Recorder!" because I was always repeating myself.

(Grandin, as cited in Ledgin, 2002, p. ix)

Friendship and belonging are critical to a student's development and form the basis for a healthy self-concept. Think back on your own experiences growing up. Most of us remember the middle and high school years as a time when we were acutely aware of ourselves in relation to others. We wanted to be cool and fit in. We were sensitive about how we looked and what our peers thought of us. We participated in school and community activities and through these experiences made friends. We were attracted to peers who communicated joy and pleasure. Their upbeat and enthusiastic personalities made them "fun to be around." They were interested in us, and over time, strong bonds developed, lasting in some cases for years after graduation.

For students diagnosed with ASD, a different school experience emerges. Many struggle to make friends and are often found alone. When opportunities to share experiences and make friends are limited, the student misses out on the most exciting and rewarding aspect of the social world: the extensive personal research and self-discovery by which typical adolescents gain expertise at relationship building and maintenance (Gutstein & Whitney, 2002).

Figure 5.1 Promote Acceptance and Belonging

Research suggests that ongoing relationships with peers have a substantial impact on the lives of adolescents. Through these relationships, adolescents practice and refine social skills, share activities, enjoy companionship, and learn peer norms and values (e.g., Hartup, 1999; Rubin, Bukowski, & Parker, 1998). As students get older, they spend proportionately more time with their peers, intensifying the influence of peer interaction on adolescent development (Hartup & Stevens, 1997). As a result, educational researchers view adolescent friendship development as an important component of inclusive education.

Despite the value of typical peer relationships, students with ASD cannot enjoy the rich and fulfilling social lives they need without a supportive school culture. In addition to student-specific challenges, many attitudinal and systemic barriers exist preventing meaningful and lasting friendship development.

The purpose of this chapter is to raise your awareness of the existing barriers to meaningful friendship formation and explore strategies to help overcome these barriers. Although we can't force friendships among students, we can help create conditions where friendship and acceptance are taught, promoted, and experienced. We can develop a school climate where the entire school community—students, teachers, administrators, staff, and parents—share the goal of nurturing each other in an atmosphere of acceptance and understanding.

BARRIERS TO FRIENDSHIP

Why do so many students with ASD struggle to make friends? If we know in our heart the student is likable, then why do her peers fail to see the same qualities and befriend her?

Tashie and Rossetti (2004) state, "The problem is a by-product of the attitudinal and educational barriers that continue to view students with disabilities in general as perpetual receivers of help. Descriptors like "less fortunate," "low functioning," "needy," "special," and "handicapped" continue to perpetuate this view. Students are unfairly viewed as tragic or lesser human beings "suffering" from their diagnosis. Out of this sense of pity comes unequal treatment and lowered expectations.

Despite a sincere desire to end the false perceptions and social isolation experienced by many students, there is still a tendency in schools to base support decisions on these broader misperceptions. Instead of seeking ways for students to connect through shared interests and common experiences, students with ASD are still segregated into separate groups. Friendship development is limited to "buddy clubs" that perpetuate unequal relationships. The typical student develops an attitude of "I who am competent and normal am helping you, the perpetually needy" (Kunc & Van der Klift, 1994).

Students with disabilities candidly report that many educational practices in schools, including schools considered inclusive, create symbolic barriers to friendship development. Studies cite the continued use of pull-out services, segregated placements, and the overreliance on adult support as contributing factors that further stigmatize the student in the eyes of his peers (Broer, Doyle, & Giangreco, 2005). We can overcome attitudinal barriers preventing the development of meaningful relationships if we understand the causes of these barriers and use strategies to minimize them.

Detrimental Effects of Adult Proximity

Students, especially during the middle and high school years, value their independence. They want to be seen as competent in the eyes of their peers. Too much help can be a disabling force interfering with friendship development and independence.

Studies show that student independence and self-esteem are compromised by the presence of an overindulgent adult hovering over the student during class. Overreliance on adult support can act as a symbolic barrier to natural peer interactions while inadvertently depriving the student of his right to independence and self-determination (Giangreco & Broer, 2007; Giangreco, Yuan, McKenzie, Cameron, & Fialka, 2005). Teachers who are assigned instructional assistants must balance their desire to assign direct support with the student's right to determine how and when support is given.

Teaching academic content cannot interfere with promoting independence and self-determination. Student dignity must not be forfeited for the sake of receiving help. The power to decide where and when help should be given, who should help, and whether in fact help is needed should not be taken away from the student. Self-reliance and personal responsibility won't develop if the adult is hovering over the student or sitting by his side to ensure full participation.

Figure 5.2 Overzealous Support

Let's examine some of the issues related to the helper-helpee trap discouraged in the literature. Giangreco, Edelman, Luiselli, and MacFarland (1997) conducted research focused on the effects of adult support across several schools and classroom settings. The following unintended detrimental effects were observed:

- Peers often held back direct engagement with the student when the instructional assistant was in close proximity.
- Instructional assistants often positioned students away from typical peers. They were observed leaving class early with students, thus preventing social contact even more.
- Students were overhelped, and prompting was seldom faded. As a result, students became prompt-dependent, relying on adults more than necessary.
- Instructional assistants frequently interfered with peer interactions. They interrupted conversations between the student and his peers

and dominated group activities. As a result, peers developed the perception that supported students were needy and incompetent.

• Instructional assistants frequently distracted class instruction, especially when starting an alternate activity with the supported student in the midst of a whole-group activity.

Giangreco and Doyle (2004) state,

Uninformed paraprofessional support and over help can interfere with peer relationships, and appropriate personal control. Inappropriate or excessive reliance on paraprofessionals can isolate the student within the classroom, establish insular paraprofessional-student relationships and create unhealthy dependencies. (p. 187)

Giangreco et al. (1997) discovered that during times when the instructional assistant was not in the classroom, peers were more likely to "fill the space the instructional assistant had vacated" (p. 13).

Be mindful of the detrimental effects of adult proximity by encouraging your instructional assistant to seek out naturally helpful peers instead of supporting the student directly. Help the instructional assistant find students you believe will be appropriate peer supporters for the student with ASD. Once the connection is made, monitor progress and encourage continued relationship development.

Pull-Out Services

Many students with ASD receive pragmatic language and social skills training to help with communication challenges stemming from the disability. These services are called *pull-out* services because the student leaves the classroom to receive the intervention. Problems arise when pull-out services interfere with in-class activities and peer interactions.

When the student is pulled out of class for services, he misses activities with his classmates while he's away. The student returns from training and rejoins the class unaware of the lesson he missed. His classmates wonder, "Where did he go?" while discussing possible reasons. "I don't know," says one student. "He went to *his* class," states another. When the student returns, his classmates are asked to explain the missed assignment while wondering why he left in the first place. Alternatively, the instructional assistant pulls the student aside to help, stigmatizing him further.

Studies show that the skills taught in pull-out sessions don't always generalize to the classroom setting (Gutstein & Whitney, 2002; Handleman, 1999; Mesibov & Lord, 1997). It's no surprise that researchers favor social skills training in natural settings over clinic-based settings. Gutstein and Whitney (2002) point out, "Without teaching within the context of meaning, there is little chance for skills to 'stick' and generalize outside the clinic setting." Despite attending social skills training, meaningful friendship development remains elusive. The student's social status continues as before, at risk for social isolation and peer victimization.

Figure 5.3 Pull-outs

Research suggests that socially isolated children may develop mental health difficulties as adults (Koegel & Koegel, 2006). Separating students from their classmates, even for short periods, can be counterproductive and should be avoided when embedded services can be developed within the classroom (Rao, Beidel, & Murray, 2008).

The ultimate goal with social skills training is for children to interact appropriately in their natural social contexts (DiSalvo & Oswald, 2002). Programmed practice in natural settings allows practice with unfamiliar adults and children (Beidel, Turner, & Morris, 2000; Krasny, Williams, Provencal, & Ozonoff, 2003) with the promise that age-appropriate friendships can develop.

Teachers and related service specialists can work together to ensure that pragmatic language and social skills training are embedded in the general education classroom. It is important to be mindful of pull-outs as a barrier to full membership in the classroom community and explore alternatives whenever possible. If your students are experiencing excessive pull-outs, discuss your concerns with the special education teacher or related service specialist.

Classroom Groupings and Peer Perceptions

Avoid seating and grouping students with autism together. When the majority of the student's social time is spent with other students with ASD, there is less opportunity for typical peer social interactions.

For students diagnosed with autism, segregated arrangements can be especially detrimental to their development. Placing students with ASD together can intensify challenging behavior and increase autistic symptoms. In the words of Dr. Philip Strain, leading researcher in the field of autism, such arrangements are "toxic" to the child's development (Strain, 2008).

The following experience helped solidify my belief in the importance of inclusion for adolescents with autism:

> *"Take a look at this picture! Aren't they cute?" our colleague beamed as she shared a special memory with us. The 3" × 5" photograph I held in my hand showed two 4-year-old boys seated together in a wheelbarrow. The picture was taken several years earlier during a preschool trip to a pumpkin patch. James and Andy, both diagnosed with autism, were now starting seventh grade. Looking at this early picture, I wondered, have these boys been together since preschool? A review of records confirmed my suspicions. Labeled autistic, they attended the autism program, always together in the same segregated placement year after year. How do they interact today? They antagonize each other. The presence of one causes anxiety in the other. Every time James makes a sound, Andy covers his ears, drops his head to his desk and screams out, "Stop it, James!" (Author)*

The first intervention we introduced into the lives of James and Andy was to separate them! For seventh grade, we scheduled the boys into different general education classes and surrounded them with typical peers. The daily routines of the classroom coupled with the presence of typical peers helped reduce the considerable anxiety the boys experienced when in the presence of each other.

Friendships develop out of shared experiences. When students work together on class projects, they must interact and cooperate to satisfy project requirements. Shared experiences provide a context for conversations, mutual respect, and friendship. Communicative competence increases and self-esteem is enhanced (Asher, Parker, & Walker, 1996; Malmgren & Causton-Theoharis, 2006).

The attitudes that typical peers develop regarding the capabilities of students with ASD strongly influence their willingness to interact with these students (Siperstein, Parker, Bardon, & Widaman, 2007). When the student is always connected to an adult or placed at a separate table with other students with disabilities, impressions are formed that the student is different, lesser, helpless, "not like us," and has little to offer on his own. These attitudes can lead to problems in and out of the classroom. Factors that discourage peer friendship include the following:

- Grouping students with autism together
- Allowing inappropriate behavior not tolerated in nondisabled students
- Using younger age materials
- Adult demeaning treatment (overhelp, Velcro aide, talking for the student)

These practices discourage typical peers from interacting with the student. Be aware how adult treatment of the student with ASD looks to his peers, especially when applying consequences for inappropriate behavior. When your expectations for behavior and performance apply equally to all students regardless of label, you serve the student with ASD well. His peers understand he is accountable and responsible for his own actions. They see that the same standards apply.

There is one important exception to this advice: If the student's behavior is out of his control, a manifestation of his disability, then alternative strategies must be employed. The determining factors: Does the student comprehend right from wrong? Is the behavior a result of sensory issues out of the student's control? For more information, see Chapter 3, Promoting Positive Behavior.

Bullying

When students are perceived as incompetent, incapable, or unintelligent there is a greater probability they will be bullied. This problem is especially concerning at the middle and high school levels where peer pressure to fit in and conform is great. Some students, in an effort to gain status from their peers, will seek recognition by bullying students they perceive as different.

Bullying can happen to academically gifted students to the same degree as it can happen to students who are intellectually challenged. The tendency for students with autism to misunderstand social encounters makes matters more challenging. Paul, a 13-year-old boy with Asperger syndrome, is an intellectually gifted and a very handsome young man. He is enrolled in honors classes at his middle school and is considered one of the top students in his class. His academic and behavioral support needs are minimal. Teachers repeatedly praise Paul for his good behavior and excellent academic performance. For the better part of the first semester, Paul seemed content. Because no concerns were brought to our attention, we assumed Paul was adjusting well to middle school. Then one day in mid-April, the poem "Paul's Lament" (Figure 5.4) was discovered by a staff member who happened to come across it in Paul's writing folder.

Bullying is an unfortunate and often tragic aspect of relationships between students, especially in middle school. Most kids are the targets of some form of abusive treatment during their school careers. Studies show that 30% of students report moderate to frequent involvement in bullying either as a victim or a perpetrator (Nansel et al., 2001). Bullying is even worse for students diagnosed with ASD. In one study, more than 400 parents of children diagnosed with ASD and other communicative disorders were surveyed about bullying. Ninety-four percent responded that a peer had bullied their child at least once during the school year (Little, 2002).

Figure 5.4 "Paul's Lament"

> ### Paul's Lament
>
> Bullies turn my happiness off, so I live with worrying.
>
> They build my hate, so I live without being safe around strangers.
>
> They paint me rude things, so I live without people knowing what I really am.
>
> They lock onto me, so I live with being a target.
>
> They take away the fact I'm smart, I live with being called a retard.
>
> They take a good day and ruin it, I live with a sore throat from yelling.
>
> They say I am gay and stupid, so I have no one who is my friend.
>
> They stop my defense, so I have no way out.
>
> They give me stupid words, so I live with idiots.
>
> They give me hate, so I live with it.
>
> They have insulted me, and I am not unhurt.
>
> They give me no reason to breathe, so I live without any fresh breath.
>
> They separate me from confidence, so I live without it.
>
> Who understands me when I say this is bad?
>
> Who understands me when I say I have not found friends?

The bullying students experience can take two forms: emotional abuse and physical abuse. Emotional abuse includes insults, teasing and name calling, threatening stares, obscene gestures, and spreading rumors about the person. Physical forms of abuse include hitting, pushing, tripping, kicking, spitting on someone, pulling hair, shouldering, and grabbing a person or their clothes or belongings. Boys are far more likely than girls to be both the targets and perpetrators of physical bullying (Olweus, 1993; Rigby, 1996). Girls are more likely to spread rumors and engage in bullying as a group (White, 2002; Wiseman, 2002). Studies show that between the ages of 8 and 14, bullying hits a peak and then tapers off in late high school (Nansel et al., 2001).

Because students with autism frequently misinterpret social cues, they miss the early signs of abuse directed at them by peers. Their naïveté opens the door for increasing and more serious mistreatment. If chronic abuse continues unchallenged, feelings of frustration and resentment can build up and then explode into physical aggression. Students with autism who experience prolonged victimization are at high risk for serious consequences, including severe anxiety, school truancy, depression, and physical health problems.

What Teachers Can Do

Awareness and proactive intervention are the best defenses against bullying behavior. If we actively help the student with friendship and belonging while educating typical peers about differences, the most serious negative consequences of bullying can be avoided. Follow these recommendations:

1. Develop a schoolwide curriculum focused on acceptance and appreciation for diversity in all its forms. Encourage classroom discussions that de-emphasize the pathology of disability in favor of understanding and appreciating the person behind the label. See "Autism Awareness" later in this chapter for more suggestions.

2. If you witness abusive behavior, stop the behavior and take appropriate disciplinary action. If you fail to act, the bully will perceive that you tacitly approve of the abuse. For victimized students, adult unresponsiveness makes them more fearful of peers. Apathy and a sense of hopelessness tend to follow (Heinrichs, 2003).

3. Pay attention and be alert for abusive behavior. Bullying is a covert activity. Many episodes are brief and verbal and occur when there is a lack of supervision (Heinrichs, 2003. p.76).

4. Gather information from students. They know who is being bullied, who the bullies are, and where the unsafe places around campus are located. Work to proactively seek out information when needed to identify the perpetrators of abuse. Work with these students to find better ways to gain status.

THE STUDENT'S ROLE IN FRIENDSHIP DEVELOPMENT

Students with autism need to be seen as likable and competent in order to make friends. There is only so much we as teachers can do. If the student is obnoxious, rude, and disrespectful; smells bad; picks his nose; dresses funny; and has poor manners, then typical peers are not going to accept him as a friend no matter how many supports we put in place. Despite the disability label, the student needs to be held accountable for behaviors and habits that get in the way of friendship and belonging. Xenia Katz, a 35-year-old woman with high-functioning autism, states,

Don't let kids get away with murder. You need to have high expectations. If you shoot for the stars, you'll get them to the stars. If you expect them to fly with eagles, they'll fly like an eagle. If you expect them to walk around on the ground like a chicken, they'll walk around on the ground like a chicken. (Hurlbutt & Chalmers, 2002)

Don't ignore inappropriate behavior in students diagnosed with ASD that you would never accept in a nondisabled student. Temple Grandin states, "Sometimes bad behavior is just bad behavior!" (personal communication, February 14, 2007). Think about what personal habits, mannerisms, and interactions with others would be considered totally unacceptable if not for the diagnosis of autism. Mindful of the student you are supporting, ask, "Is this behavior a manifestation of the disability—beyond the student's control?" If you know the student understands and can control her choices, don't expect less from her! Allowing unacceptable behavior because she has a label is fundamentally disrespectful and disempowering. If you are uncertain about what is or is not within the student's ability to control, discuss your concerns with the autism specialist or special education teacher and formulate a strategy that is person-centered and reasonable while still considering the importance of natural consequences whenever possible.

The Hidden Curriculum

The hidden curriculum is the term used to describe the unwritten social rules and expectations that most students know but were never systematically taught: things like how to dress, how to make up excuses, who to talk to, who to ignore, what to say, and what not to say. The hidden curriculum also includes understanding the difference between positive behaviors that gain approval from teachers and peers and inappropriate behaviors that are considered rude (Myles & Simpson, 2001). Students with ASD unwittingly break a lot of these rules. They're naive. It's the boy who says to his overweight aunt, "Wow, Aunt Mille, you're enormous!" While teachers vary in their expectations, certain expectations are consistent across grade levels and settings (Myles, 2005).

As teachers, we appreciate kids who follow directions, cooperate, get along with classmates, listen, complete assignments, and help out (Lane, Pierson, & Givener, 2003). Consider how your values translate into expectations for students, and then teach those expectations to the student with ASD.

Important point: Not all students with ASD are clueless about social rules. There is a wide range of competence. Some students are withdrawn, remote, socially awkward, inflexible, and flat in affect. Others are outgoing, friendly, gregarious, and enthusiastic. Keep an eye out for problems even for students who seem to "get it" most of the time. Like Paul, kids who seem well adjusted can be hiding problems from you. Pay attention to subtle cues.

Figure 5.5   Seven Personal Qualities Held in High Esteem

1. Smiling and laughing. All children enjoy seeing another child smile. It is contagious and keeps the atmosphere positive.

2. Greeting others. Encourage students to say "Hi!" to others as they pass in the hallway. It is friendly and encourages students to keep their heads up as they change classes.

3. Extending invitations. When students are leaving class together or starting an activity, encourage them to include others and to always look for additional participants.

4. Conversing. Help students understand the basic rules of communication, how to initiate a conversation and take turns, and how to interest others.

5. Sharing. No one enjoys a student who keeps things to himself. Encourage students to work together and collaborate on projects and share supplies.

6. Giving compliments. Everyone appreciates being complimented. Make a point to express appreciation when a student does a good job or shows good behavior.

7. Good appearance. Hygiene and grooming are important for self-esteem, cleanliness, and positive interactions with others.

TURNING AWKWARD ENCOUNTERS INTO TEACHABLE MOMENTS

It's like walking into a library . . . every book is different. Every feeling is a book in a big gigantic library. It's the same when looking inside someone's mind.

—Steven Kaweski

Students with ASD can stop a conversation before it gets started. The following exchange occurred at lunchtime when a nondisabled peer named Jennifer attempted to engage Vicki, a 14-year-old girl with autism, in a conversation: *Bubbly Jennifer: "Hi Vicki! How are YOU today?" Vicki: (looking down) "Fine, can you step back? I want to be left alone now, thanks."*

Some students with autism react like Vicki. Why the disinterest or discomfort with social interactions? Many students with ASD do not understand the unwritten rules of communication and are too uncomfortable to engage. Perhaps in the past, the student sought out friendship and was rejected. Regardless of a student's inclination against social encounters, developing social interaction skills is important to achieving long-term success in life (National Autism Center, 2009). Seek out opportunities for the student with ASD to share interests with an engaging peer.

Many students with ASD want to interact and make friends but are socially awkward. They laugh at inappropriate times, out of sync with the moment. Their greetings are stiff and too formal. They talk out of context in conversations. They encroach on the personal space of their peers. The following exchange took place during lunch at the start of a new school year. It serves to illustrate the type of communication breakdown that occurs when an unskilled, socially active student with ASD enters a conversation. A group of boys are talking about the high school football season:

> *Isaac: "I don't know how our team is going to pull it out this season with all the injuries. "Dirk: "Yeah, dude, it's not lookin' good!" Enter Jim, a student with Asperger's syndrome: "Do you have a ceiling fan?" Dirk, looking confused: "Say what? . . . huh? . . . uh . . . yeah, we have one." Jim: "Four blades or five?" Dirk (slightly amused): "It has five blades, man," as he turns in mock amusement to Isaac. Jim, who doesn't notice this slight aside, persists, "Does it rotate clockwise or counterclockwise?" Isaac interrupts, slightly annoyed: "Look, dude, we're talkin' football!" Jim, missing the tone of voice and body language the boys are showing, asks, "Is your washing machine a front loader or a top loader?" (Author)*

The teacher can aid the student's developing communication by making certain that communication breakdowns become lessons in conversation. After an exchange like the previous example, discuss the communication breakdown with the student. Help him or her understand what happened and offer suggestions for joining a conversation in the future.

Discuss strategies with the student's peers to help them better understand the student's challenges and how to help. Enlist their support by planning future encounters to allow the student more opportunities to practice skills. By doing so, you can turn awkward encounters into teachable moments.

Brian's Crush

Brian, a 14-year-old with ASD, was strongly attracted to a classmate named Victoria. During lunch, he would sit in close proximity to her. Brian's expressive speech is limited. In order to express himself, he sketched drawings of scenes from Disneyland showing Victoria holding his hand while standing in line for a ride.

Brian's parents discovered folders on their computer filled with pictures Brian downloaded off the Internet to share with Victoria. They contained his plans—in the form of visual images—for a dream trip to Disneyland, Paris, with Victoria! His pictures showed rides they would take and where they would stay. He could not verbally share this dream trip with her, so instead he created drawings and collected images on the computer to express his thoughts.

> *Despite his limited verbal abilities, Brian still had dreams like everyone else. His drawings and computer imagery were his means of expressing them. I realized yet again that children with autism seek to connect with classmates. Many forms of behavior are rooted in a strong desire to connect with others. (Author)*

Hygiene and Dress

Grooming, personal hygiene, and appropriate dress are common challenges for students with ASD. Unusual responses to sensory input and tactile sensitivity can cause individuals with ASD to avoid bathing and showering, washing and brushing hair, cleaning teeth, and changing clothes. Some individuals with ASD report that showering feels like standing under a hailstorm. For others, the texture of the washcloth is too rough or the smell of the soap is too strong. Clothing tags and elastic bindings can be intolerable. So, too, are clothes that are too stiff or too tight.

Some students with ASD do not consider fashion trends when choosing their clothes for the day. This can be a problem if the student is 14 but dresses like a 7-year-old. It's also a problem when the student chooses clothes that reveal too much. Clothing is chosen for comfort over style. This will help explain why some students insist on wearing the same clothes every day. These issues affect the student's appearance and interfere with the ability to make friends.

Here's one idea to consider: Ask popular, typically developing peers to serve as "fashion consultants" to the student with ASD. Enlist the help of the student's parents by requesting that they check to see how their son or daughter is dressed in the morning. Allow choice within acceptable parameters.

Figure 5.6   How Not to Act!

FROM BARRIERS TO BEST PRACTICES

Increase Teacher Engagement

Avoid the perception that adult supports in the classroom are only present to help the student with ASD. If there is an instructional assistant assigned to your classroom, encourage the person to support all students. Make yourself available to all students in the class. Encourage the instructional assistant to circulate around the room, giving help without respect to disability label. By doing this, we enhance the perception that everyone is treated equally while developing positive relationships with all students.

Studies demonstrate that teacher engagement is one of the most important contributors to student success in general education settings (Giangreco, Broer, & Edelman, 2001). Whether the student with autism is completely independent and working at grade level or needs substantial instructional accommodations, she needs an interested and engaged teacher.

With patience and gentle persistence, you will develop an appreciation for the unique qualities of the student with ASD. Positive rapport with the student contributes to successful inclusion. Giangreco (2003) states, "When teachers embrace the challenge of making the classroom a welcoming and instructionally vibrant place for all of their students, they often report that it has transformed and invigorated their teaching" (p. 1).

Avoid "The Training Trap"

Don't minimize your central role in support of students with autism because you are not an autism expert! In what Giangreco (2003) calls "The Training Trap," classroom teachers too often limit their engagement with students with disabilities because they erroneously believe they are not qualified to adequately support the students' educational needs. Not true! Don't relinquish your educational responsibilities to the instructional assistant, in essence the least qualified support personnel, just because she is assigned to the student and is "trained." Teachers have advanced degrees and years of experience. You, the professional educator, are the expert! Although training enhances the instructional assistants' ability to carry out their duties and responsibilities, it is not sufficient to prepare them to perform the instructional duties that are rightfully the responsibility of the classroom teacher. Support the principle that the instructional assistant is there to support your efforts to educate the entire class, not take control of one student's education. Most teachers are far better trained to educate a student with a disability than are most instructional assistants.

> Many students without disabilities struggle to learn. Having two adults in the classroom can improve outcomes for students who would otherwise fail without additional help. Instead of placing the aide in the position of personal assistant for one student, use him or her as a whole-class aide in support of all students in the class. See the Teaching Adolescents With Autism companion website online at www .corwin.com/adolescentautism

Enlist the Experts: Kids as Partners

As much as possible, avoid taking the student out of the classroom for extra help. Use natural supports by enlisting the help of nondisabled peers. Students naturally like to help each other. Analyze the social dynamics of the class and learn how typical kids support each other. Identify the students who are naturally helpful, and then encourage them to partner with the student with ASD.

Figure 5.7 Friendship Beyond the Classroom

Important point: Kids are the most underutilized resource in schools. By trying to be the social skills professional, we ignore the real experts, typically developing kids. For adults, it is impossible to truly know what it is like to be a middle or high school student today. It has been a long time since many of us were 13 years old (thank goodness!). The solution to this lack of connection is right there before our eyes. Classes are filled with students brimming with ideas, suggestions, and unique answers to our concerns. It is extremely valuable to receive and give information. Ask students for their perspective and share information about the student's strengths and needs.

The student's peers can provide valuable insight about what friendship is like for students their age. They can tell you how they meet, where they go, what they do, and why they like to hang out together. They can help you sort out how kids decide they want to get together, how they make time for one another, and what they consider fun. Typical peers can tell you who the student with ASD wants to spend time with. They can serve as insiders who help connect one student to another. They can share when it's appropriate for adults to step in to help and when natural peer-to-peer supports are more appropriate.

When you can't figure out how to get Cody out with some of his peers at lunch, ask the kids, "Hey guys, I'm not sure how to get Cody involved with his friends. Got any ideas?" or "I don't know what to do! I'm 47. What do you guys think?" We have learned from talks like this that typical kids have friendship problems too. Build bridges with peer groups by finding an insider. It's always better to be brought into a group by an insider than to be placed in it by an outsider.

Studies show that students with ASD benefit from involvement in activities with typical kids. In fact, significantly more social behaviors occur when students with ASD participate in cooperative learning groups, social groups during lunch and recess, and tutoring programs than for students who just receive support in social skills groups (Kamps et al., 2002).

Including students with ASD in social groups and asking kids for advice is a good start. To further relationship building, it helps to share information that will help peers better understand the student. Typical peers need to understand how he communicates, what his passions and talents are, and what causes discomfort and anxiety.

We tend to connect to others with traits and interests similar to ours (Campbell, 2007). If peers learn that the student with ASD is a lot like them, they will be more willing to accept the student. When facilitating peer support, ask yourself, "How can I help peers see the student as competent?" If we don't provide helpful information, students will form their own conclusions. Be open to peer questions and reactions and offer capacity-driven explanations. The important point to remember is this: Always be cognizant of how the student with ASD is perceived by other students. Develop an understanding beyond the context of autism. Assume competence—and then find opportunities for the student to demonstrate her talents. If the student is especially talented in art, make sure she has opportunities to display her creations.

Join Up! Promote Group Membership

It has been said that a person needs to meet 10,000 people in order to meet one friend. Students with autism need multiple chances to meet that one special friend. Encourage students to join groups based on a common interest. Sports teams, clubs, service groups, Boy and Girl Scouts, and church youth groups all provide great opportunities to connect and make friends. Shared interests form a foundation for friendship development. Many students with ASD are experts in their special interest. Is there a club that matches that interest? Can we dream up a way that a match could be created? Friendships developed around shared interests are genuine and can be lasting.

Figure 5.8   Well, It Looks Like Friendship!

Friendship Clubs

Be careful about clubs that are formed for serving the needs of students with autism. The sort of "friendship" that develops is not genuine friendship. Whenever you have two groups coming together where one is serving the needs of the other, you have a support group. There is nothing wrong with support groups! We have hundreds of them in our society: Alcoholics Anonymous, Overeaters Anonymous, and so on. The problem is, there is inequality in these types of relationships between the helper-facilitator and the helpee. There is a difference between peer support and true friendship! It is true that in the absence of friendship, peer support can sometimes lead to friendship. However, the helper-helpee relationship that develops in peer support groups can promote unequal relationships and a sense of benevolence or, worse, pity on the part of the helper. Even worse, an adult might offer a reward for helping the student with ASD. "I'll pay you to spend time with Robert." What is it called when someone is paid to be with someone? . . . Never mind!

Meaningful peer support occurs when one student helps another student just because help is needed. It's not treated as a big deal. If the focus of the relationship is reciprocity and both partners contribute, then friendship can follow. Friendship occurs when two or more people discover common interests and develop a mutually satisfying relationship. Promote reciprocal partnerships instead of helper-helpee unequal partnerships.

Be mindful of the potential risk for unequal helper-helpee relationships and unintended demeaning treatment. We don't want peers to help out of a sense of charity and then gain status as "caregivers." The student with ASD does not need charity. Typical peers need to make authentic connections based on common interests, hobbies, and experiences. They need to understand and accept the person behind the label.

The Anime Club

"We need a sponsor for our Anime Club. Would you, Mr. K?" The group of seventh and eighth graders, clustered together at lunch, stared up at me with hopeful anticipation. They were an eclectic mix of girls and boys, good kids, looking for a way to fit in somehow. Anastasia spoke up. She, the de facto president, projected confident authority. "We promise you . . . no hassles. Just need a place and a sponsor." As I mull this over, it occurs to me . . . Elaina and Jon, students with autism, like anime too. . . . Then I realize . . . an authentic social group! "Okay, I'll do it!" The first meeting is a cacophony of laughter, stories, lots of talk, and more talk about all things anime. In the middle of all this sits Elaina, sharing in the fun. Jon is playing some card game with Ms. President. Elaina makes friends with three girl members. They trade cell phone numbers and attend a weekend anime convention together. Looking back, I'm glad I agreed to sponsor. By filling a need, a group is formed and friendships develop. (Author)

Classroom Support Through Keen Observation

Closely observing how students treat each other in the classroom is an important part of your support responsibility. Every class has its own social dynamic. Who seems like the sort of student who can be a great friend? How are the seats arranged? Are disruptive students seated in close proximity? Can the student be moved to a different place in the room next to students who are supportive and nurturing?

There are qualities to look for in students who tend to be valuable peer supporters. Find students who are trusted and respected by their peers. These are the key students with a reputation for being smart due to their grades and comments in class. They are generally compliant with school rules and socially astute. They like the student with ASD and are genuinely interested in being a friend. Students who respect differences and enjoy the way persons with ASD view the world are your best candidates (Myles & Simpson, 2003).

Autism Awareness

Providing details to typical peers about the student's diagnosis is a controversial issue. Information must not be student specific unless the parent has given express permission to do so. The student's right to privacy must be respected. Carefully stated information can help peers understand the student's personality profile. Studies show that typical peers are more likely to accept a student with autism if they know the student shares similar interests and characteristics. The question is, how do you balance the need for information to bridge understanding with the student's right to confidentiality?

"Mrs. Allen, why does Hiromi rock back and forth?" The information that is shared must be discussed on a case-by-case basis, mindful of the student's right to confidentiality and the parents' wishes.

> ### Autism Myth
>
> "Children with autism cannot learn social skills."
>
> ### Fact
>
> Children with autism can learn social skills if they are included in classrooms with typical peers instead of segregated by disability label. Social skills training can also help when embedded in typical age-appropriate experiences with nondisabled peers.

Hold the Student in High Esteem

How the student with ASD is perceived and treated by adults strongly influences how his peers regard him. Be a role model for students and other adults at school by conveying through your language and actions that all students are valued. Use respectful language that emphasizes the student's strengths and talents. For example, Robert is a 14-year-old who is interested in girls and has an incredible talent for art. Don't refer to the student as "that autistic boy, Robert."

Talk to and with the student in an age-appropriate manner. If there is an issue that needs to be discussed with the class, preserve the student's dignity and work to reduce misunderstandings.

Use language that minimizes autism as pathology as much as possible. Avoid characterizations that demean the student or infer the student is ill, broken, lesser, or handicapped. False charity and benevolence do not serve the student's long-term best interests well. The unfortunate result is that lots of children and adults with disabilities like autism have scores of amateur and professional caregivers, but no friends in their lives.

Peers will be more likely to view the student as a respected and contributing member of the class when he is characterized as competent and talented. When adults model the belief that the student is not deficient, but simply "marches to the beat of a different drummer," then students are more likely to understand and accept the student. One of the many great things about kids is their willingness to accept diversity. Share enthusiastically the student's successes. Brag about the student in a sincere manner. Joke around with the student and treat him the same way you do students without disabilities.

Know and respect the student as a person. No matter what strategies the teacher decides to use to promote respect and friendship, they are meaningless unless the student is treated on equal terms with his nondisabled peers.

It is challenging to promote friendship for someone with whom you do not have a close relationship. Get to know the student. What is her story? What are her interests and dreams? What does she like? What does she dislike? What are her gifts and strengths? How does she spend her time? Who are the people in her life? What supports does she require? Can they be accomplished with help from typical peers? Most important, what does she want? Let her dreams and desires fuel the process. She is the focus. Start by helping her achieve what she wants and with whom she wants. If strategies are born out of the student's needs and interests, chances are the outcome will be student centered.

SUMMARY

Friendship and belonging are critical to a student's development and form the basis for a healthy self-concept. Students with ASD in particular need and deserve full access to the social, academic, and emotional world of their typical peers. As we have stated, students diagnosed with ASD struggle with social and emotional challenges that affect their experiences with their nondisabled peers. It is essential that despite these challenges, these students receive opportunities to socialize. Your awareness of this important need coupled with support from administration and teachers can be of great help in changing the status quo.

Situations like the many examples in this chapter perpetuate a false belief that has existed in schools and organizations for years. The peer pressure that "you must be like us in order to belong" is a long-held and deep-seated belief that is hard to reverse without informed interventions from teachers and support staff. This belief places the responsibility for changing the status quo on the person with ASD rather than identifying and then removing the barriers to acceptance, friendship, and belonging that prevent kids from having meaningful relationships.

Use the strategies in this chapter. Promote natural peer supports. Hold the student in high esteem and encourage teacher engagement. Teach the student's typical peers about how similar the student is to them. Minimize inaccurate stereotypical characterizations of autism that unfairly marginalize the student by actively working to promote friendship and belonging.

RESOURCES

Resources A–K: Inclusion Support Desired Outcomes is an 11-part set of assessment tools designed to measure the effectiveness of support practices across settings: the general education classroom, physical education class, recess, and lunch period. Based on recommended support practices, these assessment tools provide a valuable blueprint for delivering support and encouraging friendship across settings.

Resource L: Social Engagement Observation Charting
This useful form allows you to measure social interactions across settings. The easy-to-understand coding system ensures accurate recording of observations over time.

Resources M and N: Assessment of Student Participation in General Education Settings is a rubric that tracks several areas of classroom behavior and social skills.

Resource O: Student Profile
This is designed to create a snapshot of the student for general education teachers and other staff responsible for support.

FURTHER READING

The Gray Center for Social Learning and Understanding
    http://www.thegraycenter.org/
Howley, M., & Arnold, E. (2005). *Revealing the hidden social code: Social stories for people with autistic spectrum disorders.* London: Jessica Kingsley.
Moss, H. (2010). *Middle school: The stuff nobody tells you about: A teenage girl with high-functioning autism shares her experiences.* Shawnee Mission, KS: Autism Asperger Publishing Co.
Moyes, R. A. (2001). *Incorporating social goals in the classroom: A guide for teachers and parents of children with high functioning autism and Asperger's syndrome.* London: Jessica Kingsley.

6

Understanding Support

Successful Strategies for Supporting Diverse Learning Needs

Complexity creates confusion, simplicity focus.

Edward de Bono

Learning can be a complex process in which the student's learning style, experiences, values, and levels of interest affect the learning process. Each student responds to and interprets new information uniquely. Despite these complexities, a great teacher has the ability to spark student interest and the desire to learn. Great teachers make learning contagious. They create the desire in students to be lifelong learners, to ask questions, and to be curious. In order to do this, barriers to learning must be removed.

For many teachers, the thought of having a student with a disability in their class seems a completely unrealistic concept. Yet these same teachers are often unaware of the possible minor adaptations that could be made in the classroom to accommodate the needs of students with disabilities (Kunc, 1984). Educational research over the past three decades has produced a wealth of information for supporting the needs of struggling learners. The ability to adjust instruction to the needs of struggling learners is a valuable skill. Hopefully, this chapter will help expand your toolbox of ideas.

INTRODUCTION TO ADAPTATIONS

Not all students learn in the same way. Academic achievement is dependent on the student's ability to understand lesson content and apply new knowledge and skills in meaningful ways. When instructional delivery and materials create barriers to student learning, teachers develop adaptations to increase student access to instructional content. Adaptations can improve student outcomes by reducing conditions in the learning environment that interfere with learning.

Some adaptations are as simple as moving a student to the front of the class away from distractions. Other adjustments include modifying content (size, difficulty), time and pacing (more or less), type of support (peer, teacher, or instructional assistant), type of input (paper-and-pencil, word processor, visual aids, concrete examples, hands-on activities), and output (questions answered verbally, creative projects that demonstrate knowledge). The objective is to create conditions where the learning process aligns with the student's learning style to create the conditions for optimal growth.

Accommodations

Accommodations change how information is presented and how students demonstrate learning without reducing grade-level standards. Accommodations can include changes in instructional format, materials, time allowances, presentation of teaching materials, task demands, and level of staff and peer support. Tests and quizzes are modified to accommodate how the student best demonstrates knowledge. If the student struggles with pencil-and-paper tasks, a word processor may be used. Prompting strategies and physical assistance can be provided, mindful of the student's need for independence.

Modifications

Modifications are age-appropriate changes in the depth and difficulty level of instructional content. Content and task completion are simplified to match the student's level of understanding without compromising the student's dignity. Strategies used allow the student to participate with typical peers in classroom learning experiences.

Modifications may include changes in the instructional level, content, and performance requirements of lessons. The range of modifications required can vary from slight to significant depending on the student's intellectual functioning. Examples include alternative books or materials on the same theme or topic, word processor spell-check, word bank choices for answers to test questions, use of a calculator on a math test, questions reworded using simpler language, and key words and phrases highlighted.

Make Content Understandable

- Build background information and preteach vocabulary.
- Connect the lesson to the student's personal and cultural experience.

- Give the student the opportunity to choose the test format (i.e., written or oral).
- Break down concepts and key points that lead to the "big idea."
- Figure out the essential concepts students need to know and the steps to get there.
- Place a priority on practice as a means of mastering skills. Use educational software to aid lesson understanding. Give the student a chance to redo assignments.
- Provide visual support (graphic organizers, timelines, flowcharts, and pictures).

DESIGNING APPROPRIATE ADAPTATIONS

Deciding what adaptations to use depends on three factors: the age of the student, lesson objectives, and the student's needs. If a student struggles with abstract concepts, provide visual supports like graphic organizers and pictures to make the abstract concrete. Effective adaptations are age appropriate and promote successful class participation without stigmatizing the student. For example, *Sesame Street* Big Bird flash cards are not appropriate for teenagers. Effective adaptations need to be simple to make! As a teacher, you support numerous students in the course of your instructional day. Who has time to sit for hours contemplating a complex adaptation that may not work? The truth is, there is very little time to write adaptations!

SIMPLE = GOOD

If you remember one thing from this chapter, let it be this advice: Simple is almost *always* better. Consider the following "SPECIAL" suggestions when an adaptation must be made. Effective adaptations are . . .

Simple: If the adaptation is complicated and time-consuming, it's most likely not "doable" and is less likely to be implemented. Adaptations should be simple to create and use.

Practical: Consider our limited time and funds. For example, rewriting math word problems and spending hours rewriting pages of text may be desirable in helping a student read and understand, but the feasibility of rewriting texts week in and week out is not practical.

Explicit: Successful adaptations have a definite purpose and are easy to understand and use. They are explicit and direct.

Community Building: The adaptation recognizes and builds in opportunities for students to interact. Students with autism need to belong and make friends. The adaptation should never result in segregation away from peers. Good adaptations also encourage . . .

Independence Promoting: Mindful of the importance of self-determination for the person as they grow into adulthood, adaptations should lead to independence and be faded as soon as practical. Adaptations should also be . . .

Age Appropriate: The ideal adaptation capitalizes on the student's strengths while neutralizing the student's challenges. Adaptations should also be . . .

Logical and meaningful: Successful adaptations seem natural to the setting. They do not place undue attention on the student with ASD because they make sense and are logical to the time, place, and activity. They are meaningful for the student, not potentially embarrassing. The adaptation should be a normal part of the classroom routine.

STUDENT-CENTERED INSTRUCTION

When a student fails to learn, the responsibility for the failure is sometimes directed at the student. The teacher assumes the student is not capable; that he lacks the prerequisite background knowledge; or that he is lazy, disinterested, or not intellectually capable of learning the subject matter.

For inexperienced teachers, the thought of having a student with a disability in their class brings feelings of uncertainty and discomfort. "It's unrealistic," the thinking goes, for certain students to be included in general education classes. Yet these same teachers are less hesitant to accept students with diverse learning needs if introduced to the variety of adaptations and modifications possible to make learning "realistic" (Kunc, 1984).

Teachers who understand the diverse learning styles of their students focus their instructional practices on student needs, abilities, interests, and learning styles. Instead of validating false assumptions, limiting perceptions and attitudes, they focus on student-centered planning. They are willing to adjust instruction to accommodate student needs.

Student-centered instruction starts at the student's instructional level and builds on his capacities and strengths. Build supports around his areas of challenge while seeking ways for the student to demonstrate competence. Many times, all that is needed are minor curricular adaptations to remove obstacles that interfere with learning. For example, if the student struggles with reading, use pictures and graphics to bridge the gap in understanding.

Study the "Eight Questions to Consider" that follow as a starting point for determining the level of participation appropriate for the student. As we progress down the list, the student is engaging in less typical activities and experiences. Keep in mind that some level of participation in the general education setting is better than not participating at all. Think of the student with ASD as a typical student and only provide adaptations when needed to allow meaningful participation. If the student can participate without support, then encourage independence. Consider the student's learning profile from a capacity rather than deficit perspective and dwell on possible ways the student can benefit from instruction with and without support.

EIGHT QUESTIONS TO CONSIDER

1. Can the student do the same lesson as typical peers, with the same objectives, using the same materials?

   Yes! (no adaptations required) The student is involved in the same lesson as other students, has the same objectives, and is using the same materials.

   If Not—

2. Can the student do the same activity with adapted materials?

   Yes! Use materials that allow for participation in age-appropriate activities without having "prerequisite" basic communication, motor, or academic skills.

   - When other students are writing book reports, John is drawing a comic strip storyline of the plot development.
   - In math, Gabe completes fewer problems and/or uses a calculator during "math minute."
   - In language arts, key details are highlighted and more time is allowed for Josiah to complete assignments and tests.

   If Not—

3. Can the student do the same activity with physical assistance?

   Yes! Then the student is assisted to complete activities by the actual manipulation of materials, equipment, or his or her body.

   - Andrew wears headphones to block out classroom sounds that distract him from the learning activity.
   - Melissa rocks in a rocking chair to help her focus on reading.
   - James uses a MotivAider™ (a pocket-size prompting vibrator device) to periodically remind him to refocus.
   - The literature exam is given verbally instead of in writing. The inability to write does not invalidate the student's comprehension score (Neary, Halvorsen, Kronberg, & Kelly, 1992).
   - Ali is writing a story on the computer while his classmates write at their desks with pencil and paper.
   - Michelle wears an elastic deep pressure vest to reduce stress. Sometimes a weighted tube collar helps as well.

   If Not—

4. Can the student do a similar activity with modified expectations?

   Yes! Then address the same content at a different conceptual level.

   - Brian's friend Allison adapts a book chapter for Brian by paraphrasing its content, checking readability level, and recording the final version on CD.

- While students are discussing the possible motivation for the story character's actions and thoughts, Rita is using visual cues, drawings, and written words to help her match setting and character elements from a list of choices.
- Instead of taking notes, Anne fills in the blanks on the lecture guide by choosing words from a word bank.

If Not—

5. Can the student participate in this activity, with emphasis on blended skills from other areas of development written into the IEP?

   Yes! Then develop activities that address the student's needs through the content area being taught.

   - Sarah works on small-group social skills in a cooperative learning group developing a report on ancient Egypt.
   - Robert works on the computer with reading games while his peers take a literature test.
   - During history, Nadia develops her fine motor skills while building a miniature log cabin for a history project on President Lincoln.

   If Not—

6. Can the student be with the group, but working on an activity that fulfills a different purpose?

   Yes! Provide opportunities to cooperate with peers on skill areas listed in the student's IEP.

   - Frank has a goal to cooperate with peers and follow directions without losing focus. His peers need Frank to sort out a set of materials for use in their science experiment. He is reinforced for following through with experiment preparations.
   - As the Monopoly banker, Abby counts money and makes change for players in the game.

   If Not—

7. Can the student be working in class on a separate task that is related to the priorities written into the IEP?

   Yes! Plan and prepare the lesson by considering how the IEP goal can be addressed in the regular classroom setting. Use typical peers to aid the student in learning the IEP objectives.

   - Steven is learning consonant-vowel-consonant words with help from flash cards displayed in sequence by a peer tutor, who logs responses on a data sheet (+) or (−).
   - Jamie is practicing how to pay for store merchandise using the "one dollar more" systematic instruction plan in preparation for an upcoming shopping trip to the mall.

   If Not—

8. The student should be working on life skills in or outside the class related to his or her IEP goals. Possible activities include life-skills education, community-based instruction, or workability at school

or on a job site. Supported employment can begin as early as age 16. For example,

- Jory works off campus at the roller rink to meet his critical IEP goals.
- Melinda works in the campus snack bar stocking shelves and counting merchandise.
- Tara works as a volunteer at Goodwill Industries washing donated clothing items.
- Rafael volunteers at the recycle center sorting glass into like colors.

Use the following Curriculum Adaptions Flowchart as a guide to including the student.

Figure 6.1   Curriculum Adaptations Flowchart

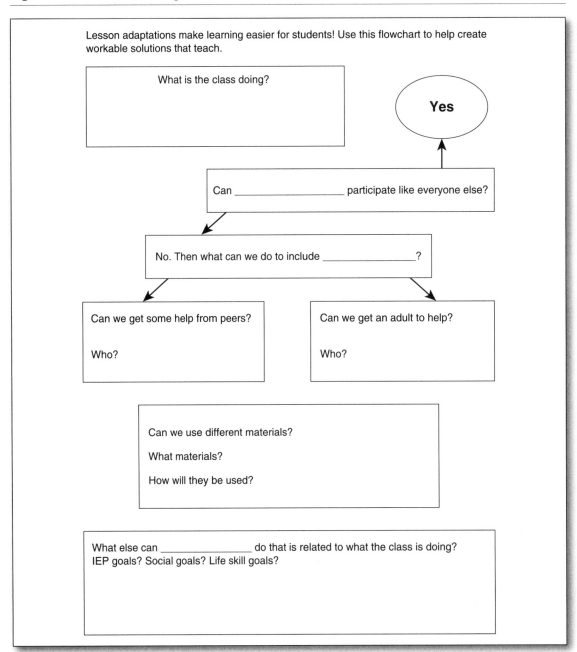

Table 6.1 Nine Adaptations

Quantity	Time	Level of Support
• Shorten task or assignment • Assign only a portion of the task • Provide credit for partial work completion • Ask the student to write key words in response to a question instead of a complete sentence • Reduce homework assignments	• Give extra time to complete tasks • Give frequent breaks • Require less time to work on frustrating tasks • Extend assignment deadlines • Provide extra time for tests • Allow more time for the student to process question before expecting a response	• Have student work cooperatively with peer • Assign a cross-age tutor or peer tutor • Provide extra help from staff • Provide positive reinforcers • Send daily or weekly progress reports home • Provide a daily assignment sheet • Facilitate regular school-home contact
Input	**Difficulty**	**Output**
• Provide visual supports • Provide additional written directions • Provide taped books or materials • Use hands-on activities and manipulatives • Provide concrete examples • Increase use of cooperative learning models • Provide prewritten notes, outline	• Use a calculator or computer • Simplify assignments and/or materials • Modify rules or expectations • Adapt skill level • Use simpler vocabulary • Provide word bank • Guide student to answer with color coding • Use matching instead of fill-in • Let student use notes for tests	• Allow verbal responses • Use multiple-choice, fill-in-the-blank, and matching instead of essay questions • Allow student to use word processing program instead of writing assignment • Underline or highlight answers instead of writing them out • Use alternate assessment
Participation	**Alternate Curriculum**	**Parallel Curriculum**
• Allow student to participate by helping others • Give alternate tasks • Allow student to participate with a partner/helper • Display student talents and capacities • Find ways to include student with peers	• Focus on IEP goals using general education activities to satisfy goals • Collaborate with special education teachers to develop alternative content goals and classwork	• Retain subject objectives but use alternate assignments appropriate for student's instructional level • Provide different instruction and materials to meet student's individual needs

Source: Adapted from Deschenes, C., Ebeling, D., & Sprague, J. (2000). *Adapting Curriculum and Instruction in Inclusive Classrooms: A Teacher's Desk Reference.* Bloomington, Indiana: The Center for School and Community Integration, Institute for the Study of Developmental Disabilities.

BLENDING IEP GOALS ACROSS SETTINGS

As we learned in Chapter 2, the IEP document is a contractual commitment between the school district and the student's parents detailing all the services and supports the student will receive. It is the collective responsibility of teachers and support staff to know the student's IEP goals and work to attain them.

Seek to support the student's IEP goals as much as possible in natural settings. Be alert for "teachable moments" that present opportunities for advancing the goals. This is easily accomplished when the IEP goal matches class assignment requirements. For example, an assigned essay can also serve to satisfy an IEP written expression goal. Vocabulary and note-taking skills can be addressed through the student's participation in a small-group history project.

The question is, how does the student accomplish goals that seem unrelated to the content of the general education class? General education settings offer numerous opportunities for the student to develop a variety of skills beyond the subject matter content.

SKILL DEVELOPMENT ACROSS SETTINGS

For students with autism, learning doesn't stop when the bell rings for lunch. Unstructured times offer valuable opportunities for social interaction and social skills development in natural settings. When the student hangs out with her peers at lunch or in between classes, she has the opportunity to develop interaction skills, personal management skills (an awareness of grooming and fashion trends), and adaptive problem solving when things don't work out as planned (e.g., learning to compromise when the student planned on playing a board game at lunch but her peers chose to walk around instead).

The school community offers multiple opportunities for the student with autism to participate alongside typical peers and learn, through the power of example and participation, a variety of life skills. The student can develop participation skills, leisure skills, domestic skills, vocational skills, independent problem-solving skills, and self-advocacy skills. Here are a few examples:

Reading Fluency

Reading fluency goals are frequently written into the IEP. The general education classroom offers numerous opportunities to read aloud. When not reading, the student benefits by tracking the words read by a fluent reader in the class. Ideas: Install a classroom suggestion box and assign the student the responsibility of reading the suggestions to the class. Ask the student to prepare a PowerPoint presentation on his topic of interest. Ask the student to draw a diagram of the class lecture or whole-group discussion. Model fluent reading for students. Use the oral CLOZE method. (Read aloud as students follow silently. Every five words, leave a word out. The students' job is to follow along and, on cue, i.e., at a snap or clap, call out the missing word in unison without missing a beat. This method is a great way to model fluent reading while compelling students to follow and respond. Monitor responses and practice the technique until the class responds on cue every time.)

Written Expression

The language arts class emphasizes note-taking skills and written expression, skills that are frequently addressed in the IEP. Ideas: Develop a class newsletter and ask students to submit articles. Ask the student to write information on the board (e.g., date, weather information, riddles, fact of the day, trivia question). Give students time to write personal notes to each other. Ask the student to write a two- or three-word note describing her impressions of the lesson. Encourage writing by tapping into the student's special interest area.

Leisure Skills

Education for students with ASD should include help in developing leisure-time activities. Participation in leisure activities can vary from full participation to partial participation, depending on the needs of the student. When searching for ways to plan for meaningful participation, consider the student's interests. Some trial and error is involved. Leisure activities include the following:

- Team sports (e.g., soccer, bowling)
- Individual sports (e.g., pool, tennis, track, swimming)
- Performing arts (e.g., music, dance, drama)
- Fine arts (e.g., ceramics, painting, sculpture)
- Attending performances (e.g., concerts, theater, movies)
- Technology (e.g., web design, Internet research, programming, blogging)
- Hobbies (e.g., photography, needlepoint, stamp and coin collecting, model building)
- Nature activities (e.g., camping, hiking, gardening)
- Participating in organized groups (e.g., church youth groups, Scouts, 4-H)
- Attending social events (e.g., dances, birthday parties, weddings, family gatherings)

Consumer Skills

Mathematics teaches the student to compute and use problem-solving skills that later translate into knowledgeable consumer skills. The student can be assigned jobs that increase student awareness of purchasing skills. For example, students can be assigned the task of analyzing the cost per ounce of various soup brands to determine the best value.

Vocational Skills

Students with autism usually require instruction in basic skills needed for the world of work. These skills are broad and overlap with several other areas. Independent adults need to have the following skills:

- Being punctual and reliable in attendance
- Following a job routine, and completing duties as assigned
- Understanding task completion
- Following safety procedures
- Accepting direction and correction
- Responding appropriately to persons in authority
- Completing a clean-up routine
- Dressing in appropriate work attire and using appropriate grooming
- Using job site leisure time appropriately (lunch, breaks)

Presentation Skills

Many classes require students to give presentations in front of their classmates. Students with ASD really benefit from these opportunities to interact with an audience of peers. The structured format is perfect for communicating the topic and answering questions.

Assign the student the task of preparing a PowerPoint presentation on his favorite topic of interest. The student can enhance the presentation by adding graphics. Using a digital camera, the student can take pictures to download into the presentation. Using the student's pictures increases audience interest while enhancing the student's ability to communicate.

Drama and Improvisation

Drama and improvisational acting are enjoyable activities that teens consider "cool." Acting is a powerful tool that teaches nonverbal language, emotion development, perspective taking, teamwork, confidence, reading others' cues, and conversation.

Use a video camera to film a short feature or film the student playing drama games. The objective is to help the student focus and develop his character, practice his role and lines, and figure out what information is vital for the scene from the perspective of other characters and the audience. When working through the appropriate body language, tone of voice, and so forth, it is so much safer getting direction on your character than receiving personal direction on social skills and behavior in a social skills training session!

Self-Advocacy Skills

Self-advocacy is best accomplished when the student develops self-awareness and uses this knowledge to approach others to negotiate desired goals. Self-advocacy can include discussions of disclosure, special interests, learning styles, learning accommodations, and even relationships with peers and adults. *These discussions build better mutual understanding and trust* (Shore, 2004). Studies show that students are more willing to accept the student with ASD if they know she is competent and shares similar interests.

Finding ways to include the student as a member of his IEP team is an important way to promote self-advocacy. Listening to the student's hopes, aspirations, and future goals and fears related to future life after school can help the IEP team gain important insight into the development of goals meaningful to the student.

SUBJECT-SPECIFIC ADAPTATIONS

Table 6.2

Math Adaptations	
1. Use peer tutors with guided instructions	13. Put number lines on desks
2. Use templates	14. Draw problems
3. Allow students to work in pairs; one student copies the problems while both students figure out the answers together	15. Use arithmetic board
	16. Use flash cards for number facts practice
4. Use a calculator to compute and check work	17. Use overhead projector and overhead calculator
5. Color-code key concepts	18. Assign fewer problems
6. Use graphic organizers	19. Use one-dollar-more strategy when counting out money
7. Cut a worksheet into segments and assign only one small section at a time	
8. Use personal and real-world examples	20. Show only one problem at a time
9. Group similar problems together	21. Use graph paper to assist in placement and alignment of numbers
10. Play Monopoly; let student with a money skills IEP goal be the banker	22. Use addition, multiplication, and division charts
11. Use computer math programs and activities	23. Give directions in small, explicit steps and break problems down into smaller steps
12. Use number stamp, number tiles, or peel-off labels to indicate answers	

Figure 6.2   Promote Opportunities for Mutual Support

Table 6.3

Reading Adaptations	
1. Teachers/peers read aloud	10. Use story maps, plot outlines
2. Use guided reading	11. Think aloud: Teacher or instructional assistant reads story aloud and models comprehension strategies (e.g., asking questions, making inferences, making connections to personal background)
3. Allow student to pass during reading aloud	
4. Limit amount to be read	
5. Preview chapter by doing a "chapter walk," pointing out new vocabulary and the meaning of pictures, charts, and graphs	
6. Highlight key words and/or key sections	12. Have a range of texts and reading levels available; investigate what types of materials students prefer (newspapers, magazines, pamphlets)
7. Use story summaries made by peers	
8. Use visual aids: pictures, graphic organizer, scatter plots, Venn diagrams, timelines	13. Allow multiple ways for student to demonstrate understanding
9. Preteach vocabulary	14. When reading, stop frequently to check for understanding: "What were the three uses for water mentioned?"

Table 6.4

Writing Adaptations	
1. Use fill-in-the-blank (with words, stickers, written label, letter or picture stamp)	9. Use riddles written on index cards: On the back side, the student writes a short answer and shares with others
2. Use graphic organizers: mapping webs, scatter plots, Venn diagrams, plot development chart, timelines	10. Use cloze notes (typed out lecture notes provided with key words left out—student fills in missing words using word bank at top of page)
3. Assign peers as note-takers	
4. Provide alternatives to written assignment: word processor, artwork, oral presentations, PowerPoint	
5. Draw a picture to demonstrate understanding	11. Use matching problems: picture-picture, picture-word, word-word, definition-word
6. Tape-record discussions or responses	12. Create a picture dictionary
7. Use modified materials (pencil grip, large-lined paper, graph paper, dry-erase board)	13. Bring a picture from home and write about it
8. Use picture sequence cards to help student develop ideas: Place in order and write one sentence on each card to develop a sequence of ideas, and later a story	14. Write oral responses dictated by peer
	15. Fill in missing word from multiple-choice list
	16. Use tracing and stencils

Table 6.5

Spelling Adaptations	
1. Create a shorter list (same words, different words, or combinations)	8. Use word family practice: Use index cards with initial consonant sounds, and manipulate them to make new words
2. Increase the number of spelling words when student reaches mastery at current modified number	9. Group words with common prefixes and suffixes; teach the meaning of common prefixes and suffixes in isolation (e.g., able = is, less = without, er = more)
3. Group spelling words into families (e.g., consonant-vowel-consonant words, "_at" words—bat, fat, rat, sat, cat, mat)	10. Color-code syllables to highlight them
4. Write initial sound of word rather than whole word	11. Use spelling games for additional practice: spelling bingo, hangman, word finds, crossword puzzles
5. Segment word into syllables and spell one part at a time	12. Practice spelling words orally: "The word is capitol. Spell it: c-a-p-i-t-o-l, capitol."
6. Do not penalize for spelling errors when test is knowledge recall and not spelling	13. Use a data sheet to track and record progress
7. Spell words with letter squares from Scrabble, magnetic letters, letter cards	14. Encourage parents to practice with student at home

Table 6.6

Listening Adaptations	
1. Pair verbal directions with visual model and written or picture outline	9. Link new facts with previous information
2. Give "alert cues" to communicate when information is especially important	10. Provide picture sequences from home of a family outing to help with class sharing
3. When reviewing lesson, present only relevant material; review and check for understanding	11. Use books on tape
4. Eliminate distractions from student desk that interfere with listening	12. Repeat back what was said in unison
5. Use cooperative peer activities: board games like "Uno," "Sorry," and "Monopoly"	13. Have sing-alongs
6. Use active learning strategies more than explaining and lecturing	14. Have a readers' theater
7. Place student near the speaker	15. Do a circle story: Go around circle and each person adds a detail to a story
8. Simplify vocabulary; speak in shorter sentences	16. Use dramatic readings
	17. Act out class skits and short one-act plays
	18. Create computer-generated stories
	19. Use partner learning: "think-pair-share"

ADAPTATIONS FOR ALL STUDENTS

Typical students vary greatly in their academic development. It is likely that the adaptations designed to benefit the student with ASD will benefit nondisabled peers as well. Consider the following questions when determining what adaptations to make:

- What is the skill or concept to be taught?
- What background knowledge is needed to master the skill or concept?
- What steps do students take to master this skill or concept?
- Can the skill be broken down into its component parts and taught systematically?
- Can the skill or concept be reinforced through practice and experience?

Many of the challenges students with ASD experience with reading comprehension, written expression, problem solving, and organization are challenges typical students experience as well. Teachers often report that many students considered "typical" actually struggle with undiagnosed learning challenges. For example, we see many students in our classrooms with ADHD who lose focus during instruction and miss concepts. These challenges frequently interfere with instruction and student success.

When you think of your class as a whole, you will discover a hierarchy of support needs among students. Some students need no support while others require significant support. These distributions fluctuate based on the subject matter and level of subject matter difficulty. Intensive individual or small-group direct instruction is necessary when students struggle to understand content. By taking a close look at content demands, you can plan adaptations and support strategies ahead of time. Enlisting academically accomplished peers as tutors can increase success for many students with ASD. In addition to focusing on the student's academic needs, the student with ASD is placed in a situation where natural interactions are built into the lesson plan.

SUMMARY

Academic adaptations are essential tools that help students with ASD succeed in the general education setting. They require careful planning and, in many instances, "thinking outside the box." In collaboration with the special education teacher, the classroom teacher develops adaptations based on his or her unique understanding of the student's strengths and challenges. The more knowledge you have of the students you integrate, the more effective the adaptations will be. When working to develop adaptations, consider the following helpful guidelines:

- Go beyond the core academic activity and consider a wide range of multilevel learning opportunities for the student.

Figure 6.3 Hierarchy of Support

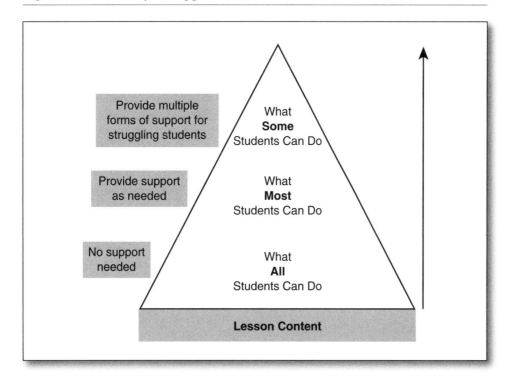

- Help design learning activities and experiences that adapt easily to the student's learning style and allow flexibility. For example, open-ended questions to explore, cooperative learning activities, peer partnering, thematic teaching units (e.g., King Tut's Tomb, the Great Wall), multi-age groupings, games, simulations, role-plays, and active experiments are ways the student with ASD can develop her learning around the way she thinks and creates meaning.
- Know the student's learning style and work to design content around that style.
- Explain content in a way that reaches the student. Know a variety of techniques for direct and indirect instruction. Keep in mind that not every student needs a different instructional delivery method. The student with ASD may respond to teaching methods that are effective for typical students.
- Provide multiple opportunities to learn the skill.
- Value the importance of activity-based group instruction. Students diagnosed with autism especially need these group activities to learn how to cooperate with others in support of a common goal.

Academic modifications can be made to all areas of the curriculum. If you are uncomfortable with a certain adaptation, consult with the special educator for alternative ideas. Determining what needs to be done to support the student involves knowledge of his IEP goals and his interests, needs, and learning style. Don't just wing it! Consult with your colleagues and together design an effective plan.

RESOURCES

Resources M and O: Assessment of Student Participation in General Education Settings

Use this form to assess the student's academic, participation, and social skills.

Resource P: Homework Summary

This form will help clarify for parents and the student the homework responsibilities, what materials are needed, and the due date.

FURTHER READING

Holden-Johns, B. (2010). *401 practical adaptations for every classroom.* Thousand Oaks, CA: Corwin.

Mazur, A. J., & Rice-Doran, P. (2010). *Teaching diverse learners: Principles for best practice.* Thousand Oaks, CA: Corwin.

Paradiz, V. (2010). *Integrated self-advocacy curriculum.* Shawnee-Mission, KS: Autism Asperger Publishing Co.

Shore, S. (2004). *Ask and tell: Self-advocacy and disclosure for people on the autism spectrum.* Shawnee-Mission, KS: Autism Asperger Publishing Co.

7

Classroom Instruction

Effective Strategies for Whole-Class Instruction

This chapter explores a variety of classroom strategies that enhance student engagement and meaningful participation. Students with ASD have enormous potential to learn academic content; however, learning can be challenging when the teacher's instructional style relies heavily on whole-class, teacher-centered instruction.

No specific cognitive profile adequately describes how students with autism learn. However, it is safe to say that most students with and without autism struggle to stay engaged if instructional delivery is not matched to the student's learning style. Research shows that many of the recommended practices for educating students with ASD benefit typically developing students as well. The educational practices included in this chapter will support learning for all students, not just students with autism and other disabilities.

When considering what instructional approach to use, be mindful of the importance of differentiated instruction. Research suggests that many of the academic and emotional challenges students experience disappear when the teacher is mindful of each student's learning modality

(Ellis, Gable, Gregg, & Rock, 2008). Bravmann (2004) states that differentiated instruction is based on three beliefs:

1. Everyone learns differently.

2. Quality is more important than quantity.

3. "One-size-fits-all" curriculum and instruction presumes that content is more important than the learning needs of students.

These beliefs require that every teacher answer three specific questions:

1. What is most important for students to know?

2. How can each student's specific learning needs be met?

3. How can each student best demonstrate what he or she has learned?

Emphasize activity-based instruction over passive listening. Encourage peer-to-peer interaction. Regarding students with ASD, be knowledgeable of the student's IEP and embed instruction that supports IEP goals. Appropriate instruction, a comfortable setting, and informed support can lead to greater achievement.

The following "Common Recommendations of National Curriculum Reports" (Zemelman, Daniels, & Hyde, 2005) illustrate how closely aligned best practices for educating students with disabilities complement what experts across the country define as best practices for general classroom instruction for all students.

"Common Recommendations of National Curriculum Reports" represent the conclusions of experts and practitioners from a wide variety of educational fields, including science, mathematics, language arts, and social science. Considering the widely diverse backgrounds of the experts, the following fundamental insights into teaching and learning are remarkably congruent. It is especially noteworthy that, on many key issues, the recommendations from these diverse organizations are unanimous (Zemelman et al., 2005).

COMMON RECOMMENDATIONS OF NATIONAL CURRICULUM REPORTS

- LESS whole-class, teacher-directed instruction (e.g., lecturing)
- LESS student passivity: sitting, listening, receiving, and absorbing information
- LESS presentational, one-way transmission of information from teacher to student

- LESS prizing and rewarding of silence in the classroom
- LESS classroom time devoted to fill-in-the-blank worksheets, dittos, workbooks, and other "seatwork"
- LESS student time spent reading textbooks and basal readers
- LESS attempts by teachers to thinly "cover" large amounts of material in every subject area
- LESS rote memorization of facts and details
- LESS emphasis on the competition and grades in school
- LESS tracking or leveling of students into "ability groups"
- LESS use of pull-out special programs
- LESS use of and reliance on standardized tests

- MORE experiential, inductive, hands-on learning
- MORE active learning with all the attendant noise and movement of students doing, talking, and collaborating
- MORE diverse roles for teachers, including coaching, demonstrating, and modeling
- MORE emphasis on higher-order thinking: learning a field's key concepts and principles
- MORE deep study of a smaller number of topics, so that students internalize the field's way of inquiry
- MORE reading of real texts: whole books, primary sources, and nonfiction materials
- MORE responsibility transferred to students for their work: goal setting, record keeping, monitoring, sharing, exhibiting, and evaluating
- MORE choice for students (e.g., choosing their own books, writing topics, team partners, and research projects)
- MORE enacting and modeling of the principles of democracy in school
- MORE attention to affective needs and the varying cognitive styles of individual students
- MORE cooperative, collaborative activity: developing the classroom as an interdependent community
- MORE heterogeneous classrooms where individual needs are met through individualized activities, not segregation of bodies
- MORE delivery of special help to students in regular classrooms
- MORE varied and cooperative roles for teachers, parents, and administrators
- MORE reliance on descriptive evaluations of student growth, including observation/anecdotal records, conference notes, and performance assessment rubrics

OVERCOMING LANGUAGE AND COMMUNICATION CHALLENGES

Students with ASD may be inattentive, easily distracted, and anxious during classroom instruction due to their challenges with expressive and receptive language. Although we covered communication in detail in Chapter 4, it is important to remember the value of explicit directions. Too many words confuse. Keep your directions short and succinct. Also, be on the alert for conversation breakdowns caused by the student's inability to effectively communicate his or her ideas.

The following chart identifies specific challenges students with ASD may experience when communicating in class and some ideas to help them.

Table 7.1 Communication Challenge–Meet Solution

Communication Challenges	Solution
<ul><li>Tendency to make irrelevant comments</li><li>Tendency to interrupt</li><li>Tendency to talk over the speech of others without giving partner a turn to speak</li><li>Difficulty understanding complex language</li><li>Challenges with following multistep directions</li><li>Misunderstands the intent of words with multiple meanings</li><li>Processing incoming language may take extra time; wait longer for a response</li><li>Doesn't catch the drift of group conversation and will switch topic to special interest</li><li>Does not understand nuanced forms of communication like subtle cues, tone of voice, sarcasm, and body language</li><li>Applies social rules too literally—rule-bound; comes off as contrived and rehearsed</li></ul>	<ul><li>Teach appropriate opening comments</li><li>Teach conversation skills in small-group settings</li><li>Teach rules and cues for conversation turn-taking and when to reply, interrupt, or change the topic</li><li>Audiotape conversations and play back for student; emphasize positives</li><li>Explain metaphors and words with double meanings</li><li>Encourage student to ask for instructions to be repeated, simplified, or written down if confused</li><li>Pause between instructions and check for understanding</li><li>Limit oral questions to a number the student can manage</li><li>Watch videos to identify nonverbal expressions and their meanings</li></ul>

Provide Explicit Instructions

Students with ASD interpret language literally and have difficulty interpreting figures of speech and other forms of nuanced expression. Speak clearly and to the point in short phrases. Be concrete. A sarcastic "Oh, THAT was great!" may unwittingly cause misunderstandings. Students with ASD do not understand "meaningful looks" that attempt to convey disapproval. If the student is doing something inappropriate, tell the student in clear, short statements what he *should* do. Learn the student's best form of receptive communication and use it whenever possible. When speaking to the student, consider the following suggestions:

1. Make sure you have the student's attention before delivering instruction. Remember—that does not necessarily mean the student has eye contact!

2. Check for understanding. Ask the student to respond to make sure she understands.

3. Review previous learning before giving new directions.

4. Be clear and specific. Keep instructions to the point and without asides that confuse meaning.

5. Use positive directions. Tell students what you want, not what you don't want.

6. Model with physical gesturing.

7. Avoid drawn-out explanations and frequently check for understanding. If the student makes an error, give the correct answer immediately; then ask again. Avoid "moralizing."

Wrong Way:

Teacher: Now get ready for the multiplication question! I hope all that work we did can help you answer right! . . . Sam, keep your attention up here . . . Jennifer, get back to work now . . . Okay, here we go: What is 9 times 9?

Student: 34.

Teacher: No, that's wrong! How many times do we need to go over this? If I've told you once I've told you a thousand times! The answer is 81! [With a sigh] Remember we went over this yesterday! Now listen carefully and let's really try hard to finally get it right this time! What is 9 times 9?

Student: I don't know.

Right Way:

Teacher: What is 9 times 9?

Student: 34.

Teacher: The answer is 81. What is 9 times 9?

Student: 81.

Teacher: Yes, 81. Excellent!

What Not to Say!

- **Avoid overuse of pronouns:** "Now do *that* again so we can get it!"

  In favor of: *"Do problems 1, 2, and 3. Practicing the steps in these three problems will help you get right answers."*

- **Avoid confusing word order:** "Before placing your worksheet in the 'done' box on my desk, make sure it is complete and your name is written on the top."

  In favor of: *"Write your name on the top. Then make sure you complete the entire worksheet. Finally, place your completed work in the 'done' box on my desk."*

- **Avoid words with multiple meanings:** "Let me spell it out for you."

  In favor of: *"Here are the rules of the game."*

- **Avoid idioms and figurative speech:** "I'm feeling under the weather today."

  In favor of: *"I feel sick today."*

- **Avoid using abstract concepts:** "This task will help change your overall impressions."

  In favor of: *"Read this chapter and you will know why life is hard for people without jobs."*

- **Avoid long lectures and complicated directions:** "Now, when we finish this part, go to page 45 and complete the four questions on that page, but remember that they are only a part of the rest of the work we'll be doing on the next page, so if you have questions, go back to page 15 and read over the glossary. That's a good place to find alternative answers to your questions. Okay?"

  In favor of: *"Look at your checklist and follow each step. Check off each step when completed. If you need help, raise your hand."*

Depending on the language skill of the student, it may be necessary to provide instructions one at a time, waiting for the student to finish each step before providing additional direction.

Keep in mind the autism diagnosis and its effect on communication. When you experience challenges communicating instructions to students with ASD, remember the characteristics of the diagnosis. The following quote from McGinnity and Negri (2005) is illuminating:

> "I was rarely able to hear sentences because my hearing distorted them. I was sometimes able to hear a word or two at the start and understand it and then the next lot of words sort of merged into one another and I could not make head or tail of it." (p. 28)

Figure 7.1 Too Much Verbal Information

Active Engagement: Learning to Listen

Students with ASD tend to daydream during oral instruction. Understand that active listening is not an automatic behavior for students with ASD. Teach active listening skills systematically by breaking down listening into its component parts, and then reinforce each component.

1. Teach the student to face the speaker.

2. Look at one spot (which does not mean he or she must make eye contact).

3. Place hands in a planned position.

4. Praise and reward each step.

VISUAL SUPPORTS

Words are a barrier to communication. There's a reason why it is said that a picture is worth a thousand words. When you first picked up this book, what caught your eye? I'm betting it was the pictures!

Telling students with words is never as powerful as showing them.

Most students with ASD respond more positively to what they see than what they hear or read. Visual supports like graphic organizers, schedules, pictures, drawings, and photos help the student process, organize, remember, and respond to information more effectively. Students respond appropriately when they understand expectations. Their stress levels and challenging behaviors decline. When spoken or written words fail to communicate, a visual support can bridge the gap in understanding.

All of us use visual supports in our daily lives to remember things, find places, and organize our thoughts. If you boot up your computer and click on icons, use GPS navigation, write to-do lists, or display a calendar on the wall, you are using a visual support. The next time you enter your vehicle, take a minute to notice all the visual cues the automaker has designed into the instrument panel. For students with ASD, visual supports capitalize on the student's tendency to see the world in concrete, literal terms.

To illustrate the power of visual supports, compare the following two methods for providing instructions for setting a table. Read over the directions contained in Figure 7.2; then "read" the directions visually in Figure 7.3. Consider which example best communicates the intended purpose in the most clearly understood mode.

Get the point? It is reasonable to assume that most people would choose the photo to teach how to set a table. The picture renders Figure 7.2 unnecessary. The picture is clear and succinct, leaving little chance for error.

When you are trying to decide between written instructions and visuals, try to solve the problem visually if you can. Visuals translate better than words.

Figure 7.2 Directions for Setting the Table

Put the dinner fork on the left side of where the dinner plate will be. The handle of the fork should be closest to the person, with the tines of the fork pointing straight ahead, away from the person. In many home cutlery sets, there are two sizes of fork. The larger one is the dinner fork. The smaller one is for salads and dessert.

Leave enough room on the placemat for the dinner plate, or set the dinner plate down on the mat beside the fork, depending on how the cook is planning to dish out the dinner. If dinner will be served from the stove or a sideboard, the plates can start there, and everyone can carry his own plate to the table after serving himself. If dinner will be served from serving dishes and platters on the table, then place a dinner plate in the center of the place setting. Also, if bread is to be served, a separate bread plate is placed to the left and above the dinner plate at about the same height as the glass.

On the right-hand side of the dinner plate, first put the knife. The handle should be placed vertically in front of the person. The teaspoon goes to the right of the knife, very close to it at the widest part of the spoon. The handles of the knife, fork, and spoon should be parallel to each other.

A basic place setting includes a glass. This goes above the teaspoon, just off to the right of the top of the knife. Each person should also have a folded napkin. The easiest thing to do is fold the napkin flat and put it neatly in the center of the plate.

This is a very basic way to set a table, and it will never fail to look neat and tidy.

Figure 7.3 Directions for Setting the Table

Remember: Visual supports need to be age appropriate and relevant to the student's needs. The layout and content of the visual should be user-friendly, containing only information the student needs and nothing more. Do not add extra decoration and artwork not relevant to the purpose of the visual support.

While most people on the autism spectrum are visually based, not all are. However, whatever the student's learning style, it will most likely be to an extreme and to the exclusion or near exclusion of other learning modalities.

Graphic Organizers

Graphic organizers help students understand abstract concepts by turning the abstract into visual form. Graphic organizers come in a variety of forms, each type serving a different function. The following examples illustrate types and uses for graphic organizers.

Concept mapping (Figure 7.4) helps students understand the relationships between concepts, images, and words. Concepts, usually enclosed in boxes or circles, are connected with arrows in a branching pattern. Concept mapping helps students visualize the relationships among different concepts that would otherwise be hard to understand. Concept mapping also helps students structure their writing ideas.

Autism Myth

"All children with autism think in pictures."

Fact

While visual thinking may be more common in students with autism, it is also common in people who are not autistic. Each person experiences learning uniquely; therefore, not every person with autism is a visual thinker.

Figure 7.4 Concept Mapping

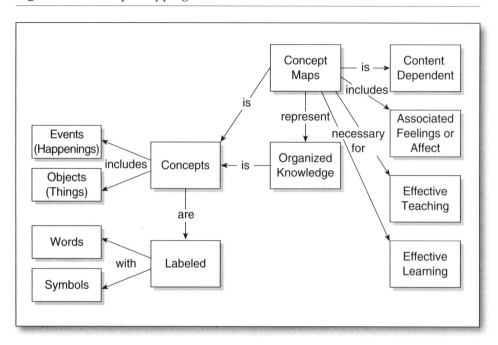

Figure 7.5 Cause-Effect

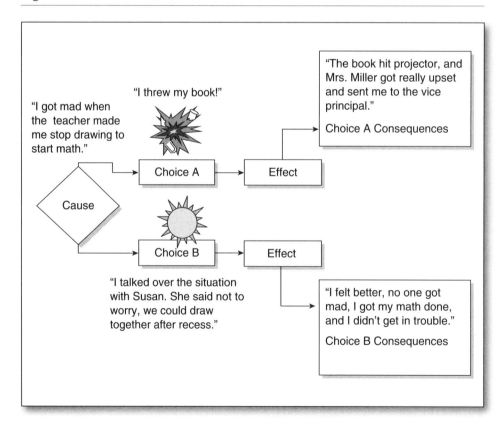

Cause-and-effect graphic organizers (Figure 7.5) are useful for helping students understand how their response to situations (upsetting changes, bullying, teasing, angry person) causes a result or consequence. A typical

Choice A response is listed (e.g., "I yelled," "I hit," etc.), followed by consequences (loss of privilege, punishment, parents were called). More favorable responses and resulting consequences are filled in next and compared. Ask the student, "What if we tried this way next time?" Share with the student all the possible positive things that could happen as a result.

Goal setting graphic organizers (Figure 7.6) help students visualize, and then organize, their goals. List things they do well and enter this information into the symbols labeled "What I already do well." Repeat with "Areas to develop" and "What I need to do." Help students determine where they can find assistance for each problem and list them in "Resources." As students discuss their ideas for improvement, they can begin to focus their energies and set priorities—the first step to goal attainment.

Venn diagrams (Figure 7.7) are useful for comparing the logical relationships between sets of things. Simple Venn diagrams consist of two or three circles that intersect at a common point. Shared characteristics are listed in the overlapping area, allowing for easy identification of shared and unshared characteristics. Venn diagrams help students with ASD better understand the relationship between different elements.

Inspiration Software™: Go to the Inspiration Software website for computer software designed for supporting students in organizing ideas. Teachers can create graphic organizers like the example in Figure 7.8 using this program. Go to http://inspiration.com/ for information.

Figure 7.6   Goal Setting

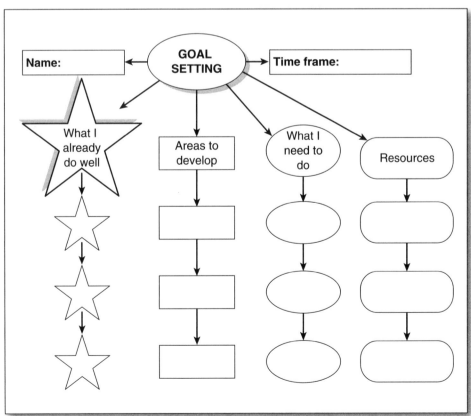

Figure 7.7   Venn Diagrams

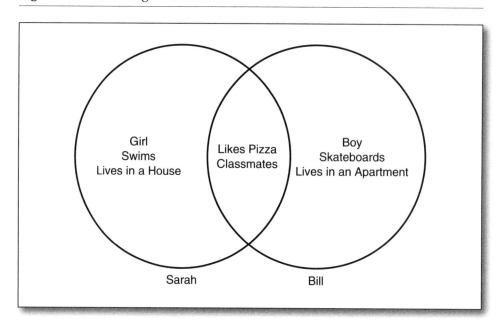

Figure 7.8   Planning Map

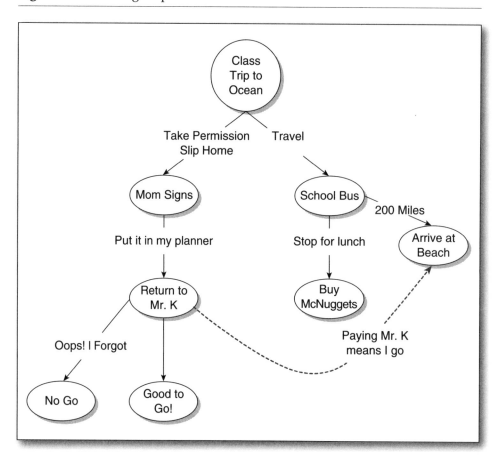

ACTIVITY-BASED INSTRUCTION

Activity-based instruction emphasizes experiential learning over whole-class large-group instruction and individual task completion. Many students learn better by doing than by passively listening and taking notes. The activity should (1) include the student with ASD and a partner or small group of typical peers, and (2) be meaningful and age appropriate for all the students involved in the activity.

Instruction in small groups increases the amount of instructional time the teacher can spend with each student during the lesson. This allows for increased interaction between students as well. Students feel more comfortable asking questions in small groups. They respond more frequently and receive more corrective feedback. Students are more focused when they are actively engaged and less likely to be distracted.

Teaching Students to Work in Groups

Students with ASD need to learn how to work cooperatively in small groups. They may understand the lesson but struggle to work with their peers. Teach students appropriate group behavior and give them adequate time to practice. The ability to work cooperatively with others is a valuable workplace skill students will need as adults.

Caution: There is a strong likelihood the student with ASD will be left out if students get to pick their own group members. Whatever strategy you use to form groups, be careful not to set the student up for rejection. Taking into account each student's unique skill set, organize groups in advance, mindful of the need for diversity. When considering who should work alongside the student with ASD, pick typical peers who are nurturing and who demonstrate tolerance for differences. Avoid putting students with ASD together in the same group.

Figure 7.9   Activity-Based Instruction

Developing Group Skills

Students will learn to do the following:

1. Follow directions while complying with group rules and procedures.

2. Fulfill assigned roles.

3. Take turns and work cooperatively.

4. Correct errors without issue.

5. Provide supportive comments and assistance to other group members.

Explicit Instructions

Provide clear and explicit directions. Developing group skills requires specific instruction and practice. Use visual support to reinforce group skills and provide ample opportunity to learn skills in steps.

1. Identify and explain the skills necessary to work in groups.

2. Model cooperative behavior.

3. Practice working in small groups with well-defined activities before more complex projects.

4. Provide explicit end goals or outcomes for the group activity.

5. Praise students for demonstrating appropriate group skills.

6. Have students move to larger and more complex groups as skills increase.

Simple Rules

Students will follow directions that make sense and are not complicated. Keep rules to a minimum. Make rules simple to understand and follow. Give students the reasons for rules.

Group members should understand and do the following:

1. Know the purpose of the group.

2. Know the rules for the group activity.

3. Contribute to the group in a way that showcases the student's strengths.

4. Have skills for working in groups or the opportunity to learn and practice these skills.

Involve All Group Members

Group activities can be challenging for students with ASD, who tend to "march to a different drummer." These students do not always work cooperatively and share ideas. Increase the student's interactions with peers while instructing the student on cooperation and teamwork. Explain the student's needs to his peers and teach them how to assist. Consider the following components that contribute to effective group activities:

- All members of the group are assigned a defined role.
- Leadership of the group is shared (when it is a peer group activity).
- The success of the group is dependent on all members of the group.

The literature on cooperative learning (Thousand, Villa, & Nevin, 2002) informs us that groups should be set up to create positive interdependence by establishing mutual goals, dividing the work among all members of the group, dividing materials and resources among group members, assigning different roles to individuals in the group, and providing group rewards. The following suggestions contribute to the involvement of students with ASD in group activities:

- Question students frequently. This increases their opportunity to respond.
- Ask students to respond in unison. Ask them to respond randomly. If the student with ASD engages in compulsive questioning that interferes with group instruction, tell the student to write his questions down. Explain that you will meet with him after class to answer his

Figure 7.10 Assign Tasks that Highlight Student Thinking

questions. You could incorporate a private visual signal reminding him to wait.

- Ensure that all students participate.
- Use signals and prompts to indicate transitions to new activities.
- Be enthusiastic and involved.
- Frequently reward correct student responses with praise.

Avoid promising the reward of time off task for completing assignments. For example, at the start of a period, the teacher says, "Okay, group, when you finish this lesson, you can have free computer game time! Now let's get this done, so we can play!" The student motivation for task completion is off-task time. As a result, instead of concentrating on understanding the lesson and learning, the goal becomes getting it done as fast as possible in order to play computer games. Not a good thing!

Instead, focus on accomplishment by celebrating learning. Say, "I am so proud of your hard work and hope you know that learning these skills will help you better understand what you are reading." This way, the focus builds a valuing for the learning process, instead of an extrinsic reward.

STRUCTURED SETTING, PREDICTABLE SCHEDULE

The classroom should be structured to provide consistency and clarity. Students with ASD like to know where things belong and what is expected. They gain comfort from routine and like to know in advance when changes will occur. Planned activities should be displayed in visual form and in clear view. The student can be helped to learn to use the schedule independently. Peers can remind the student to look at the schedule when it is time to transition to the next activity or lesson.

Provide a daily visual schedule individualized for the student and designed to fit with the overall classroom routine. Vary tasks to prevent boredom and alternate activities to reduce anxiety and prevent inappropriate challenges. Alternate familiar, successful experiences with less preferred activities. If anxiety develops, allow a break from the large-group activity.

Allow the student to move around if she needs to. A break from passive sitting could help prevent challenging behavior. See Chapter 8 for more information on visual schedules.

- Provide a structured, predictable, and welcoming classroom environment.
- Prepare a visual schedule and place it where its easily visible to the student.
- Adapt the classroom setting to reduce stimuli that trigger challenging behavior.

- Minimize the effect of stimuli that cannot be eliminated.
- Adapt tasks and materials to avoid student anxiety and frustration.
- Provide a relaxation area.
- Connect the student with peers who model class routines and are willing to prompt the student when needed.

PEER SUPPORT

Peer tutoring is a wonderful way to connect students to each other and promote peer-to-peer interactions. We see immediate improvements in academics when students work in pairs. Tutoring sessions must be structured, with both students having assigned roles. Ideally, the relationship between the two students is reciprocal, where both benefit from the experience.

Examine the needs and interests of students you plan to support. Provide opportunities for interaction between these students and their peers so that they reach a comfort level before starting. Peers must understand the basic diagnosis of autism in order to best help. Be sure to match the peer tutor's academic and personal strengths with the needs of the student he or she supports. Here are some other strategies to consider:

- Pair students together who have a positive relationship or have a desire to work together.
- Pair students together who have similar interests.
- Use well-connected students who are popular and can potentially expand the student's social network.
- Teach the tutor what tasks and materials to use in tutoring, how to give directions, how to provide positive reinforcement, and what to do when encountering inappropriate behavior.

Encourage respect for every person, regardless of ability. Peer tutors need to value relationships while respecting every person's unique talents, strengths, and interests. Don't create "benevolent helpers" by placing certain students in permanent positions of authority and status. Encourage students who are usually on the receiving end of the helper-helpee relationship to demonstrate competence whenever possible. Encourage students with ASD to use their skills to serve the needs of their teacher and classmates. The cartoon illustrations found throughout this book were created by Devon, a student with ASD who attended our school. Devon gained positive notoriety around campus for his incredible artistic talent and pleasing personality. The students in Devon's advanced art class admired his abilities and looked to him for help. They saw Devon as a gifted artist who helped them better their skills, not as a student with a disability.

Figure 7.11 Peer Tutoring

SPECIAL INTERESTS AND MOTIVATION

> *Scott, a seventh-grade boy with Asperger syndrome, was passionate about medieval history. Whenever Scott got the chance, he would head to the library to check out books dealing with fiefs, castles, knights, and the black plague. Scott's passion for history gained him respect from his teachers and fellow students. At the conclusion of the school year, Scott was awarded the Top History Student Award. After receiving his plaque, his favorite teacher, Mr. Thompson, knighted Scott with a crown for his achievements. (Author)*

This vignette is an example that illustrates the importance of motivation to learning. When students are motivated to learn, they are more interested and engaged. If motivation can be improved, then overall improvement is increased. If the student's special interest can serve to motivate classroom participation, then think of ways for the student to use his special interest to access content learning.

Scott's award brought his family great pride and joy. His mother, after attending Award Night, stated that it was the first time her son received public recognition. This accomplishment helped boost Scott's self-esteem. Koegel and Koegel (2006) identified five components that reliably improve motivation:

1. **Choice:** Strive to give students choice for assignment completion. Choices include materials to use, peer partners, the order of task completion, and how the assignment is presented.

2. **Alternate between easy and hard tasks:** The drill-and-kill method is not very motivating. Give students several easy tasks to build confidence, and then slip in a challenging one. Because they have momentum going, the harder task will more likely be accomplished.

3. **Natural reinforcers:** When rewards are directly connected to student behavior, it is likely the behavior will be repeated. Students often spend hours texting their friends but struggle to complete writing assignments. It is not hard to understand that text messaging is rewarding and therefore motivating. Look for things the student enjoys and find ways to embed them in the learning activity.

4. **Task variation:** Learning is much easier if tasks are varied frequently between easy and challenging. That way the student can mentally relax after a task requiring a lot of thought.

5. **Reward attempts:** If the student is making an honest effort, she needs to be rewarded. Many students with ASD have experienced so much repeated failure that when they reach middle school, they give up trying. If we reward them for every attempt, no matter the outcome, their willingness to try again will greatly increase (p. 23).

TEACHING INDEPENDENCE

Learned helplessness and prompt dependency are unfortunate learned behaviors that many students with ASD acquire after years of segregated placements and overzealous support. Starting when they enter school, many students who are labeled as special ed are unfairly viewed as less capable than their peers. They receive extra help and assistance without first getting the opportunity to try things on their own.

Many students are shielded from consequences that would naturally occur if the student did not have a disability. For example, the teacher cleans up after the child with a disability but expects the nondisabled child to clean up on his own. Inappropriate behavior is ignored because "He can't help it!"

Well-intentioned teachers and other staff members who overhelp these students may unconsciously be underestimating their potential abilities and, as a result, inadvertently denying them opportunities to make choices. The compounding effect of such treatment over years of excessive help causes prompt dependency and learned helplessness that is hard to undo. In the words of Van der Klift and Kunc, 1994, "Help outside the context of choice and self-determination is disrespectful."

View the student as a typical, nondisabled person and go as far as possible in the direction of building competence *despite the label.* This doesn't mean you ignore the student's challenges that are a manifestation of the disability. It means that the driving force behind support is the potential of the individual, not the perceived limitations stemming from the label. Do not be afraid to ask when you are uncertain about the student's potential. The highest compliment you can give persons with disabilities is to believe in their potential by striving for a higher standard instead of assuming incompetence.

Prompts, Modeling, and Chaining[1]

Prompting is a process of providing verbal or physical assistance in a way that encourages participation. Prompting is extremely beneficial if used in a systematic way. Prompting works well with promoting social conversation and learning multistep tasks.

The mastery of a task or skill requires careful analysis of the steps leading to task completion. Each strategy provides the student with opportunity and practice: the basic building blocks of learning and task mastery. Remember to value independence and the principle that all prompting strategies are temporary. There are three types of prompts:

1. Auditory prompting includes verbal statements—"Hey Kyle, let's get to work"—and sound signals, including a timer buzzer or beeper.

2. Visual prompting includes gestures, hand signals, reminder cards, pictures, and drawings designed to assist the student with task completion or alert the student to stay on task.

3. Physical prompting includes lightly tapping the student on the shoulder to gain attention.

The essential concept behind prompting is to give as little assistance as possible. Assistance is increased or decreased according the student's level of need. The ultimate goal for all instruction is for the student to perform as independently as possible.

When a prompt is provided, there needs to be a plan for how the prompt will be reduced. Reducing a prompt is called fading. Consider the prompting hierarchy, that is, the system of prompts to be given and how they will be reduced or changed as the student approaches mastery.

Deciding on the prompts to use will depend on how the student learns and on the demands of the instructional task. Prompts can start with most to least or least to most. What follows is a list of the types of prompts teachers use to assist students to successfully complete a task:

- Increase assistance
- Decrease assistance
- Provide graduated guidance

Providing Guidance

- Exert no more force than is needed to move the student's hand in a desired direction.

---

[1]Adapted from Saskatchewan Learning (2001). *Creating opportunities for students with intellectual or multiple disabilities: The Evergreen Curriculum.* Regina, SK. Used by permission of the Ministry of Education.

- At the start of each prompt, use the minimum force needed (a light touch), building slowly until the student's hand starts moving.
- Decrease guidance when movement begins and continue decreasing as long as movement continues.
- If movement stops, increase gradually until it begins again.
- If the student resists or pulls away, apply enough pressure to keep the hand motionless. When resistance ceases, gradually apply enough pressure to guide the hand.
- Provide verbal praise during guidance only when the student is actively participating, not when the student is resistant or uninvolved in the desired task or activity.
- Follow the exercise through; do not quit or interrupt before the final step.
- Use either shadowing or spatial fading once guidance has been reduced to a touch.

Peer-Delivered Prompting

Prompting is a good way to encourage peer interaction. Instead of the adult delivering the prompt, the classroom teacher arranges in advance for a typical peer to help. For example, if the student with ASD tends to daydream, a peer sitting next to her could say, "Hey, Michelle, I need your help with this problem. Can we work together?" or "Steven, listen to Mr. K, he has an idea for you." Another way to prompt might be during an activity where the student's peer reminds the student with ASD to complete a five-step task using a checklist. "OK, Ishmael, now do step three and check off when done, please."

Modeling

Modeling is physically demonstrating the desired behavior or response. For students with ASD, it is a powerful tool because the student is provided a picture of what the desired response looks like. Modeling can be used alone or with prompting. The following are procedures for using modeling:

- Get the student's attention.
- Ask the student to demonstrate the desired behavior.
- If the student cannot perform the behavior, model it.
- Have the student try to imitate the model.
- Reinforce appropriate imitation (it need not be perfect).

Note: If the student does not begin to imitate, use prompts to get the student started. Do not expect a perfect performance at first. Reinforce each progressively better attempt to imitate until the target behavior is performed.

Chaining

Chaining is a great tool for teaching multistep tasks. Most procedures, routines, duties, chores, and assignments break down to component steps. By identifying the smaller steps, it is possible to list each step in the chain, teach it, and then move up the chain until the student can perform the entire multistep task. There are two ways to teach a student a task using a chaining strategy:

1. Forward Chaining: The teacher begins with the first step of the multistep task and gradually helps the student learn each step, working forward toward mastery of the complete task.

2. Backward Chaining: The teacher breaks down the steps of a task and teaches them in reverse order. This gives the student the satisfaction of completing the task successfully with every attempt. Instead of the student starting at the beginning and getting lost in the process, the teacher does all but the last step and lets the student complete the work. The teacher fades back, doing less and less while the student does more and more, always ending with the student performing the final step.

The process of using prompts, modeling, and chaining is part of a larger strategy used to support students who would otherwise struggle to master tasks and content subject matter independently. This instructional practice is called systematic instruction. For more information, search the Internet for sites that specialize in this effective practice. Most likely, your special education colleagues can share more information on systematic instruction. When someone says, "Abigail can't learn!" share the process of breaking the learning down into smaller units and then systematically teaching each subunit.

Here's one final cautionary note to consider: Skipping steps or moving too quickly through the task sequence can cause frustration and loss of interest in the task. For the student with ASD who obsesses over perfection, missing steps can cause an emotional episode. Reinforce step completion using pictures, diagrams, checklists, and concrete examples.

Independent Practice

Independent practice must be designed to reinforce the learning goals of the lesson and promote interest and involvement. For some students, it is necessary to increase practice, reinforce, and review more often. Make sure to practice respect for the student's needs.

- Allow independent practice after supervised practice.
- Make sure the student can do all components before letting him practice alone.
- Provide work that is challenging, but not frustrating.

- Do not give unnecessary "busy work" to occupy time.
- Use peer tutoring and small-group activities to keep the student's attention on task.

EXPERIENTIAL LEARNING

Learning From Experience Beyond the Classroom

There are numerous opportunities beyond the classroom for group and individual learning experiences. Experiential learning is an important strategy for helping students understand through hands-on doing.

The following ideas provide an activity-based approach to learning while promoting peer interaction. Before starting a group activity, make sure that each student has a role to play. Consider the student's strengths and interests when assigning group roles. For example, if the student is a talented artist, he could be assigned the task of creating illustrations.

Here's a word of advice: If you let students form their own groups, plan in advance to ensure that students with ASD are not left out. Prearrange groups in advance and develop an understanding among students about the student with ASD. Work with group members to increase the student's participation.

Study Teams: Students are seated in teams and given a set of materials or specific content to study. Teams tutor each other on the information. The complexity of the material can be individualized for each team member. Students are tested on the material individually or as a group.

Research Teams: As questions come up during class, students write questions into a community class notebook. Small groups of students form research teams (two to three students, including the student with ASD), who are assigned to investigate information during the class period by interviewing knowledgeable students or school staff, or researching the subject on the Internet and through other sources of information to clarify the concepts. The presentation of the information takes advantage of each research team member's strengths. Perhaps the student with ASD is an excellent illustrator who contributes by developing a poster that illustrates the team's findings. Or the student may be a computer expert who has the ability to develop a PowerPoint presentation with embedded media, pictures, and illustrations. Another team member might add text to the presentation, while another student might be responsible for orally presenting the team's findings.

Classroom, Grade Level, or Schoolwide Survey Teams: Select a weekly question related to the instructional content or school issue and poll or survey the student body. This can be done in a cooperative format with role assignments that include the interviewer, transcriber, data analyzer, illustrator, presenter, and so on. Interview questions can be recorded on audiotape to be played back and answers recorded to be transcribed later.

Community Outreach Teams: Identify community members who have expertise in the subject area, conduct an interview, gather relevant materials or information, and make a presentation to the class.

Classroom Newsletter: Use a computer for a small group of students to generate topics, illustrations, and layout for an ongoing class newsletter. The preparation of the newsletter may include collecting stories from classmates, taking digital photos, word processing, printing, editing, copying, collating, stapling, and delivering the newsletter to other classes in the school.

Performing Arts Performance Analysis: The student with ASD is grouped with members of the school band, dance class, and drama class. Using a video camera, the student films the performance for the group. The video is played back for group enjoyment and analysis.

The student with ASD assists the class by developing a performance library, documenting performances over time. The same procedure could be applied to the visual arts class. The student takes digital photographs of peer-created works of art and displays the work through a variety of media, including a PowerPoint presentation. If the student is computer and Internet savvy, he or she could develop a website dedicated to the class artwork.

Lecture Service: A student attends and video- or audiotapes lectures in classes for students who are absent. The tapes are logged and filed in the library and then made available to students. This activity could be a group project for a student media class or leadership class. A checkout system could be developed, as well as a written introduction and synopsis of the lecture that is included in the CD or tape storage case.

Paraphrased Chapter Reading: For students with ASD who are unable to comprehend grade-level reading content, a peer who is nondisabled may be assigned to read a chapter in the text one day in advance of the class. The student paraphrases the content into a shortened version. This activity can be done orally for the student with ASD or placed in shortened, easier-to-read written form, enhanced with pictures and graphic organizers. In exchange for the nondisabled student doing the added work, he would be excused from the chapter test. The process of summarizing the chapter is a powerful learning tool for the student without disabilities equal to or greater in value than studying for the test alone.

SUMMARY

Teachers can do a great deal to strengthen the instructional process for students with ASD. The teacher can provide the optimal learning environment for most students by providing explicit instructions, effectively carrying out large- and small-group instruction, and using strategies that enhance participation and learning.

When planning instruction, consider the student's learning style. Connect instruction to previously learned content while ensuring that new concepts are logically sequenced and connected. Key decisions about instructional content, curriculum, and adaptations are the responsibility of the general education teacher in partnership with the special education staff and members of the IEP team.

The amount and quality of instruction has a major influence on student learning. Making a commitment to respect student on-task time is important to the realization of successful learning outcomes. Keep students interested and engaged. Idle time causes boredom. When the teacher is actively involved in delivering instruction and monitoring progress, more learning occurs. Express your sincere belief in the student's capacity to learn, and establish high expectations for achievement.

The use of graphic organizers and other support strategies can help reinforce concepts, not just for students with ASD, but for any student who is a visual learner. Visual information is concrete and comes in many forms. Teachers may choose to use one of the strategies featured in this chapter or make up their own. Pictures are helpful tools for teaching concepts as well. Graphic organizers can be used to help the student with ASD make visual connections to abstract information.

The finding, handling, and distribution of materials in the classroom can take a significant amount of time away from instruction. Keep the work area organized so that time is not lost looking for materials. Establish procedures for handing out and picking up learning materials and store frequently used materials in an easy-to-find place.

If the student requires prompting, give as little assistance as needed for the student to accomplish the task. Assistance is increased or decreased according to the level of need, mindful of the student's need for independence. Most prompting strategies, along with support in general, should not be a permanent condition. Fade or decrease assistance as soon as appropriate.

Students with ASD learn best by doing. Concrete experiences are especially valuable for these students. Participating in the activity is tangible and involving. Learning in small cooperative learning groups also allows students opportunities to interact and learn from one another. There is reason to communicate.

RESOURCES

The following resources are especially helpful in assessing the effectiveness of your classroom routines and instructional practices:

> Resource A: General Education Classroom—Goals and Desired Outcomes
>
> Resource B: Secondary General Education Classes—Lecture
>
> Resource J: Instruction and Group Management Goals and Desired Outcomes

Resource K: Inclusion Support Teacher Role Management Areas

Resource M: Assessment of Student Participation in General Education Settings

FURTHER READING

Farrell, S. C. T. (2009). *Talking, listening, and teaching: A guide to classroom communication.* Thousand Oaks, CA: Corwin.

Gangwer, T. (2009). *Visual impact, visual teaching: Using images to strengthen learning* (2nd ed.). Thousand Oaks, CA: Corwin.

Goldstein, H., Kaczmarek, L. A., & English, K. M. (2002). *Promoting social communication: Children with developmental disabilities from birth to adolescence.* Baltimore, MD: Paul H. Brookes.

Koegel, R. L., & Koegel, L. (2006). *Pivotal response treatments for autism; Communication, social & academic development.* Baltimore, MD: Paul H. Brookes.

Thousand, J., Villa, R. A., & Nevin, A. I. (Eds.). (2002). *Creativity and collaborative learning.* Baltimore, MD: Paul H. Brookes.

8

Organization

Many kids struggle with disorganization. With the developing brain, it is a natural part of being a young person. Differences in organizational abilities are also a basic personality preference that does not necessarily improve with age. If you saw my workspace, you might wonder how anything gets accomplished. There are books and journals randomly strewn about and stacks of papers piled high, topped off with a half-eaten sandwich on a plate balancing precariously on top of the pile. Somehow, I manage to get by, unless of course I misplace my cell phone and keys.

Students with ASD and their neurotypical peers cannot be allowed to behave this way. Disorganization can cause big problems and, if not corrected, may impact the student's ability to function at school, at home, or socially.

We are living in the age of accountability. Due to federal and state legislation, students today face higher expectations and more accountability than did students a few years ago. They are accountable to as many as seven different teachers, all with their own assignments, tests, and project requirements. When the school day ends, and the student returns home, there is homework to complete. Many kids become stressed and disorganized while struggling to keep pace. These multiple challenges can cause emotional anxiety and academic failure.

Unlike in elementary school, where the watchful eyes of teachers provide organizational guidance, older students are expected to be independent and organized. Life is painful for students who do not meet the expectations of their teachers and parents.

Every year teachers see the same pattern: Students start the new school year committed to earning good grades. They arrive the first day of school equipped with new spiral-ringed binders filled with supplies. The air is filled with new attitudes and hopes for success. After a few weeks, however, concerns begin to surface. We start to notice crumpled papers, unwashed gym clothes, and long-overdue, unfinished homework at the bottom of backpacks. Not surprisingly, lost assignments are not turned in and grades, along with those high aspirations, begin to drop. These issues can be devastating to student self-esteem and stressful to parents.

The state of the backpack is a sign of a larger problem. Despite the student's potential to learn, many students with ASD struggle with understanding, planning, and organizing information. If students are to reach their potential, strategies for teaching organization need to be pursued and included in the curriculum.

ORGANIZATION DEFINED

We will discuss two forms of organization in this chapter: physical organization (managing materials) and thought organization (organizing one's thoughts). The term "executive functioning" refers to the student's ability to organize information in his mind in a way that allows him to access, manipulate, and use the information to generate new ideas.

Establish a daily routine for school organization starting the first day of school. Include a written explanation to parents listing required supplies and how the home-school connection will be established. Develop a positive rapport with parents starting the first day. Gain parental support for setting a high priority on school organization. Typical student organizational tasks to master include the following:

1. Turn in homework at the beginning of class.

2. Get out paper, text, pencil, or pen.

3. Check board for assignment.

4. When work is completed, place handouts and other course material in their designated binder location, write homework assignment in planner, close binder, and place neatly in backpack.

5. Prepare to leave class three minutes before it ends (pack books and materials).

Encourage parents to use the same approach at home (e.g., check planner, do homework at a specified time, have parent initial homework, clean out book bag, check for necessary supplies for school).

Learn through collaborating with the special education teacher, student, and support staff how the student best receives new information. Read over the student's IEP goals and purposely observe the student for clues to his or her organizational challenges. Ask the student how he or she best remembers things. Learning the student's routines will help you connect with the person and together seek solutions to organization problems. The more you can learn in advance, the less you will need to rely on trial and error.

Figure 8.1   Being Organized Is Important

EXECUTIVE FUNCTIONING

Executive functioning refers to a person's ability to internally think through information and organize it efficiently in order to achieve a goal. People with well-developed executive functioning possess the ability to

- sequence tasks into a logical order of steps,
- categorize information into groups or classes,
- prioritize goals according to predetermined priorities,
- understand the consequences for choices in a way that alters behavior,
- apply lessons learned from an experience to a similar situation,
- stay focused on a task in spite of distractions,
- anticipate transitions and adjust the current activity in anticipation of the next activity, and
- apply previously learned information to a new or expanded concept.

Students with ASD struggle with these skills. They have difficulty with organization and planning. They struggle to process information, make transitions, and anticipate problems before they occur. Before you can help, understand the nature of the student's challenges. As stated, learn about the student's challenges so that you can provide effective strategies to help.

MANAGING INFORMATION

Just as Post-it Notes and reminder boards help us remember our daily responsibilities, providing organization supports that are visual can help students with ASD stay organized. Student planners, checklists, schedules, and graphic organizers are concrete and easy to follow.

STUDENT PLANNER

The student planner is where all assignments are recorded. Checking the planner reminds the student of upcoming assignments and test deadlines. The planner is the starting point for long-term planning.

Teach the student to write down assignments in the planner. Check to make sure the assignments are recorded properly. Make sure the student has the due date for each assignment written in the appropriate place. See Figure 8.2 for an example.

Highlighters and colored markers emphasize or distinguish different activities (e.g., class, work, study, and practice). Help the student develop the habit of using the planner to track assignments and projects.

Student Planner Checklist

✓ Does the school require the student to have a specific planner?
✓ How well does the student use her planner?
✓ Do parents follow through by checking the planner and signing off?
✓ Does the student have a classmate she can call if she forgets to write the assignment in her planner?

If the student is not turning in homework, is earning low grades, or is forgetting to return school forms with a parent signature, she may not be using her planner. Use the following questions; rate the student on her performance. Use "always," "sometimes," or "never'" for the statements below; then check recommended actions to take on the next page. The student . . .

1. Does not know due dates for assignments.

2. Is unprepared for tests and quizzes.

3. Asks for help at the last minute; for example, the volcano project is due tomorrow, first period, and the student is not prepared.

4. Starts long-term projects the night before they are due.

Figure 8.2   Planner Basics

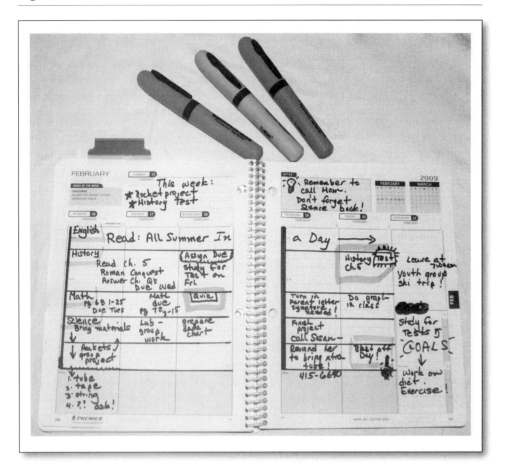

Answers/Recommended Actions

If the answer is "never" to all four statements, you can most likely spend your energy supporting students that are more needy. Check in on the student to make sure good habits are maintained.

If the answer is "sometimes" to two statements, the student needs to be praised for the areas of strength. Teach the student to use the planner as a useful tool for keeping his information in one place. Monitor progress.

If the answer is "always" to three or more statements, the student needs significant support to learn how to manage his responsibilities. Establish a home-school connection and work out a plan to teach the student how to organize his responsibilities. With parent input, develop a system for home and school that ensures the student follows through on his school responsibilities. Monitor closely and chart progress.

VISUAL SCHEDULES

Visual schedules turn abstract concepts of time into concrete images. The schedule communicates to the student when events will take place and what will come next in a clear and uncluttered manner. Visual schedules decrease challenging behaviors by reducing unanticipated changes.

The first step in developing an effective visual schedule is to assess the student's understanding of different forms of visual communication. If, for example, the individual understands some photos, but generally is at an object level, the schedule may consist of a combination of objects and photos. As the individual demonstrates understanding of the objects, they may be paired with the photos to teach the individual the meaning of the photos. An object may be faded or removed when the individual is able to demonstrate understanding of the photo. Always pair the written word with photos and picture symbols. The hierarchy of visual communication (least abstract to most abstract) is as follows:

- Objects (whole object, miniature object, partial object)
- Photos
- Picture symbols (line drawings such as Mayer-Johnson Picture Communication symbols)
- Written words

Visual schedules organize class activities in symbols (pictures, photographs, words, icons) in the order they will occur. They help students with ASD understand what is going to happen and make expectations clear during a specific time or activity. Visual schedules help reduce anxiety because the visuals turn the unknown into something tangible the student understands.

Students with ASD do best when their schedule is structured and predictable. You will find this true for students across the spectrum. Printed schedules that are written or typed with an emphasis on the student's needs, as opposed to generic schedules, work best. The schedule should be easily accessible to the student. Some students will insert their schedule in the front of their binder. Others tape it to the inside cover of their planner. Including the start and end times is a good idea as long as the student is not rigid about time. If the student stresses when times don't follow exactly, then just show the sequence of events instead, leaving times out.

The visual information should be simple and clear. Choose the activities that are the most important to the student. Use whatever combination of words, symbols, or pictures the student best understands. Highlighting or circling key words to gain attention to the most important details is a good idea as well. Schedules can be revised "on the spot." If the student is prone to anxiety over schedule changes, explain the change in a neutral tone of voice while you cross out or add something to the schedule. The idea you want to remember is to pair visual information (writing in the change) with verbal information (explaining the change).

If the student is prone to perseverate about being exact with time schedules, you could develop an undefined schedule (see Figure 8.3). In addition, you might also want to build in flexibility by using a symbol to represent "I don't know." For example, a question mark may be used. You could then delay making a decision about an activity. For greater success, the schedule should be followed consistently. "Make it an essential part of the daily routine. Continually refer back to it when communicating about its information" (Hodgdon, 1999, p. 38).

Figure 8.3 Undefined Schedules

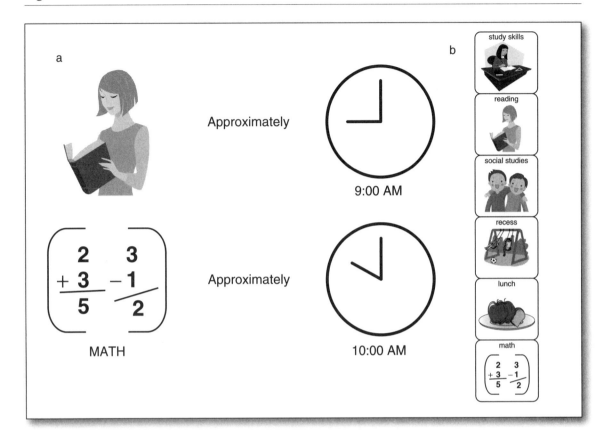

Strategies for Using Visual Schedules

Not all students need visual schedules in order to make sense of school expectations and time frames. There is no need to use visuals if the student is doing fine. Use visual schedules to

- provide structure and predictability (effective in reducing anxiety that's leading to challenging behaviors);
- make abstract time concepts, such as "later," "next," or "last," more concrete;
- reduce anxiety when unexpected changes will occur in the regular schedule;
- help the student transition from one activity to the next;
- increase independence;
- provide structure for students with limited attention spans; and
- support successful inclusion in the general education classrooms.

CHECKLISTS

We find that students who use checklists need less prompting. Using checklists takes advantage of the student's visual strengths, promotes independence, and makes directions more concrete. As items are completed, they can be marked off. This process helps build a sense of accomplishment for students.

Include items that, for example, remind the student to get out pencil and paper, put name on paper, put due date on paper, read directions, complete work, put work away in appropriate notebook section (e.g., to do tonight, to do this week), write assignment on assignment sheet, get teacher to sign, take home and complete work. See Figure 8.4 for an example.

Meet with the student after a week to evaluate her progress. Don't just focus on areas that need improvement. Focus on what the student is doing right and praise.

Color Coding

Encourage the student to use color coding to organize study notes, handouts, school supplies, and the planner. Color coding is a good way to organize paperwork after class. Colors can help students understand in which order assignments should be completed and where and when to turn in assignments.

During free time, teach the student to organize notes using color coding. First, review the handouts with the student and compare the major topics covered. Assign a highlighter color to each of the major topics, and highlight all the information in each topic using its assigned color. The notes then may be reorganized according to the major topics. This strategy helps the student incorporate textbook material into notes, resulting in more complete and accurate notes to use for exam preparation.

Figure 8.4   A Checklist

After School — Monday

☑ Snack

☑ Alone time

☑ 4:00 Feed fish

☑ Take out garbage

☑ Put dishes in dishwasher

☑ Show Mom homework list

☐ Homework — Math pg. 56—59 then English

☐ Dinner

☐ Finish homework

☐ Open binder — put my homework stuff in turn-in folder. <u>Don't forget!</u>

☐ <u>My free time</u>

☐ <u>Get ready for bed</u>

Color coding can also be used in a variety of ways to prepare for tests. The student can make flash cards about different topics in different colors of ink or on different colors of index cards. Another way is to use different colors of ink to arrange information in outline form. To show the difference between main points from supporting details, write in different colors. To distinguish information related to different topics, write the main points and supporting details for each topic in different colors. Also, identify important information in the notes by using colored highlighters. Be creative! Think of other ways to use colors to indicate relationships and associations among information to be learned for the test.

HOMEWORK CHALLENGES

Students with ASD need to decompress and escape to their special safe zone when they get home from school. For many, this is a critical survival strategy. Many times, homework is not completed because the medication the student is taking has worn off. The student has managed to "keep it together" all day. Now he is rebounding from the reduced effects of the medication. One more demand or task may be too much.

In the words of one mother,

> Many of these kids are really struggling to stay up with the demands of the homework. Getting through the day leaves little energy at night for homework completion. Many are taking medication that wears off in the late afternoon, leaving the "rebound effect." This impairs their ability to reason at night.

Homework must be viewed as it relates to the student's level of challenge after school. Do not set the student up for an emotional episode at home by insisting he do all his homework. As always, approach homework issues as a team that includes teachers, parents, the instructional assistant, and the student.

MANAGING MATERIALS

Many students with ASD do not manage materials well. They lose handouts and forget to turn in assignments. Their backpack may look like a jumbled, disorganized mess of wadded-up papers and loose items. They cannot find the permission slip they were supposed to bring back to school or the assignment that was due last week. Important homework assignments are marked incomplete. One of our students with ASD aced all his science tests but received a C in the class because he repeatedly forgot to turn in assignments. The following are a few tips to remember:

- The student needs to be responsible for his personal school supplies. Avoid giving out pencils and pens when the student "forgets" to bring his own.

- A three-ring binder with organized sections marked off with color-coded tabs for each subject area works best. Additional headings could include "Assignments Due/Date," "To Do Tonight," and "Ongoing Work."
- The student can use a supply pouch that opens and closes with a zipper filled with pencils, markers, erasers, and a hand-held plastic pencil sharpener.
- Color-code materials. Cover the textbook for one course in the same color as the notebook for that course. Use the same color coding to prioritize assignments.
- If possible, obtain two copies of each textbook. Mark one "To be left in school" and the other "To be left at home."
- Schedule a weekly time to help the student clean out his backpack at school. Fade this support when the student has learned the routine. Monitor to ensure the student follows through when support has been discontinued.

THREE-RING BINDERS

Three-ring binders with dividers are highly recommended for organizing and storing information. Materials like handouts, notes, and assignments are frequently lost due to the student's lack of an organized system for storing papers. Three-ring binders allow the student with ASD to organize class materials in one place by subject. The binder is easy for the student to carry in his backpack.

Three-ring binders offer four advantages over spiral notebooks: First, notes may be easily inserted and removed for reorganizing, recopying, or reviewing. Second, extra papers can easily be organized and added using a three-hole punch. This puts all course materials in one place for easy access. Third, dividers may be inserted for separating class materials by major topic or for separating notes from handouts, homework, and other class papers. Finally, most three-ring binders include inner pockets for storing extra paper and materials. The following are three instructions to tell the student:

- Tell the student to write a note to her parent requesting the purchase of divider pages to place in a three-ring binder. The student will use the dividers to separate each class.
- Help the student put the notes and handouts in the proper sections of the binder. Fade this support over time. Continue to monitor, however, to make certain the student really develops the habit of putting papers in their proper place.
- Encourage the student to use a three-hole punch for papers not already punched. Then train the student to insert homework and handouts in the correct binder sections. This habit is an important skill for the student to learn.

Figure 8.5 Three-Ring Binder Supply Pouch

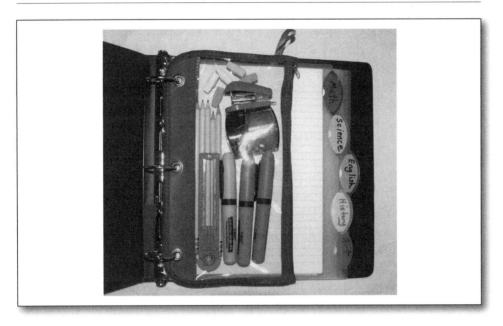

TOOLS

It seems reasonable to expect students to have a pencil, eraser, and paper to write on. However, veteran teachers are not surprised by the number of students who come to class without these basic tools. Instill early on that *the student* is responsible for his school supplies. Do not always give in by providing the student with needed items. Remember the importance of independence and self-determination. This includes being responsible for one's own materials.

Figure 8.6 Tools of the Trade

SUMMARY

Organization is an important survival skill for all students, but it is especially important for students with ASD. Teachers expect middle and high school students to be organized. Most general education teachers stress organization and will help students develop organizational skills. However, expectations are higher at the middle and high school levels, and there is less tolerance when students fail to follow recommended strategies.

Many students with ASD have difficulty finding their materials and homework and need help completing tasks and organizing papers and information. Strategies like the ideas shared in this chapter need to be established early and consistently reinforced. To begin this process, teachers should incorporate visual prompts and picture cues in their classroom. Visual supports like student planners, schedules, and checklists help the student process, organize, and remember information more effectively. In the absence of organization, these students run the risk of school failure.

In addition to helping the student organize information, the teacher needs to help the student learn how to manage school supplies and materials. A well-organized three-ring binder equipped with a supply pouch filled with everyday supplies like pencils, erasers, and colored highlighters will help the student better manage the demands of the classroom. Students should have subject-specific materials for classes as well. Math might include a calculator and ruler, while English may require a dictionary and thesaurus. Pictures of the materials students need for class will help them determine the supplies to bring from home.

In addition, colors and symbols can help students learn in which order assignments should be completed and where and when to turn in assignments. For example, teachers can establish color-coded folders for homework in each subject area. If students finish their work early, they can place the finished assignment in the appropriate folder immediately or as soon as they get to school in the morning.

For these processes to work, students with ASD need consistent practice and home support to learn organizational skills. Establishing a consistent routine or process for assigning and collecting classwork and homework is important as well.

Teachers can also help students understand the best way to make "to-do" lists in their calendar and how these lists help them complete assignments. Large assignments should be broken down into manageable chunks or separate subtasks. Students should schedule time in their assignment books to work on each task. When they have completed a task or assignment, they should check it off.

Students live in their own parallel realities of fantasies, dreams, and fears. Oftentimes, their internal thoughts are consumed with priorities we may not share. It is hard for school organization and homework completion to compete with Xbox 360™ in the student's mind. Teachers and parents need to understand how kids think and guide them toward making room for the things that matter.

RESOURCES

Resource P: Homework Summary

This provides the teacher with a form that will help clarify for parents the student's homework responsibilities, what materials are needed, and the due date.

FURTHER READING

Burke, J., Steinkamp, B., & Charron, C. (2010). *The planner guide: An organizational and reference system for people with social and cognitive challenges.* Williamston, MI: The Planner Guide LLC. On the web: info@theplannerguide.com

Goldberg, D. (2005). *The organized student: Teaching children the skills for success in school and beyond.* New York: Fireside.

Gore, M. C., & Dowd, J. F. (1999). *Taming the time stealers: Tricks of the trade from organized teachers.* Thousand Oaks, CA: Corwin.

Appendix 1

Glossary of Frequently Used Terms

Accommodations: Alterations to the environment, equipment, or format of a curriculum to allow equal access to the content. Unlike modifications, accommodations do not alter the actual content of the material being taught.

Adaptations: Involve an adjustment to the instructional content or performance expectations of students with disabilities from what is expected or taught to students in general education. Adaptations are usually included as part of a student's IEP. Examples of adaptations include decreasing the number of exercises the student is expected to complete or allowing extra time to complete work.

Adaptive behavior: "Practical intelligence." An individual's manner of dealing with the demands of daily life, including self-care skills, organizational skills, basic interpersonal skills, and managing in community settings (obeying rules, taking responsibility, etc.).

ADHD: Attention deficit hyperactivity disorder.

Advocate: An individual who is not an attorney, but who assists parents and students in their dealings with school districts regarding the student's special education programs.

Affective: A term that refers to emotions and attitudes.

Age appropriate: At the chronological (actual) age of the student. The term can be applied to materials, curriculum, and modifications for the student or to the student's behavior.

Annual goals: A required component of an IEP. Goals are written for the individual student and can be for a maximum of one year.

Antecedent: An event that precedes a behavior.

Attention: The ability to concentrate as needed.

Auditory processing: How the brain processes and interprets what is heard through the ear.

157

Baseline: Beginning observations prior to intervention; level of functioning established or measured without any active intervention from the observer.

Body language: Information about a person's thoughts or feelings that is unconsciously conveyed through physical mannerisms.

Central coherence: The brain's ability to process multiple chunks of information in a global way, connecting them and viewing them in context, in order to determine a higher level of meaning. Poor central coherence can make it difficult to generalize.

Circle of Friends: A technique used to enlist the involvement and commitment of peers in developing and supporting effective inclusion (also called Circle of Support).

CLOZE procedure: A teaching technique that involves deleting words from the text and leaving blank spaces. Measurement is made by rating the number of blanks that can be correctly filled. The oral CLOZE method is also useful when directing whole-class reading. The teacher reads a passage and periodically leaves one word out. Students chorally respond with the missing word on a predetermined cue (snap of fingers, arm movement, etc.).

COACH: An assessment and planning tool designed to help educators identify family-centered priorities for their students, define the educational program components, and address these components in an inclusive setting.

Cognition: Conscious mental activity, including thinking, perceiving, reasoning, and learning.

Cognitive: A term that refers to reasoning or intellectual capacity.

Collaboration: Individuals working together for a common goal.

Community-based instruction (CBI): Skills are taught at varied locations in the community (supermarket, library, mall, restaurant) rather than in the classroom in order to help the student learn independence in the community.

Conference: Generic term that may refer to a multidisciplinary conference, IEP meeting, annual review, or other type of meeting. When in doubt, it is important to clarify the purpose of any conference.

Consonant: A basic speech sound that, when combined with a vowel, creates a syllable or whole word.

Continuum of services: The range of services that must be available to the students of a school district so they may be served in the least restrictive environment.

Curriculum: The subject matter that is to be learned. A curriculum is usually described in terms of its scope and sequence. For example, a teacher or parent might evaluate the curriculum in a given class to determine if it matches the student's IEP goals.

Curriculum-based assessment: Measuring a student's progress in the curriculum to determine if the adaptations designed for the student are working or need to be adjusted.

Deficit: Inadequacy in functioning due to developmental delay.

Delay: Development that does not occur within expected time ranges.

Differentiated instruction: Recognizing the student's varying background knowledge, readiness, language, and preferences in learning and interests, and reacting responsively. Differentiated instruction is a process to approach teaching and learning for students of differing abilities in the same class. The intent of differentiating instruction is to maximize each student's growth and individual success by meeting each student where he or she is, and assisting in the learning process.

Disability: A physical, sensory, cognitive, or affective impairment that causes the student to need special education.

Due process: In special education, due process refers to a specific set of procedures designed to settle disputes between school districts and parents.

Echolalia: The immediate or delayed echoing or repetition of complete verbal expressions heard at an earlier time. Possible functions of echolalia include conversation maintenance, communication, self-soothing, and verbal rehearsal. Echolalia can be functional (using the phrase in an appropriate context to aid communication) or nonfunctional (vocalizing without relationship to the context of the situation).

Empathy: A projection of one's thoughts and feelings into the personality of another in order to understand him better.

Extended school year: A service for a special education student to receive instruction during ordinary school "vacation" periods.

Fading: A technique for errorless learning whereby the teacher cues the student with multiple stimuli to make the correct response. Gradually, the number of cues are reduced, or "faded," until only one stimulus comes to exert control over the responding.

Fine motor: Muscle functions that require tiny muscle movements. For example, writing or typing would require fine motor movement.

Free appropriate public education (FAPE): Special education and related services that (1) have been provided at public expense, under public supervision and direction, and without charge; (2) meet the standards of the State educational agency; (3) include an appropriate preschool, elementary school, or secondary school education in the State involved; and (4) are provided in conformity with the individualized education program. (20 U.S.C. §1401)

Functional behavioral assessment (FBA): A problem-solving process for addressing a student's challenging behavior. FBA relies on a variety of techniques and strategies to identify the purposes of specific behavior and to help IEP teams select interventions to directly address the challenging behavior. It looks beyond the behavior itself, focusing on identifying significant, pupil-specific social, affective, cognitive, and/or environmental factors associated with the occurrence (and nonoccurrence) of specific behaviors.

Generalization: In concept formation, problem solving, and transfer of training, the detection by the learner of a characteristic or principle common to a class of objects, events, or problems. Also, in conditioning, the principle that once a conditioned response has been established for a given stimulus, other similar stimuli will also evoke that response.

Gross motor: Muscle functions require large muscle movements. For example, walking or jumping would require gross motor movement.

Heterogeneous grouping: An educational practice in which students of diverse abilities are placed within the same instructional groups. This practice is usually helpful in the inclusion of students with disabilities.

Homogeneous grouping: An educational practice in which students of similar abilities are placed within the same instructional groups. This practice usually serves as a barrier to the inclusion of students with disabilities. The practice is helpful, however, for small-group direct instruction where students are all in need of the same intervention strategy.

IEP meeting: A gathering required at least annually under IDEA in which an Individualized Educational Program (IEP) is developed or revised for a student receiving special education.

Inclusion: Full inclusion refers to the inclusion of a student with a disability in an age-appropriate regular classroom at the student's neighborhood school. The student moves with peers to subsequent grades. All related services are provided in the regular classroom through a collaborative approach, except where privacy is an issue. Curriculum may be district core curriculum as for the other students or modified core curriculum to provide physical assistance, adapted content or material, multilevel curriculum, curriculum overlapping (same activity, same goals), or substitute curriculum.

Individualized Educational Program (IEP): A written educational prescription developed by a school for each student with a disability. An IEP must contain the student's present levels of educational performance, annual and short-term educational goals, the specific education program and related services that will be provided to the student, and the extent to which the student will participate in the regular education program with nondisabled students.

Individuals With Disabilities Education Act (IDEA): Public Law 108-446 is called the "Individuals with Disabilities Education Improvement Act of 2004." Its "short title" is Individuals With Disabilities Education Act.

Integration: Integration refers to the inclusion and interaction of students with special needs in an age-appropriate regular education program and/or classroom from which they are able to derive educational benefit in a variety of areas, including social skills and interactions, communication and language skills, classroom skills, independent living/vocational skills, and academic skills. Integration is an ongoing process related to the individual needs of students.

LEA: Local educational agency; that is, a local public school district.

Least restrictive environment (LRE): Provisions for LRE appear in IDEA regulations. LRE requires that "to the maximum extent appropriate, students with disabilities are educated with students who are non-disabled; and special classes, separate schooling, or other removal of students with disabilities from the regular educational environment occurs only if the nature or severity of the disability is such that education in regular classes with the use of supplementary aids and services cannot be achieved satisfactorily."

Mainstreaming: This is an outmoded term referring to the practice of returning students with disabilities to a regular classroom for a portion of the school day. The student, however, is a "drop-in" and not a full member of the classroom. Students who were mainstreamed into regular education classes were considered visitors who did not appear on the general education teacher's role. As a result, the general education teacher perceived the student as not part of the class and oftentimes was reluctant to take responsibility for the student's learning outcomes. This practice also created symbolic barriers between the student and his or her peers because the student was not considered a full member of the class.

MAPS (Making Action Plans): A person-centered planning process used before major life transitions (leaving high school to enter a work environment) to help the student and family focus on dreams for the student's future. MAPS is carried out in a meeting with the student's family and friends. They gather to share their positive beliefs for the person's future and express affirming statements regarding the student's talents and strengths. Facilitators and participants must believe in the person's capacity to reach his or her goals. The end result of MAPS is to have a plan for the person's future, keeping in mind the student's interests, strengths, and dreams while addressing challenges that may interfere with progress toward goals and how to overcome them.

Mean: The arithmetical average; the sum of all scores divided by the number of scores.

Modality: An avenue of acquiring sensation; the visual, auditory (hearing), tactile, kinesthetic (motion and balance), olfactory (smell), and gustatory (taste) modalities are the most common sense modalities.

Modeling: A procedure for learning in which the individual observes a model perform some task and then imitates the performance of the model. Modeling accounts for much verbal and motor learning in young children.

Modifications: Changes to what a student is expected to learn. They are provided to students with disabilities who are working below grade level and who may require modified expectations within a given activity to meet their individual needs. Alternative curriculum goals can be used to make the content more relevant and functional to the individual's needs. Requirements for a student may be partially adapted, with the student expected to master some, but not all, of the expectations. Or the level of mastery that is expected for a student may be altered.

Natural proportions: Ensuring that the proportions, or ratios, of students with disabilities in any given class represent the natural proportions that occur in the community. This would mean there is not overrepresentation in one class and underrepresentation in another, but all classes reflect the naturally occurring proportions of the general population in the community. Typically, no more than 1% to 2% of a school's population will have significant disabilities, and there should be no more than one student with a significant disability in a regular classroom. In general, 10% to 15% of students may have some type of disability, and so for classes of 30 students, for example, there would be 3 to 5 students with disabilities.

Negative feedback: Communication to the subject that his or her response was incorrect. It tends to reduce the chances of repetition of the behavior.

Negative reinforcement: A procedure for strengthening behavior when the consequence of that behavior is the termination or avoidance of an aversive stimulus. That is, the response is followed by the avoidance or termination of some event noxious to the individual.

Norm: An average, common, or standard performance under specified conditions (e.g., the average achievement test score of 9-year-old children or the average birth weight of male children).

Objective observation: Audiotape, videotape, or written notation of behaviors. Can include tallies for frequency, duration, or speed; can be a narrative transcription of the actions and verbalizations observed.

Occupational therapy (OT): A special education–related service that is usually focused on the development of a student's fine motor skills and/ or the identification of adapted ways of accomplishing activities of daily living when a student's disabilities preclude doing those tasks in typical ways (e.g., modifying clothing so a person without arms can dress himself or herself).

PATH (Planning Alternative Tomorrows With Hope): A group planning tool that transition planners can use to develop long- and short-range goals by encouraging students with the help of family and friends to think about their hopes for the future.

Perseveration: The tendency for one to persist on without interruption on a specific thought, act, or behavior to the exclusion of other thoughts.

Person-centered planning: Person-centered planning is a process whereby students with disabilities, with the support of families, direct the planning and allocation of resources to meet their own life vision and goals.

Person-first language: A method of description that is used when referring to people with disabilities. The guiding principle is to refer to the person first, not the disability. In place of saying "autistic student," it is preferable to say "student with autism." This way, the emphasis is placed on the person, not the disability.

Phonics: The study of speech sounds with special reference to reading.

Primary reinforcer: Those stimuli that can strengthen behaviors they follow without prior learning. These reinforcing stimuli derive their reinforcing power from the fact that they satisfy physiological needs of the organism (e.g., food, water).

Program specialist: A program specialist is a specialist who holds a valid special education credential, health services credential, or school psychologist authorization, and who has advanced training and related experience in the education of individuals with exceptional needs and a specialized, in-depth knowledge of special education services.

Rapport: A relationship of ease, harmony, and accord between the subject and examiner or therapist.

Regression: The return to a previous or earlier developmental phase.

Reinforcement: A procedure to strengthen or weaken a response by the administration of immediate rewards (positive reinforcement) or punishment (negative reinforcement).

Reinforcer: Any stimulus event that can be used to strengthen a behavior it follows.

Related services: Related services include developmental, corrective, and other supportive services as are required to assist a student with a disability to benefit from special education. Examples of related services include speech-language pathology, psychological services, and occupational therapy.

Resource Specialist Program (RSP): Students receiving special education instruction for less than 50% of the school day are enrolled in RSP. These students may be "pulled out" of the general classroom for special assistance during specific periods of the day or week and are taught by credentialed special education resource specialists.

Resource teacher: A specialist who works with students with special learning needs and acts as a consultant to other teachers, providing materials and methods to help students who are having difficulty within the regular classroom. The resource teacher may work from a centralized resource room within a school where appropriate materials are housed.

Self-determination: Individuals making the choices that allow them to exercise control over their own lives, to achieve their personal goals and to acquire the skills and resources necessary to participate fully and meaningfully in school and society.

Sensory integration: Sensory integration refers to the management of multiple sense perceptions entering the mind all at once. The ability to manage the senses helps individuals respond and behave accordingly. Some individuals with autism struggle to sort out multiple sensory inputs and may find certain sensations aversive. If the person is unable to filter out certain sensory stimuli, an emotional response may result.

Social perception: The ability to interpret stimuli in the social environment and appropriately relate such interpretations to the social situation.

Socialization: Shaping of individual characteristics and behaviors through the stimuli and reinforcements that the social environment provides.

Special day class (SDC): A self-contained classroom in which only students who require special education instruction are enrolled.

Special education: The individually planned and systematically monitored teaching procedures and other interventions designed to help learners with special needs achieve the greatest possible personal self-sufficiency and success in school and community.

Special education local plan area (SELPA): The geographical service area that is responsible for administering special education programs and services.

Splinter skill: A skill that is not an integral part of an orderly sequential development. It is a skill mastered ahead of the usual developmental sequence or is advanced compared with the student's overall developmental level.

Stereotypical behavior: A repetitive motor behavior with no obvious purpose. These behaviors are common with individuals on the autism spectrum. Many refer to them as "self-stimulating" behaviors, as they appear to be motivated by something in the self. Stereotypical behaviors can interfere with learning and attending to tasks.

Stereotyping: A biased generalization, usually about a social or national group, in which individuals are falsely assigned traits they do not possess.

Stimulus: An external event, act, or influence that causes physiological change in a sense organ.

Student study team (SST): A general education process designed to make preliminary modifications within the general education program of a student not succeeding in class (sometimes referred to as a "student success team").

Supplementary aids and services: Aids, services, and other supports that are provided in regular education classes, other education-related settings, and extracurricular and nonacademic settings, to enable students with disabilities to be educated with nondisabled students to the maximum extent possible.

Syndrome: A complex set of symptoms; a set of symptoms or characteristics occurring together. This contrasts with disease, which is a disorder of structure or function in the person.

Transition: The period of adjustment from school to working life that is outcome oriented encompassing a broad array of services and experiences that lead to employment and adult life.

Transition services: A coordinated set of activities for a student with a disability that is designed to facilitate the student's movement from school to postschool activities.

Workability: A program that promotes independent living and provides comprehensive preemployment worksite training, employment, and follow-up services for youth in special education who are making the transition from school to work, postsecondary education, or training.

Others:

_____

_____

_____

_____

_____

_____

_____

_____

_____

_____

_____

_____

_____

Appendix 2

Special Education Acronyms

ADA: Americans With Disabilities Act

ADD: Attention deficit disorder

ADHD: Attention deficit hyperactivity disorder

APE: Adaptive physical education

AS: Asperger syndrome (sometimes referred to as Asperger's syndrome)

ASD: Autism spectrum disorder

AVID: Advancement Via Individual Determination (AVID) is a college preparatory program for students in the middle who are often economically disadvantaged and underachieving.

DSM-IV: *Diagnostic and Statistical Manual of Mental Disorders, 4th edition*

ED: Emotional disturbance

FBA: Functional behavioral assessment

IDEA: Individuals With Disabilities Education Act

IEP: Individualized Educational Program

IFSP: Individualized family service plan

LRE: Least restrictive environment

NCLB: No Child Left Behind Act

OT: Occupational therapy

PBSP: Positive behavior support plan

PDD-NOS: Pervasive developmental disorder not otherwise specified

PT: Physical therapy or therapist

RTI: Response to intervention

SELPA: Special education local plan area

SIP: School improvement program

SPT: Speech pathologist services

TBI: Traumatic brain injury

Others:

_____

_____

_____

_____

_____

_____

_____

_____

_____

_____

_____

_____

_____

_____

_____

_____

_____

_____

Resources Part I

Inclusion Support Resources

Resource A

Date: Setting: Student(s):   Support Staff:

General Education Classroom—Goals and Desired Outcomes

Support Staff		Class Teacher	
Support Role		**Class Membership/Teacher Ownership**	
☐	Arrives on time	☐	Talks to the *Ss throughout class
☐	Helps ALL students	☐	Shares information to help others positively understand differences
☐	Supports and fades, roving room whenever possible	☐	Highlights what *Ss do well, strengths
☐	Helps all students follow teacher directions, expectations	**Seating/Physical Class Arrangement**	
☐	Takes initiative to help where needed	☐	Seats *Ss next to peers not other *Ss
☐	Shares information to help others positively understand differences	☐	Directs/praises peers to work with and help *Ss
☐	Helps highlight *S's strengths, be seen as able	☐	Seats *Ss near teacher and by compassionate peers who help
☐	Interprets unusual *S behavior, S differences and actions	☐	Rotates peers to work with *Ss
Peer Support		**Active Participation**	
☐	Talks to peers, establishes meaningful relationships	☐	Calls on the *Ss during class discussion
☐	Recruits peers to help *Ss	☐	Assigns *Ss class role, responsibilities
☐	Tells peers how to help *Ss: "Show___ how to"	☐	Finds ways to help the student participate
☐	Tells peers how to help *Ss: "Show___ how to"	☐	Provides activity-based learning tasks

Active Participation		Active Participation	
☐	Helps simplify work; develops adaptations; makes on-the-spot changes	☐	Helps simplify/modify activities, homework, tests for *Ss
☐	Assists *Ss to raise hand, give answer, contribute	**Direct Instruction to *Ss**	
Direct Instruction to *Ss		☐	Praises *Ss often for desirable actions, behavior, successes
☐	Praises *Ss often for desirable actions, behavior, successes	☐	Helps the *Ss with class activities, content
☐	Focuses on supporting, teaching *S's IEP goals	☐	Checks *Ss' work frequently
☐	Attends to *Ss, checking in regularly	☐	Knows, teaches, and reinforces IEP goals to *Ss
☐	Helps *Ss interact with peers, class teacher	**Collaboration With Support Staff**	
☐	Tracks student performance (data, work samples)	☐	Assigns support staff to lead small groups
Collaboration With Class Teacher		☐	Directs support staff to meet *S and class needs
☐	Connects with class teacher	☐	Identifies students at risk for support staff to help
☐	Advocates for *Ss (makes suggestions, intervenes, responds to needs)	☐	Acknowledges support staff as another "teacher" in classroom
☐	Takes initiative to find out about class activities, homework, tests, field trips, projects, presentations	**Positive Teacher Contributions:**	
*Student		**Peers**	
☐	Talks to peers	☐	Talks to *Ss
☐	Talks to class teacher	☐	Helps *Ss
☐	Participates actively in class activities, groups, pair work	☐	Acts in a positive, respectful way toward *Ss
☐	Works on IEP goals	☐	Initiates including *Ss in class activities
☐	Practices academic skills within class activities	☐	Includes *Ss in conversations, discussion
☐	Uses choice boards, picture routines as needed	☐	Finds ways to help *Ss complete class work
☐	Uses motivating and meaningful learning materials to acquire academic skills	☐	Accepts *Ss' differences

*S(s) = student(s) with disabilities.

Source: Doering, K. (2010). *Reflection Tools for Facilitating Positive Student Outcomes.* San Francisco State University, California Research Institute (CRI), Department of Special Education. Used with permission.

Resource B

Date: Setting: Student(s):   Support Staff:

Secondary General Education Classes—Lecture

Check all that are occurring	
Class Teacher	
☐	Ensures that the *Ss get a copy of all handouts that are passed out during class
☐	Calls on *Ss and adapts question format to *Ss' ability level (e.g., "yes/no" question; gives two different answers for *Ss to select)
☐	Provides copy of lecture overheads and/or notes for *Ss to use, highlight, add information
☐	Provides support staff with curricular plan, tests, CDs, lessons, project descriptions, etc., for the instructional unit
☐	Shares daily activities with support staff (classwork, homework, handouts; collecting student work; returning papers/homework)
☐	Checks for comprehension when relevant
☐	Simplifies work for *Ss to increase understanding and/or reduce amount of work to be performed
☐	Gives *Ss a role and responsibilities (e.g., passing out supplies, handouts; collecting student work; returning papers/homework)
Student Participation – The *S:	
☐	Looks at and listens to teacher
☐	Copies down what is on the board or overhead
☐	Writes key words and/or phrases he or she hears throughout the lesson
☐	Uses modified materials to learn key concepts
☐	With individualized support, *S is engaged (e.g., taking notes, listening and tallying key words and/or concepts, highlighting copies of lecture notes)
☐	Asks questions and/or makes lecture-related comments

☐	Comments in class discussions and activities (reads aloud, shares journal entry, presents book report, raises hands to respond to teacher question)

Support Staff	
☐	Checks in with class teacher before class to determine day's activities, homework, supplemental materials that could be obtained to help teach key concepts
☐	Helps *S to greet class teacher and peers
☐	Asks peer to assist with note taking (e.g., carbon paper, two-ply paper)
☐	Redirects *S to attend to teacher (as needed)
☐	Listens to lecture and writes down key concepts every 5–10 minutes for *S to copy when relevant
☐	Gathers and/or records all pertinent information (e.g., handouts, homework, project description, tests, essays, upcoming field trips information)
☐	Facilitates *S's independence and completion of goals and daily routine and tasks (e.g., gets out materials, takes out homework, participates in back-and-forth conversation with peers)
☐	Assists the class teacher in the preparation of lesson plans, instructional materials, and modifying work
☐	Together with the class teacher, identifies and unobtrusively works with and supports any student who needs assistance
☐	Records progress on *S's goals, preferably <u>with</u> *S
☐	Contacts class teacher (before class, during their prep period) to identify curricular units, to target academic concepts, and to get handouts that will be disseminated to all *Ss
☐	Contacts class teacher to share ideas and modified materials that have been developed
☐	Creates modified handouts to meet *Ss ability level (e.g., who, what, why focus; highlights the answers in sentence and reference with the page number or question number)
☐	Shares student interests with peers, teacher to assist others to know more and interact with *S
☐	Helps *S to start conversations with peers, then fades

Peers	
☐	Greet *S
☐	Talk to *S and engage in friendly conversation during free time
☐	Direct *S to raise hand and provide *S with answers to share during class discussion, as appropriate
☐	Redirect *S to attend to teacher, as needed
☐	Treat *S in a positive, respectful manner

*S(s) = student(s) with disabilities.

Source: Doering, K. (2010). *Reflection Tools for Facilitating Positive Student Outcomes.* San Francisco State University, California Research Institute (CRI), Department of Special Education. Used with permission.

Resource C

Date: Setting: Student(s):   Support Staff:

Instructional Assistants Supporting Students

In General Education Classrooms

Check all that are occurring		Notes
☐	Arrives on time and takes initiative to find out about day's activities (greets teacher, peers; checks in with teacher)	
☐	Works with ALL students (*Ss, other Ss with IEPs, Ss at risk, classmates)	
☐	Helps out the class teacher (helps all Ss follow teacher directions, class rules, and expectations; leads small-group activities; provides 1:1 support to students who need it)	
☐	Develops modifications, simplifies work, makes on-the-spot adaptations	
☐	Interacts with and praises peers as often as possible	
☐	Tells the peers to help *Ss ("Show _____ what book to get out," "Tell _____ to get in line," etc.)	
☐	Provides assistance and instruction to *Ss (teaches IEP goals, provides needed modifications, identifies ways to increase participation)	
☐	Highlights *Ss' strengths (points out successes and abilities as often as possible. Also, tells *Ss what to do vs. what not to do)	

Check all that are occurring		Notes
☐	Collects behavioral data, work samples on *Ss' work during class	
☐	Involves *Ss in interactions with peers and class teacher as much as possible	
☐	Moves around the class, while keeping an eye on *Ss and returning as needed	
☐	Provides information and explanation to peers and class teacher to help them understand differences	
☐	Follows assigned schedule and completes key responsibilities	

*S(s) = student(s) with disabilities.

Source: Doering, K. (2010). *Reflection Tools for Facilitating Positive Student Outcomes.* San Francisco State University, California Research Institute (CRI), Department of Special Education. Used with permission.

Strengths   Target Areas:

Resource D

Date: Setting: Student(s):   Support Staff:

Instructional Assistants— Providing Quality Support

Within General Education Classrooms

Check all that are occurring		Notes
Be Another "Teacher"		
☐	Develop trusting relationship with peers	
☐	Help ALL students follow teacher directions, expectations	
☐	Lead small-group activities	
☐	Support, fade, and return to *Ss when necessary; work with all students who need assistance	
☐	Take initiative to help where needed	
☐	Follow through with teacher requests	
Provide Information ALL the Time		
☐	Describe each *S's learning goals to class teacher	
☐	Help others understand the *Ss' actions, behaviors—be positive	
Help Others View *Ss Positively		
☐	Help others understand and accept *Ss	
☐	Highlight *Ss' strengths, abilities, successes	

Check all that are occurring	Notes
☐ Comment on what the *Ss are doing well	
☐ Help others see *Ss as competent	
Help *Ss Participate/Make Modifications	
☐ Encourage *Ss to raise their hands to contribute; give them an answer to share	
☐ Make on-the-spot adaptations to help the *Ss participate and be successful	
☐ Help simplify work, make modifications	
Tell Peers How to Help, What to Do (Peer Supports)	
☐ Help *Ss interact with their peers	
☐ Help *Ss interact with their class teacher	
☐ Recruit peers to help *Ss	
☐ Tell peers how to help *Ss—"Could you tell ___ to get out . . ."	
☐ Praise peers for helping	
Direct Instruction to *Ss	
☐ Praise *Ss often for desirable actions, successes, positive progress	
☐ Focus on supporting, teaching *Ss IEP goals	
☐ Check *Ss' work frequently	
☐ Help *Ss be as independent as possible	
Document Student Performance	
☐ Record student progress on IEP goals	
☐ Obtain and save important student work, work samples, behavioral data, tests	

*S(s) = student(s) with disabilities.

Source: Doering, K. (2010). *Reflection Tools for Facilitating Positive Student Outcomes.* San Francisco State University, California Research Institute (CRI), Department of Special Education. Used with permission.

Resource E

Date: Setting: Student(s):   Support Staff:

Recess

Check all that are occurring	Notes
Planning/Preparation	
☐ A peer buddy system is in place and is regularly utilized when needed	
☐ *Ss' interests and desired materials are used to plan activities	
☐ Fun, motivating materials are available for *Ss to choose from and use	
☐ Structured activities are selected in advance and regularly taught	
☐ Choice boards or communication devices are available as needed	
Transition to Yard	
☐ *Ss transition to and from yard at the same time as their peers	
☐ *Ss walk to/from yard with peers versus separate from them	
Routine, Schedule	
☐ *Ss attend the recess that their same-aged peers attend	
☐ *Ss follow recess rules	
☐ *Ss line up with peers and return to class at the same time as peers	
Socially Connected	
☐ *Ss interact with their peers (initiation and responding)	
☐ *Ss receive assistance from peers	

☐	Multiple peers approach *Ss during recess
☐	Meaningful interactions occur throughout recess between *Ss and peers
☐	Peers naturally include *Ss in recess activities, conversation, etc.

Meaningful Yard Participation	
☐	*Ss are participating in age-appropriate activities, using age-appropriate materials
☐	*Ss are actively engaged in recess activities versus passively watching
☐	*Ss make choices of desired free-time activities
☐	Ratio of time: *Ss spend more time in proximity to peers than to only support staff or by themselves

Desirable Staff Instruction	
☐	Staff arrive at yard with or before *Ss
☐	Staff set up and run structured activities for a portion of the recess time
☐	Staff actively recruit peers to interact with and support *Ss
☐	Staff focus on teaching social, play skills to *Ss
☐	Staff prompt peers to support *Ss and praise peer involvement
☐	Staff teach game rules, activity steps to all students
☐	Staff resolve conflicts as needed and positively impact on the social success of all students
☐	Staff share information to help peers understand *Ss' differences and how to best support *Ss

*S(s) = student(s) with disabilities.

Source: Doering, K. (2010). *Reflection Tools for Facilitating Positive Student Outcomes.* San Francisco State University, California Research Institute (CRI), Department of Special Education. Used with permission.

Strengths: Targets:

Resource F

Date: Setting: Student(s):   Support Staff:

Lunch/Yard

Check all that are occurring	Notes
Cafeteria Access/Arrival	
☐ ALL *Ss eat in the cafeteria	
☐ *Ss are dispersed throughout cafeteria, not clustered	
☐ *Ss arrive with, not before or after, their peers	
Routine	
☐ *Ss follow cafeteria protocol, stand in line; *Ss do not cut into the line	
☐ *Ss greet cafeteria staff	
☐ *Ss are sitting <u>with</u> peers during lunch	
☐ *Ss ask for help, or are prompted to ask for assistance	
Eating Skills/Independence	
☐ *Ss make choices of what they want to eat/drink	
☐ *Ss take appropriate bites, liquid intake	
☐ *Ss eat healthy lunch items before dessert	
☐ *Ss feed themselves as independently as possible	
☐ *Ss throw away trash	
☐ *Ss return uneaten food to backpack/lunch bag	
Appearance/Age Appropriateness	
☐ *Ss use age-appropriate lunch box, utensils, equipment	
☐ *Ss monitor their appearance (wipe mouth; tuck clothing in; change clothing to address drooling, food spillage, etc.)	
☐ *Ss bring age-appropriate materials at lunchtime (newspapers, magazines, ball, Frisbee, photo albums, etc.)	

Socially Connected	
☐ *Ss interact with their peers (initiation, responding)	
☐ *Ss receive assistance from peers	
☐ Multiple peers approach *Ss during lunch/yard	
Transition to Yard	
☐ *Ss transition with peers versus are last to leave cafeteria	
☐ Peer(s) accompany *Ss from cafeteria to yard	
Meaningful Yard Participation	
☐ *Ss are engaged in age-appropriate, meaningful activities with peers	
☐ *Ss make choices of desired free-time activities	
☐ *Ss remain engaged versus passively watching	

*S(s) = student(s) with disabilities.

Source: Doering, K. (2010). *Reflection Tools for Facilitating Positive Student Outcomes.* San Francisco State University, California Research Institute (CRI), Department of Special Education. Used with permission.

Resource G

Date: Setting: Student(s):   Support Staff:

Physical Education Class

Goals and Desired Outcomes

Check all that are occurring		Notes
Schedule		
☐	*Ss attend the P.E. class that their same-age typical peers attend	
☐	*Ss' IEP goals for P.E. have been clearly identified and are being taught	
Transition to Class		
☐	*Ss transition to/from the gym/locker room at the same time as their peers	
☐	*Ss arrive at P.E. location *with* peers versus separate from them	
Dress/Changing		
☐	*Ss have been assigned lockers next to peers, not other *Ss	
☐	*Ss use a combination or key lock to secure their clothing, valuables	
☐	*Ss are expected to dress for class and have the necessary P.E. clothes	
Teacher Ownership/Class Membership – The P.E Teacher:		
☐	Talks to *Ss throughout the class; shares information with peers to help them positively understand *Ss' differences	
☐	Highlights what *Ss do well, strengths, successes, positive progress	
☐	Directs support staff to run class activity and meet all *Ss' needs	
☐	Directs peers to partner with *Ss	
☐	Adapts activities, games to allow for meaningful *S participation	

Meaningful Participation	
☐	*Ss line up with peers and follow the designated roll call procedure
☐	*Ss sit next to and around typical peers, not other *Ss
☐	*Ss follow class rules and teacher directions
☐	*Ss are participating in age-appropriate activities, using age-appropriate materials
☐	*Ss spend more time in proximity to peers than to only support staff or by themselves
Peer Interactions and Support	
☐	*Ss interact with their peers (initiation, responding)
☐	Students receive assistance from peers
☐	Multiple peers approach *Ss during class
☐	Meaningful interactions occur throughout class between *Ss and peers
☐	Peers naturally include *Ss in class activities, conversations, etc.
Desirable Staff Support – The Support Staff:	
☐	Arrives at class on time with or before *Ss
☐	Sets up and runs structured activities
☐	Teaches game rules, activity steps to all *Ss
☐	Actively recruits peers to interact with and support *Ss
☐	Focuses on teaching IEP goals to *Ss
☐	Prompts peers to support *Ss and praises peer involvement
☐	Resolves conflicts as needed and has a positive impact on the social success of all *Ss
☐	Shares information to help peers understand differences and how to best support *Ss

*S(s) = student(s) with disabilities.

Source: Doering, K. (2010). *Reflection Tools for Facilitating Positive Student Outcomes.* San Francisco State University, California Research Institute (CRI), Department of Special Education. Used with permission.

Resource H

Date: Setting: Student(s):   Support Staff:

Structured Social Opportunities

Social Activities and Social Clubs

Goals and Desired Outcomes			
Preparation		**Social Activity**	
☐	Has an activity structure in mind	☐	Starts at targeted time
☐	Gathers needed materials in advance to utilize time efficiently	☐	Assists all students to greet one another
☐	Recruits peers earlier in the day of the time for the club meeting or activity	☐	Follows the planned structure for the meeting or activity
		☐	Organizes and directs the activity
☐	Reminds peers earlier in the day of the time for the club meeting or activity	☐	Assigns peer partners when relevant
☐	Interviews peers to determine activities that they prefer	☐	Promotes creative problem solving as a means to increase participation, engagement, and peer empowerment
☐	Identifies fun, motivating, and interactive materials and activities that are age appropriate	☐	Facilitates *S independence, interdependence, and group participation
☐	Generates a written list of varied interactive toys, games, computer programs, and activities that students choose from to allow for student choice and to avoid repetition and loss of involvement/motivation	☐	Coaches peers to assist and support the *Ss Tells peers what to say, ask, do (e.g., "Tell [student name] to open the box." "Show [student name] how to set up the game")
☐	Arranges to have snack items that will provide additional motivation for peers to participate	☐	Redirects conversation to *Ss
		☐	Highlights the competency of all students

Goals and Desired Outcomes		
Student	**Peers**	
☐ Greets peers	☐ Talk to and interact with *Ss	
☐ Communicates with peers and uses AAC devices when needed	☐ Assist and support *Ss	
☐ Participates actively in class activities, groups, conversations	☐ Act in a positive, respectful way toward *Ss	
☐ Works on social goals: greetings, turn-taking, social exchanges	☐ Initiate including *Ss in social activities	
☐ Practices targeted skills within social activities	☐ Include *Ss in conversations, discussion	
☐ Uses choice boards, AAC devices, conversation books, communication boards, social stories, albums, joke cards, etc., to communicate and socialize with peers	☐ Find ways to help *Ss participate	
	☐ Multiple peers interact with *Ss	
	☐ Accept *Ss' differences	

Support Staff Role as "Social Facilitators"
☐ Gets to know the peers and develops a meaningful rapport
☐ Learns the names of peers and personalizes conversations with them
☐ Learns important likes and preferences of *Ss and peers
☐ Prompts and facilitates *S greetings, interactions, manners
☐ Facilitates group discussions and problem solving
☐ Supports student-to-student interactions
☐ Constantly shares information with peers
☐ Anticipates unspoken questions and/or answers questions
☐ Models age-appropriate interactions with all students
☐ Positively interprets *Ss' behavior
☐ Ensures *Ss are the focus of any social interaction
☐ Fades immediate support, intervening as needed: "Get in, get out"

Clean-Up and Closure
☐ Provides transitional cues (e.g., "5 more minutes and then we need to clean up")
☐ Assigns roles that allow all students to participate in clean-up
☐ *Ss and peers leave area together, not separately
☐ Solicits ideas for the next group meeting/activity
☐ Cleans up before bell rings

*S(s) = student(s) with disabilities.

Source: Doering, K. (2010). *Reflection Tools for Facilitating Positive Student Outcomes.* San Francisco State University, California Research Institute (CRI), Department of Special Education. Used with permission.

Resource I

Date: Setting: Student(s):   Support Staff:

School Jobs

Check all that are occurring	Comments
Schedule	
☐ Meaningful work has been secured and is being performed ☐ Job tasks are performed on a regular basis ☐ The same students leave for and finish the job at set times ☐ Job tasks are taught in natural contexts ☐ Students work next to and/or in view of nondisabled peers, coworkers ☐ The number of students participating makes sense for work being performed	
Routine	
☐ *S obtains, carries, and takes responsibilities for work materials ☐ *S checks in with "boss" (if appropriate) ☐ A consistent flow of work is provided ☐ *S follows the same route, routine to complete the job ☐ A picture schedule/routine is used to guide *S through job activities ☐ Strategies are used to allow the *S to work as independently as possible	
Social Opportunities	
☐ *S has opportunities to interact with others (peers, class teachers, staff) ☐ *S initiates/responds to social greetings, conversation ☐ Staff ensure that student is the primary receiver of interactions ☐ *S works alongside peers (if possible) ☐ Staff prompt *S to greet, thank, talk to peers, teachers, staff, ask questions, ask for help, etc.	
Work Quality	
☐ Work is performed correctly ☐ Staff and *S actions do not jeopardize relations with site, needs, concerns ☐ Staff respond with quickness, sensitivity to site needs, concerns ☐ All materials are properly returned to their correct location	

Perception of Competence, Positive Contribution	
☐ Statements are positive when speaking of *S's abilities ☐ Undesirable actions are interpreted positively ☐ *S makes a positive contribution to assist teachers, staff, the school community by completing the job	
Desirable Staff Instruction	
☐ Staff praise students often for desirable actions ☐ Staff provide relevant information and reinforcement to site personnel ☐ Staff demonstrate enthusiasm regarding the job and *S's potential ☐ Staff engage in brief social conversation with site personnel	
Documentation of Student Performance, Job Procedures	
☐ Data on *S's performance is collected during or immediately following job ☐ A written checklist of job procedures is delineated to guide staff ☐ Data is analyzed periodically to determine student progress, need areas	

*S(s)=student(s) with disabilities.

Source: Doering, K. (2010). *Reflection Tools for Facilitating Positive Student Outcomes.* San Francisco State University, California Research Institute (CRI), Department of Special Education. Used with permission.

Resource J

Date: Setting: Student(s):   Support Staff:

Instruction and Group Management Goals and Desired Outcomes

Lesson/Group Management		Systematic Instruction	
☐	Effectively positions *Ss to manage behaviors, group	☐	Establishes *Ss' attention before speaking
☐	Provides clear introduction specific to lesson/activity	☐	Gives clear, simple directions
☐	Creates a motivating context for learning	☐	Knows and teaches skills targeted for instruction
☐	Maintains participation of all *Ss throughout activities	☐	Applies consistent and accurate use of prompt procedures
☐	Praises students for all desirable behavior	☐	Gives *Ss time to respond
☐	Provides relevant information and rationale to peers	☐	Delivers positive reinforcement for correct responses
☐	Enables *Ss to make choices throughout the activity	☐	Provides consistent feedback for incorrect responses
☐	Scans area to anticipate behavior, provide intervention	☐	Avoids multiple, repetitive directives and excessive talk
☐	Adapts activity so all *Ss can participate meaningfully		
☐	Facilitates interactions between *Ss and peers		
☐	Designs/follows written plans, outlines to guide instruction		

		Tracking Student Performance	
☐	Provides closure to wrap up activity, lesson		
☐	Cleans up, returns materials	☐	Collects student performance data regularly and consistently
☐	Allows sufficient time for and facilitates smooth transitions	☐	Obtains and saves important student work samples
☐	Follows schedule—adheres to start/end times	☐	Documents how much help *Ss received to complete work
Classroom Management		☐	Includes *Ss in the discussion/summary of their performance
☐	Helps enforce class expectations	☐	Completes and upgrades graphs of behavioral data
☐	Creates and/or uses modifications to help *Ss participate		
☐	Reacts appropriately to unexpected situations		
☐	Uses positive strategies versus punitive procedures		
☐	Takes initiative to provide support as needed		
☐	Makes on-the-spot decisions that demonstrate common sense	**Advocates for *Ss**	
☐	Provides support to *Ss, moves around class, and returns as needed	☐	Helps *Ss to be as independent of adult assistance as possible
☐	Works with ALL students	☐	Positively interprets unusual *S behavior, differences, actions
☐	Directs peers to support *Ss	☐	Helps others understand *Ss' communication attempts
☐	Models positive and age-appropriate interactions	☐	Responds appropriately to questions asked about the *Ss
☐	Points out *Ss' successes and positive progress	☐	Identifies key moments to provide information to help others better understand the *Ss

*S(s) = student(s) with disabilities.

Source: Doering, K. (2010). *Reflection Tools for Facilitating Positive Student Outcomes.* San Francisco State University, California Research Institute (CRI), Department of Special Education. Used with permission.

Resource K

Date: Setting: Student(s):   Support Staff:

Inclusion Support Teacher Role Management Areas

Are These Indicators Present?	Comments
Be Another "Teacher"	
☐ Be present in general education settings ☐ Develop trust with peers, school, and community staff ☐ Be present in general education classes the majority of the school day ☐ Lead small-group activities in general education classrooms ☐ Coteach lessons when desirable	
Collaborate With General Education Teachers	
☐ Communicate each *S's learning goals to class teacher ☐ Organize learning opportunities for peers (lunch clubs, lessons) ☐ Ask class teachers for ideas on how to bring about desired outcomes ☐ Share information about what the *Ss are learning (academic, social, behavior, communication, independence, etc.) with class teacher, peers, administration ☐ Identify activities that allow peers to work together	
Give Information and Help Others Learn About Disabilities	
☐ Help others understand, accept *Ss ☐ Highlight *Ss' strengths, abilities, successes ☐ Comment on what the *Ss are doing well ☐ Help others understand the *Ss' actions, behaviors—be positive ☐ Help others see the *Ss as competent	
Design Adaptations	
☐ Develop creative materials to teach academic skills ☐ Create to-do lists that help staff know what materials to make	

Help Establish Peer Connections and Foster Relationships	
☐ Recruit peers ☐ Set up opportunities for structured peer interactions ☐ Collaborate with class teachers to determine effective peer supports ☐ Tell peers how to help *Ss—"Could you tell____ to get out . . ."	
Create Systems to Evaluate Student Progress	
☐ Develop simple systems for systematically collecting student progress data ☐ Train staff how to implement the system ☐ Monitor whether staff are consistently gathering student performance data	
Train and Monitor Staff	
☐ Model and teach effective strategies for supporting the *Ss ☐ Provide positive feedback (areas of strength) and identify areas to work on ☐ Work with class teachers to develop and assess instructional assistant roles	
Question ALL That Is Going On, Identify Creative Solutions	
☐ Identify what is going well, as well as areas that need to be improved ☐ Identify new skills to teach *Ss ☐ Make suggestions for change ☐ Make on-the-spot changes to help *Ss be successful	

*S(s)=student(s) with disabilities.

Source: Doering, K. (2010). *Reflection Tools for Facilitating Positive Student Outcomes.* San Francisco State University. California Research Institute (CRI), Department of Special Education. Used with permission.

Resource L.1

Social Engagement Observation

INTRODUCTION

Use the following observation charting rubric (Resource L.2) titled "Social Engagement Observation Charting" to measure progress toward social goals. Observations should accurately reflect student progress. It's important to take data not only to be accountable for IEP goals but to learn what techniques work best in achieving goals.

Chart Explained: The Social Engagement Observation Chart is divided into 40 separate boxes, each designed to measure one interaction. The chart can accommodate a total of 40 possible interactions. From the completed chart, the IEP team can determine the amount of progress the student is making and in what areas. Accurate reporting reveals areas of strength as well as areas that challenge the student. For example, consider a nonverbal student who, prior to the current placement, avoided contact with his peers. With the coding system, an observer can record if the student participated with peers in an activity and if the interaction was a positive or negative encounter. Remember: A student does not have to talk to interact! Just being in proximity to peers is a form of interaction. For some students, if they join in on an activity, that behavior may be considered significant!

Explanation of Coding: Each code represents a clearly defined observable behavior that can be defined as communication in some form. Use the following descriptions as guidelines only.

Verb (Verbal Interaction): The student uses vocalizations to express an emotion. Vocalization includes common speech and other vocalized sound that communicates something.

If the direct result of the verbalization results in a positive outcome (e.g., peer approval, attainment of needs that leads toward the identified goal), mark (+). If the vocalization leads to a negative outcome (e.g., student gains negative attention, leaves an unfavorable impression with others), then mark (–). We have now recorded what the student did (verbalized) and the outcome, negative or positive.

Act (Activity): The student engaged in an activity involving another individual or group without prompting. "Activity engagement" is broadly defined as seeking out an activity that involves others for some purpose. Being around people does not have to be the motivation for engaging in the activity. Just doing something with others because of a mutual interest is enough. If the activity was generally positive in nature, mark (+). If the activity resulted in some negative outcome (e.g., student is rejected for inappropriate behavior, poor sportsmanship, etc.), mark (–)

PI (Peer Interaction): This is defined as an interaction between the observed student and his or her peer. The interaction can be initiated by either the peer or the student with ASD. The interaction must be reciprocal (both conversation partners contribute to the interaction) to earn a (+). For example, if a typical peer asks the student a question, and the student says, "Leave me alone, I don't want to talk," the interaction would be marked (+) because the student with ASD did initiate and communicated his feelings. However, if the typical peer engages the student in conversation and the student runs off without commenting, the score would be (–) because no interaction occurred. Hopefully, you will observe interactions that sustain conversation beyond a short question and answer. If this happens, it's a big deal and should be noted!

TI (Target Initiation): This type of initiated response is defined in the IEP or is part of a broader set of skills. It is targeted for a reason. Based on previous interventions, the targeted initiation is a priority to the child's family or in response to a social deficit. For example, if a student tends to enter a social conversation with off-topic remarks that cause the student to appear socially inept, the intervention may target the student's ability to appropriately enter a conversation by making relevant comments that fit what the group is talking about. If the student enters a group conversation and mentions something totally off topic, the score would be marked (–). in another example, a student enters a room and fails to state a proper greeting. The targeted response would be to seek opportunities for the student to enter a room for the purpose of appropriately greeting someone. If the student successfully greets a person, the student would earn a (+). If the student fails to greet as planned, he would earn a (–).

B (Inappropriate Interaction): If the student is observed acting inappropriately toward his peers or staff, (B) is an appropriate code to circle. For example, if the student kicks someone or hits another person, the score would be marked B. This code is appropriate when measuring the behaviors of students who use challenging behavior to communicate. Another example is the student who shouts out or screams. He or she is not engaged in a social situation but is communicating through inappropriate behavior.

Calculate the percentages of each response to better understand the student's preferred mode of communication and to gauge if a targeted communication is increasing or reducing.

Here's how: (1) Count the total the number of boxes used; (2) count the total number of one type of communication—for example (Verb) verbal; and (3) count the total number of (+) verbal and (−) verbal. To determine how many verbal responses out of all responses, divide the total number of boxes by the total number of verbal (+) or (−). You get the idea!

Resource L.2

Student: Date(s):   Observer(s):

Social Engagement Observation Charting

Instructions: Each numbered box on the following page represents one interaction opportunity. Circle if interaction was verbal (Verb) or activity (Act). Activity interactions include group projects, board games, team sports, and group presentations.

1	2	3	4	5	6	7	8
Verb Act	Verb Act	Verb Act	Verb Act	Verb Act	Verb Act	Verb Act	Verb Act
PI TI B + −	PI TI B + −	PI TI B + −	PI TI B + −	PI TI B + −	PI TI B + −	PI TI B + −	PI TI B + −
9	**10**	**11**	**12**	**13**	**14**	**15**	**16**
Verb Act	Verb Act	Verb Act	Verb Act	Verb Act	Verb Act	Verb Act	Verb Act
PI TI B + −	PI TI B + −	PI TI B + −	PI TI B + −	PI TI B + −	PI TI B + −	PI TI B + −	PI TI B + −
17	**18**	**19**	**20**	**21**	**22**	**23**	**24**
Verb Act	Verb Act	Verb Act	Verb Act	Verb Act	Verb Act	Verb Act	Verb Act
PI TI B + −	PI TI B + −	PI TI B + −	PI TI B + −	PI TI B + −	PI TI B + −	PI TI B + −	PI TI B + −
25	**26**	**27**	**28**	**29**	**30**	**31**	**32**
Verb Act	Verb Act	Verb Act	Verb Act	Verb Act	Verb Act	Verb Act	Verb Act
PI TI B + −	PI TI B + −	PI TI B + −	PI TI B + −	PI TI B + −	PI TI B + −	PI TI B + −	PI TI B + −

Verb—Verbal Interaction ____%

Act—Activity Interaction ____%

PI—Peer Interaction ____%

TI—Target Interaction*

B—Inappropriate Interaction

(+) = Engaged in positive social interactions

(−) = Not engaged in social interaction

---

*The student's interaction goal

Notes:

Resource M

Assessment of Student Participation in General Education Settings

FORM 1

Student: _____ Grade, Subject, and Class Period:

_____

Classroom Teacher: _____ Prep Period: _____

Room Number: _____ # of Students in Class: _____

Observation completed by: _____

Instructions:

1. After the student attends the specific general education class for approximately one week, the team reviews all the skills identified in Resources M and N of this assessment tool.

2. Circle about five items that the team identifies as priorities for instructional emphasis for the individual student.

3. Write objectives for each of the circled items; then design related instructional programs.

4. Review student progress on all items at least two more times during the school year. Revise as needed.

Score:
+ for items the student consistently performs

+/− for items the student does some of the time but not consistently

− for items the student never or very rarely performs

NA for items that are not appropriate for the student/class

CLASSROOM ROUTINES AND ACTIVITIES

DATE:				DATE:			
1. Gets to class on time				11. Shares materials with peers when appropriate			
2. Gets seated in class on time				12. Uses materials for their intended purpose			
3. Performs transitional activities during class in response to situational cues (e.g., changes in seating, activity)				13. Puts materials away after use			
4. Begins tasks				14. Uses classroom materials and equipment safely			
5. Stays on task				15. Works cooperatively with partner			
6. Participates in some regular class activities without adaptations				16. Works cooperatively in small group			
7. Terminates tasks				17. Takes notes			
8. Tolerates out-of-the-ordinary changes in routine				18. Accepts assistance			
9. Follows class rules				19. Evaluates quality of own work (given a model)			
10. Locates/brings materials to class as needed				20. Copes with criticism/correction without incident and tries an alternative behavior			

Source: Reformatted and reprinted with permission: Figure 5.2 Classroom assessment tool. From Macdonald, C., & York, J. Regular class integration: Assessment, objectives, instructional programs. In J. York, T. Vandercook, C. Macdonald, & S. Wolff (Eds.), *Strategies for full inclusion* (pp. 83–116). Minneapolis, MN: University of Minnesota, Institute on Community Integration.

Resource N

Assessment of Student Participation in General Education Settings

FORM 2

Student: _____ Grade, Subject, and Class Period:

_____

Classroom Teacher: _____ Prep Period: _____

Room Number: _____ # of Students in Class: _____

Observation completed by: _____

Instructions:

1. After the student attends the specific general education class for approximately one week, the team reviews all the skills identified in Resources M and N of this assessment tool.

2. Circle about five items that the team identifies as priorities for instructional emphasis for the individual student.

3. Write objectives for each of the circled items; then design related instructional programs.

4. Review student progress on all items at least two more times during the school year. Revise as needed.

Score: +   for items the student consistently performs

      +/−   for items the student does some of the time but not consistently

      −   for items the student never or very rarely performs

      NA   for items that are not appropriate for the student/class

SOCIAL AND COMMUNICATION SKILLS

DATE:				DATE:			
Interacts with peers				**States or indicates**			
a. Responds to others b. Initiates				a. Don't know b. When finished with an activity			
Interacts with the classroom teacher				**Orientation**			
a. Responds to others b. Initiates				a. Orients toward the speaker or other source of input b. Secures listener's attention before communicating c. Maintains eye contact with listener when speaking			
Uses social greetings							
a. Responds to others b. Initiates				**Gestures**			
Uses farewells				Uses appropriate gestures and body movements when interacting with others			
a. Responds to others b. Initiates							
Uses expressions of politeness (e.g., please, thank you, excuse me)				**Conversation**			
a. Responds to others b. Initiates				a. Uses intelligible speech (volume, rate, articulation, etc.) b. Uses appropriate language/vocabulary/topic conversation c. Takes turns communicating in conversion with others			
Participates in joking or teasing							
a. Responds to others b. Initiates				Comments			
Asks questions							
a. Asks to help b. Asks for information (e.g., clarification, feedback)							
Follows directions							
a. For curricular tasks b. For helping tasks, errands c. Given to the student individually d. Given to the student as part of a group							

Source: Reformatted and reprinted with permission: Figure 5.2 Classroom assessment tool. From Macdonald, C., & York, J. Regular class integration: Assessment, objectives, instructional programs. In J. York, T. Vandercook, C. Macdonald, & S. Wolff (Eds.), *Strategies for full inclusion* (pp. 83–116). Minneapolis, MN: University of Minnesota, Institute on Community Integration.

Resource O

Student Profile Information

Student: _____ DOB: _____

Age: _____

Parent/Guardian(s): _____

Address: _____

Class Schedule: Class Teacher Room #	Related Services:	Time	Provider	Contact
	SPT: M Tu W Th F	_____	_____	_____
1				
2	APE: M Tu W Th F	_____	_____	_____
3				
4	OT: M Tu W Th F	_____	_____	_____
5				
6	Other: M Tu W Th F	_____	_____	_____

Reading:	Phonemic Awareness	Phonics/ Decoding	Fluency	Comprehension	Vocabulary
Math:	Basic Operations + − ×	Word Problems	Time/ Money	Fractions Decimals Ratios	Geometry Pre-Algebra
Writing:	Spelling	Grammar	Sentence Structure	Topic Sentence Supporting Information	Handwriting Keyboarding (circle)

IEP Goals:

Method of Communication:

      How student expresses information:

      How student receives information:

Environmental Challenges:

Behavior Considerations:

Resource P

Homework Summary

Student: _____ Week of: _____

Subject	Monday	✓	Tuesday	✓	Wednesday	✓	Thursday	✓	Friday	✓
	Homework:	☐	Homework:	☐	Homework:	☐	Homework:	☐	Homework:	☐
	Due Date:		Due Date:		Due Date:		Due Date:		Due Date:	
	Materials:		Materials:		Materials:		Materials:		Materials:	
	Homework:	☐	Homework:	☐	Homework:	☐	Homework:	☐	Homework:	☐
	Due Date:		Due Date:		Due Date:		Due Date:		Due Date:	
	Materials:		Materials:		Materials:		Materials:		Materials:	
	Homework:	☐	Homework:	☐	Homework:	☐	Homework:	☐	Homework:	☐
	Due Date:		Due Date:		Due Date:		Due Date:		Due Date:	
	Materials:		Materials:		Materials:		Materials:		Materials:	
	Homework:	☐	Homework:	☐	Homework:	☐	Homework:	☐	Homework:	☐
	Due Date:		Due Date:		Due Date:		Due Date:		Due Date:	
	Materials:		Materials:		Materials:		Materials:		Materials:	

Homework Notes:

Resources Part II

Behavior Support Resources

Resource Q

Behavior Support Tools

Introduction

When a student is not complying with directions or is acting out, avoiding tasks, being the class clown, and so forth, it may be time to intervene with a behavior support plan. Before jumping to conclusions and giving your opinion, a little scientific inquiry is in order. Observe the student across settings to determine where the challenging behavior is most likely to occur. Jot down the situation and activities as the period progresses. Rate the student's performance level using the "Situational Analysis" (Resource R) or "Scatter Plot Analysis" (Resources S.1 and S.2) or "Positive Behavior Support Analysis" (Resource T) to chart the relationship between factors affecting behavior and the student's response. These techniques will be useful in identifying possible environmental factors (seating arrangements), interpersonal issues (the presence of certain people), activities (independent task completion, disliked subjects), or sensory factors (noise level) and time of day that may contribute to an increase in challenging behavior.

You are encouraged to modify these tools to meet your needs. They can be customized to analyze specific behaviors and situations. For example, you can change the Scatter Plot increments of 5 minutes to 10, 20, or 30 minutes, 1 hour, or a few days. You can alter the Situational Analysis by filling in different behaviors and activity arrangements.

Make sure you describe behaviors in concrete terms that are easy to communicate and simple to measure and record. If descriptions are vague—"Sherry has a poor attitude" or "Sam is inappropriate"—it is difficult for two observers to interpret the same behavior in measurable terms. What is inappropriate to one person may be acceptable behavior for someone else. As an example of a concrete description of a problem behavior, if you see Sam gaining approval from his classmates after he calls out during instruction, you might decide the function of the behavior is to gain favor from his peers.

When the function of the behavior is understood, a behavior intervention plan can be developed. Once you understand why the challenging behavior is occurring, you can change conditions to reduce anxiety while working to satisfy the student's needs in more acceptable ways.

Consider a few examples: If Sherry has been working on a class assignment for a long time and is becoming restless, instead of punishing her for "escaping tasks," allow for more breaks between tasks. Perhaps do more activity-based peer partner work. If you know Tom struggles with math and notice a pattern where every time he's asked to engage in a difficult math assignment, he acts out to avoid instruction, modify the instruction to fit Tom's needs.

It's helpful to observe the student across settings and during different types of activities to see if a challenging behavior is present. To further validate your conclusion, conduct interviews with other teachers to see if they agree.

Source: Adapted from Magee-Quinn, M., Gable, R. A., Rutherford, R. B., Nelson, & Howell, K. W. (1998). *Addressing student problem behavior: An IEP team's introduction to functional behavioral assessment and behavior intervention plans.* Washington, DC: Center for Effective Collaboration and Practice, American Institutes for Research. Used with permission.

Resource R

Situational Analysis Form

Student Name: _____   Starting Date: _____

Observer*: _____   Class Period: _____

*Relationship to student: _____ Describe on back how well you know this person (see below) and why you are qualified to provide this assessment.

Observed Behaviors	Transition	Worksheet/Workbook	Read Aloud	Read Silently	Instructional Activity	Computer Time	Large-Group Lecture	Independent Work	Paper-Pencil	Small-Group Project/Lab	
Off Task											
Withdrawal											
Fidgeting, Tense											
Daydreaming											
Distracted											
Agitated/Irritable											

Special note: This form is intended for use by individuals who know the student well (i.e., student history, background, and challenges). This form is not intended for use by individuals who are unfamiliar with the student.

Resource S.1

Scatter Plot Analysis

Sample

Student Name:	Sue Smith	Starting Date:	4/5
Observer:	Sarah	Time Period:	History 2nd period

	4/5	4/6	4/7	4/8	4/9	4/12	4/13	4/14	4/15	4/16
9:00	■					■	■			■
9:05	■									■
9:10										
9:15	■				■					■
9:20	■				■					■
9:25					■					
9:30										■
9:35										
9:40					■					■
9:45					■					■
9:50					■					
9:55					■					■
10:00	■	■	■		■	■	■			■

Notes: Sue has the most trouble on Mondays and Fridays. Worried about seeing Dad? She also has trouble settling in to start class. Every day she was prompted to start her lessons. Also, it seems like she shuts down at the end of the period except short Thursdays! Periods too long.

Resource S.2

Scatter Plot Analysis

Form

Student Name: Starting Date:

Observer: Time Period:

☐ actively involved   ◢ partially involved   ■ not involved

Date:											

Notes:

Resource T

Student: Date: Observer:

Positive Behavior Support Analysis

Areas of concern:

- ❒ The student is unsuccessful with relationships; has few friends.
- ❒ The student feels threatened, teased, or harassed by others.
- ❒ The student struggles to understand concepts. When?_____
- ❒ The student does not contribute to class discussions and activities.
- ❒ The student's behavior interferes with the learning of others.
- ❒ The student does not participate in class lessons and activities.
- ❒ The student struggles to cope with sensory input like loud noises and bright lights.

In boxes below, define up to three of the student's most challenging behaviors, using words your grandmother could understand. Avoid vague and/or clinical descriptions of behavior (e.g., "off-task behavior" or "inappropriate"); use precise descriptions (e.g., "continuously taps foot and daydreams" or "pokes student beside him").

Challenging Behavior 1	Challenging Behavior 2	Challenging Behavior 3

Possible reasons for behavior:

- ❒ Environmental stressors (odors, touch, loud noises, bright lights, crowded rooms)
  Comments:
- ❒ Social stressors (confusing social situations, annoying people, abusive treatment)
  Comments:
- ❒ Internal stressors (student is lonely and unhappy, fearful, anxious, stuck on one thought, overly stimulated, tired, hungry, sick, too warm or cold)
- ❒ Other possible reason? If yes, what?

When Where Who

1. Are there times during the week when the behavior is most likely to occur? If so, when?

2. Where is the behavior most likely to occur? Who is present? Do you notice a pattern?

3. What was happening just before the behavior occurred? What happened next?

References

Adreon, D., & Stella, J. (2001). Transition to middle and high school: Increasing the success of students with Asperger syndrome. *Intervention in School and Clinic, 36*(5), 266–271.

Affleck, J., Edgar, E., Levine, P., & Kortering, L. (1990). Postschool status of students classified as mildly mentally retarded, learning disabled, or non-handicapped: Does it get better with time? *Education and Training in Mental Retardation, 25,* 315–324.

American Psychiatric Association. (2000). *Diagnostic and statistical manual of mental disorders* (4th ed., text rev.). Washington, DC: Author.

Asher, S. R., Parker, J. G., & Walker, D. (1996). Distinguishing friendship from acceptance: Implications for intervention and assessment. In W. Bukowski, A. Newcomb, & W. Hartup (Eds.), *The company they keep: Friendship in childhood and adolescence* (pp. 366–407). Cambridge, England: Cambridge University Press.

Asperger, H. (1944). Die "Autistischen Psychopathen" im Kindesalter. *Archiv für Psychiatrie und Nervenkrankheiten, 117,* 76–136.

Attwood, T. (2008). An overview of autism spectrum disorders. In K. D. Buron & P. Wolfberg (Eds.), *Learners on the autism spectrum: Preparing highly qualified educators* (pp. 19–43). Shawnee Mission, KS: Autism Asperger Publishing Co.

Baker, J. (2003). *Social skills training: For children and adolescents with Asperger syndrome and social-communication problems.* Mission, KS: Autism Asperger Publishing Co.

Baker, M. J., Koegel, R. L., & Koegel, L. K. (1998). Increasing the social behavior of young children with autism using their obsessive behaviors. *Journal of the Association of Persons With Severe Handicaps, 23*(4), 300–308.

Baltaxe, C., & Simmons, J. (1977). Bedtime soliloquies and linguistic competence in autism. *Journal of Speech and Hearing Disorders, 42,* 376–393.

Barnhill, G. (2001). What is Asperger syndrome? *Intervention in School and Clinic, 36,* 258–266.

Baron-Cohen, S. (1992). Out of sight or out of mind: Another look at deception in autism. *Journal of Child Psychology and Psychiatry, 33,* 1141–1155.

Baron-Cohen, S. (2007). I cannot tell a lie. *In Character, 3,* 52–59.

Baron-Cohen, S. (2009). Autism: The empathizing-systemizing (E-S) theory. In A. Kingstone & M. B. Miller (Eds.), *The year in cognitive neuroscience, 2009: Annals of the New York Academy of Sciences, 1156,* 68–80.

Bauer, S. (1999). *Asperger syndrome.* Retrieved February 11, 2011, from http://www.aspergersyndrome.org/Articles/kelley.aspx

Beidel, D. C., Turner, S. M., & Morris, T. L. (2000). Behavioral treatment of childhood social phobia. *Journal of Consulting and Clinical Psychology, 68,* 1072–1080.

Bellamy, G. T., Rhodes, L., Bourbeau, P., & Mank, D. (1986). Mental retardation services in sheltered workshops and day activity programs: Consumer benefits

213

and policy alternatives. In F. Rusch (Ed.), *Competitive employment issues and strategies* (pp. 257–271). Baltimore, MD: Paul H. Brookes.

Bellini, S. (2006). The development of social anxiety in adolescents with autism spectrum disorders. *Focus on Autism and Other Developmental Disabilities, 21*(3), 138–145.

Blackorby, J., & Wagner, M. (1996). Longitudinal postschool outcomes of youth with disabilities: Findings from the National Longitudinal Transition Study. *Exceptional Children, 62*(5), 399–413.

Bravmann, S. (2004). *Two, four, six, eight, let's all differentiate: Differential education yesterday, today, and tomorrow.* Retrieved June 25, 2010, from http://education .jhu.edu/newhorizons

Broer, S. M., Doyle, M. B., & Giangreco, M. F. (2005). Perspectives of students with intellectual disabilities about their experiences with paraprofessional support. *Exceptional Children, 71*(4), 415–430.

Campbell, J. M. (2007). Middle school students' response to the self-introduction of a student with autism: Effects of perceived similarity, prior awareness, and educational message. *Remedial and Special Education, 28*(3), 163–173.

Carothers, D. E., & Taylor, R. L. (2004). Social cognitive processing in elementary school children with Asperger syndrome. *Education & Training in Developmental Disabilities, 39*(2), 177–187.

Carter, E. W., & Hughes, C. (2006). Including high school students with severe disabilities in general education classes: Perspectives of general and special educators, paraprofessionals, and administrators. *Research and Practice for Persons With Severe Disabilities, 31*(2), 174–185.

Centers for Disease Control and Prevention. (2007). Prevalence of autism spectrum disorders: Autism and developmental disabilities monitoring network, six sites, United States, 2002. In *Surveillance Summaries*, MMWR 2007, 56. Retrieved May 3, 2008, from http://www.cdc.gov/mmwr/preview/ mmwrhtml/ss5601a2.htm

Centers for Disease Control and Prevention. Autism Information Center. (2010). Retrieved May 31, 2010, from http://www.cdc.gov/ncbddd/autism/index .html

Chandler-Olcott, K., & Kluth, P. (2009). Why everyone benefits from including students with autism in literary classrooms. *Reading Teacher, 62*(7), 548–557.

Church, C., Alisanski, S., & Amanullah, S. (2000). The social behavioral and academic experiences of children with Asperger syndrome. *Focus on Autism and Other Developmental Disabilities, 15*, 12–20.

Cole, D. A., & Meyer, L. H. (1991). Social integration and severe disabilities: A longitudinal analysis of child outcomes. *Journal of Special Education, 25*(3), 340–351.

Copeland, S. R., Hughes, C., Carter, E. W., Guth, C., Presley, J., Williams, C. R., et al. (2004). Increasing access to general education: Perspectives of participants in a high school peer support program. *Remedial and Special Education, 26*, 342–352.

Crone, D. A., & Horner, R. H. (2003). *Building positive behavior support systems in schools: Functional behavior assessment.* New York: Guilford Press.

Curie, E. (1939). *Madame Curie: A biography by Eve Curie.* New York: Doubleday.

Dales, L., Hammer, S. J., & Smith, N. J. (2001). Time trends in autism and in MMR immunization coverage in California. *Journal of the American Medical Association, 285*, 1183–1185.

DeStefano, L., & Wagner, M. (1991). *Outcome assessment in special education: Lessons learned.* Menlo Park, CA: SRI International.

DiSalvo, D. A., & Oswald, D. P. (2002). Peer-mediated interventions to increase the social interaction of children with autism: Consideration of peer expectancies. *Focus on Autism and Other Developmental Disabilities, 17*(4), 198–208.

Doering, K. (2005). *Reflection tools for facilitating positive student outcomes.* San Francisco: San Francisco State University, California Research Institute (CRI), Department of Special Education.

Dunlap, G., & Kern, L. (1993). Assessment and intervention for children within the instructional curriculum. In S. F. Warren, J. Reichle, & D. P. Wacker (Vol. Eds.), *Communication and language intervention series: Vol. 3. Communicative alternatives to challenging behavior: Integrating functional assessment and intervention strategies* (pp. 177–203). Baltimore, MD: Paul H. Brookes.

Edelson, M. G. (2005). A car goes in the garage like a can of peas goes in the refrigerator: Do deficits in real-world knowledge affect the assessment of intelligence in individuals with autism? *Focus on Autism and Other Developmental Disabilities, 20*(1), 2–9.

Ellaway, C., & Christodoulou, J. (1999). Rett syndrome: Clinical update and review of recent genetic advances. *Journal of Pediatric and Child Health, 35,* 419–426.

Ellis, E., Gable, R. A., Gregg, M., & Rock, M. L. (2008). REACH: A framework for differentiating classroom instruction. *Preventing School Failure, 52*(2), 31–47.

Farrugia, S., & Hudson, J. (2006). Anxiety in adolescents with Asperger syndrome: Negative thoughts, behavioral problems, and life interference. *Focus on Autism and Other Developmental Disabilities, 21,* 25–35.

Folstein, S., & Rutter, M. (1977). Infantile autism: A genetic study of 21 twin pairs. *Journal of Child Psychology and Psychiatry, 18*(4), 297–321.

Fombonne, E. (2005). Epidemiological surveys of autism and other pervasive developmental disorders. In F. R. Volkmar, R. Paul, A. Klin, & D. Cohen (Eds.), *Handbook of autism and pervasive developmental disorders* (3rd ed., pp. 42–69). New York: Wiley.

Friend, M., & Cook, L. (1998). *Interventions: Collaboration skills for school professionals* (3rd ed.). White Plains, NY: Longman.

Frith, U. (2001). Mind blindness and the brain in autism. *Neuron, 32*(6), 969–979.

Fryxell, D., & Kennedy, C. H. (1995). Placement along the continuum of services and its impact in students' social relationships. *Journal of the Association for Persons With Severe Handicaps, 20,* 259–269.

Gahran, A. (2005). *Why communicate at all?* Retrieved June 17, 2010, from http://www.contentious.com/2005/05/30/why-communicate-at-all/

Ghaziuddin, M., & Butler, E. (1998). Clumsiness in autism and Asperger syndrome: A further report. *Journal of Intellectual Disability Research, 42*(1), 43–48.

Giangreco, M. F. (2003). Working with paraprofessionals. *Educational Leadership, 61,* 50–53.

Giangreco, M. F., & Broer, S. M. (2005). Questionable utilization of paraprofessionals in inclusive schools: Are we addressing symptoms or causes? *Focus on Autism and Other Developmental Disabilities, 20*(1), 10–26.

Giangreco, M. F., & Broer, S. M. (2007). School-based screening to determine overreliance on paraprofessionals. *Focus on Autism and Other Developmental Disabilities, 22*(3), 149–158.

Giangreco, M. F., Broer, S. M., & Edelman, S. W. (2001). Teacher engagement with students with disabilities: Differences between paraprofessional service delivery models. *Journal of the Association for Persons With Severe Handicaps, 26,* 75–86.

Giangreco, M. F., & Doyle, M. B. (2004). Directing paraprofessional work. In C. Kennedy & E. Horn (Eds.), *Including students with severe disabilities* (pp. 185–204). Boston: Allyn & Bacon.

Giangreco, M. F., Edelman, S., Luiselli, T. E., & MacFarland, S. Z. C. (1997). Helping or hovering? Effects of instructional assistant proximity on students with disabilities. *Exceptional Children, 64,* 7–18.

Giangreco, M. F., Smith, C. S., & Pinckney, E. (2006). Addressing the paraprofessional dilemma in an inclusive school: A program description. *Research & Practice for Persons With Severe Disabilities, 31*(3), 215–229.

Giangreco, M. F., Yuan, S., McKenzie, B., Cameron, P., & Fialka, J. (2005). "Be careful what you wish for . . .": Five reasons to be concerned about the assignment of individual paraprofessionals. *Teaching Exceptional Children, 37*(5), 28–34.

Grandin, T. (1995). *Thinking in pictures: And other reports from my life with autism.* New York: Vintage Press.

Grandin, T. (2000). *My experiences with visual thinking, sensory problems, and communication difficulties.* San Diego, CA: Autism Research Institute.

Grandin, T., & Barron, S. (2005). *Unwritten rules of social relationships: Decoding social mysteries through the unique perspectives of autism.* Arlington, TX: Future Horizons.

Gutstein, S. E., & Whitney, T. (2002). Asperger syndrome and the development of social competence. *Focus on Autism and Other Developmental Disabilities, 17*(3), 161–171.

Handleman, J. (1999). Assessment for curriculum planning. In D. Berkell-Zager (Ed.), *Autism: Identification, education & treatment* (2nd ed., pp. 99–110). Mahwah, NJ: Lawrence Erlbaum.

Harrower, J. K., & Dunlap, G. (2001). Including children with autism in general education classrooms: A review of effective strategies. *Behavior Modification, 25,* 762–784.

Hartup, W. W. (1999). Peer experience and its developmental significance. In M. Bennett (Ed.), *Developmental psychology: Achievements and prospects* (pp. 106–125). Philadelphia, PA: Psychology Press.

Hartup, W. W., & Stevens, N. (1997). Friendships and adaptation in the life course. *Psychological Bulletin, 121,* 355–370.

Heinrichs, R. (2003). *Perfect targets: Asperger syndrome and bullying: Practical solutions for surviving the social world.* Shawnee Mission, KS: Autism Asperger Publishing Co.

Hines, R. A., & Johnston, J. H. (1996). Inclusive classrooms: The principal's role in promoting achievement. *Schools in the Middle, 5*(3), 6–10.

Hoch, H., Taylor, B. A., & Rodriguez, A. (2009). Teaching teenagers with autism to answer cell phones and seek assistance when lost. *Behavior Analysis in Practice, 2*(1), 14–20.

Hodgdon, L. A. (1999). *Visual strategies for improving visual communication: Vol. 1. Practical support for school and home.* Troy, MI: Quirk Roberts.

Howlin, P., & Asgharian, A. (1999). The diagnosis of autism and Asperger syndrome: Findings from a survey of 770 families. *Developmental Medicine and Child Neurology, 41,* 834–839.

Hunt, P., Farron-Davis, F., Beckstead, S., Curtis, D., & Goetz, L. (1994). Evaluating the effects of placement of students with severe disabilities in general education versus special classes. *Journal of the Association for Persons With Severe Handicaps, 19,* 200–214.

Hurlbutt, K., & Chalmers, L. (2002). Adults with autism speak out: Perceptions of their life experiences. *Focus on Autism and Other Developmental Disabilities, 17,* 103.

Jackson, L. (2002). *Freaks, geeks, and Asperger syndrome: A user guide to adolescence.* London: Jessica Kingsley.

Jackson-Brewin, B., Renwick, R., & Schormans, A. F. (2008). Parental perspectives of the quality of life in school environments for children with Asperger syndrome. *Focus on Autism and Other Developmental Disabilities, 23,* 242.

Kaland, N., Møller-Nielsen, A., Callesen, K., Mortensen, E. L., Gottlieb, D., & Smith, L. (2002). A new "advanced" test of theory of mind: Evidence from children and adolescents with Asperger syndrome. *Journal of Child Psychology and Psychiatry, 43,* 517–528.

Kamps, D., Royer, J., Dugan, E., Kravits, T., Gonzalez-Lopez, A., Garcia, J., et al. (2002). Peer training to facilitate social interaction for elementary students with autism and their peers. *Exceptional Children, 68*(2), 173–187.

Kanner, L. (1943). Autistic disturbances of affective contact. *Nervous Child, 2,* 217–250.

Koegel, R. L., & Koegel, L. (2006). *Pivotal response treatments for autism: Communication, social, & academic development.* Baltimore, MD: Paul H. Brookes.

Koegel, R. L., Koegel, L. K., & Surratt, A. V. (1992). Language intervention and disruptive behavior in preschool children with autism. *Journal of Autism and Developmental Disorders, 22,* 141–153.

Kohn, A. (1995). *Discipline is the problem—not the solution.* Retrieved September 11, 2010, from http://www.alfiekohn.org/articles_subject.htm#null

Koning, C., & McGill-Evans, J. (2001). Social and language skills in adolescent boys with Asperger syndrome. *Autism: The International Journal of Research & Practice, 5,* 23–36.

Krasny, L., Williams, B. J., Provencal, S., & Ozonoff, S. (2003). Social skills interventions for the autism spectrum: Essential ingredients and a model curriculum. *Child and Adolescent Psychiatric Clinics in North America, 12*(1), 107–122.

Kunc, N. (1984). Integration: Being realistic isn't realistic. *Canadian Journal for Exceptional Children, 1*(1).

Kunc, N., & Van der Klift, E. (1994). Hell-bent on helping: Benevolence, friendship, and the politics of help. In J. Thousand, R. Villa, & A. Nevin (Eds.), *Creativity and collaborative learning: A practical guide to empowering students and teachers* (pp. 21–28). Baltimore, MD: Paul H. Brookes.

Lane, K. L., Pierson, M. R., & Givener, C. C. (2003). Teacher expectations of student behavior: Which skills do elementary and secondary teachers deem necessary for success in the classroom? *Education and Treatment of Children, 26,* 413–418.

Laurent, A. C., & Rubin, E. (2004). Emotional regulation challenges in Asperger's syndrome and high functioning autism. *Topics in Language Disorders, 24*(4), 286–297.

Ledgin, N. (2002). *Asperger's and self esteem, insight and hope through famous role models.* Arlington, TX: Future Horizons.

Lenhart, A., Ling, L., Campbell, S., & Purcell, K. (2010). *Teens and mobile phones. Pew Internet & American Life Project.* Washington, DC: Pew Research Institute. Retrieved June 23, 2010, from www.pewinternet.org/~/media//Files PIP-Teens-and-Mobile-2010.pdf

Lewis, S. (1994). Full inclusion: An option or a system? *Journal of Visual Impairment and Blindness, 88,* 293–294.

Lipsky, D. K. (1994). National survey gives insight into inclusive movement. *Inclusive Education Programs, 1*(3), 4–7.

Little, L. (2002). Middle class mothers' perceptions of peer and sibling victimization among children with Asperger's syndrome and nonverbal learning disorders. *Issues in Comprehensive Pediatric Nursing, 25,* 43–57.

Malmgren, K. W., & Causton-Theoharis, J. N. (2006). Boy in the bubble: Effects of paraprofessional proximity and other pedagogical decisions on the interactions of a student with behavioral disorders. *Journal of Research in Childhood Education, 20*(4), 301–312.

McGinnity, K., & Negri, N. (2005). *Walk awhile in my autism: A manual of sensitivity to promote understanding of people on the autism spectrum.* Cambridge, WI: Cambridge Book Review Press.

McGregor, G. (1993, Fall). Inclusion: A powerful pedagogy. *Front Line, 2*(1), 8–10.

Mesibov, G., & Lord, K. (1997). *Some thoughts on social skills training for children, adolescents and adults with autism.* Unpublished manuscript.

Mirenda, P. (2001). Autism, augmentative communication, and assistive technology: What do we really know? *Focus on Autism and Other Developmental Disabilities, 16*(3), 141–151.

Mullins, E. R., & Irvin, J. L. (2000). Transition into middle School: What research says. *Middle School Journal, 31*(3), 57–60.

Myles, B. S. (2005). *Children and youth with Asperger syndrome: Strategies for success in inclusive settings.* Thousand Oaks, CA: Corwin.

Myles, B. S., Hagiwara, R., Dunn, W., Rinner, L., Reese, M., Huggins, A., et al. (2004). Sensory issues in children with Asperger syndrome and autism. *Education and Training in Developmental Disabilities, 39,* 283–290.

Myles, B. S., & Simpson, R. L. (2001). Understanding the hidden curriculum: An essential social skill for children and youth with Asperger syndrome. *Intervention in School and Clinic, 36*(5), 279–286.

Myles, B. S., & Simpson, R. L. (2003). *Students with Asperger syndrome: A guide for educators and parents* (2nd ed.). Austin, TX: Pro-Ed.

Myles, B. S., & Southwick, J. (2005). *Asperger syndrome and difficult moments: Practical strategies for tantrums, rage, and meltdowns.* Shawnee Mission, KS: Autism Asperger Publishing.

Nansel, T., Overpeck, M., Pilla, R., Ruan, W., Simons-Morton, B., & Scheidt, P. (2001). Bullying behaviors among U.S. youth: Prevalence and association with psychosocial adjustment. *Journal of the American Medical Association, 285,* 2094–2100.

National Autism Center. (2009). *Evidence-based practice and autism in the schools: A guide to providing appropriate interventions to students with autism spectrum disorders.* Randolph, MA: National Autism Center.

National Research Council. (2001). *Educating children with autism.* Washington, DC: National Academy Press.

Neary, T., Halvorsen, A. T., Kronberg, R., & Kelly, D. (1992, December). *Curricular adaptations for inclusive classrooms.* San Francisco: California Research Institute for the Integration of Students With Severe Disabilities.

Newman, L. (2007). *Secondary school experiences of students with autism.* Menlo Park, CA: SRI International. Retrieved April 25, 2010, from http://ies.ed.gov/ncser/pubs/20073005/index.asp

Odom, S. L., & Strain, P. S. (1984). Peer-mediated approaches to promoting children's social interaction: A review. *American Journal of Orthopsychiatry, 54,* 544–557.

Olweus, D. (1993). *Bullying at school: What we know and what we can do.* Oxford: Blackwell.

Pardini, P. (2002). The history of special education: Rethinking schools. *Urban Education Journal, 16*(3).

Picket, A. L., Gerlach, K., Morgan, R., Likins, M., & Wallace, T. (2007). *Paraeducators in schools: Strengthening educational teams.* Austin, TX: Pro-Ed.

Pitonyak, D. (2005, November 1). *10 things you can do to support a person with difficult behaviors.* Retrieved September 7, 2010, from http://www.dimagine.com/

Pitonyak, D., & O'Brien, J. (2009, January 19). *Effective behavior support, version 2.* Retrieved September 7, 2010, from http://www.dimagine.com/

Premack, D. G., & Woodruff, G. (1978). Does the chimpanzee have a theory of mind? *Behavioral and Brain Sciences, 1,* 515–526.

Rao, P. A. C., Beidel, D. C., & Murray, M. J. (2008). Social skills interventions for children with Asperger's syndrome or high-functioning autism: A review and recommendations. *Journal of Autism and Developmental Disorders, 38*(2), 353–361.

Rigby, K. (1996). *Bullying in schools: And what to do about it.* London: Jessica Kingsley.

Roberts, E. M., English, P. B., Grether, J. K., Windham, G. C., Somberg, L., & Wolff, C. D. (2007, October). Maternal residence near agricultural pesticide applications and autism spectrum disorders among children in the California central valley. *Environmental Health Perspectives, 115*(10), 1482–1489.

Robertson, T. S., & Valentine, J. W. (1998). *Research summary: The impact of inclusion on students and staff.* Retrieved March 24, 2010, from http://www.nmsa.org/Research/ResearchSummaries/Summary14/tabid/268/Default.aspx

Rubin, K. H., Bukowski, W., & Parker, J. G. (1998). Peer interactions, relationships, and groups. In W. Damon (Ed.), *Handbook of child psychology* (5th ed.). New York: Wiley.

Sands, D. J., Kozleski, E. B., & French, N. K. (2000). *Inclusive education for the 21st century: A new introduction to special education.* Belmont, CA: Wadsworth/Thompson Learning.

Saskatchewan Learning. (2001). *Creating opportunities for students with intellectual or multiple disabilities: The Evergreen Curriculum.* Regina, SK, Canada: Author.

Sears, R. W. (2007). *The vaccine book: Making the right decision for your child.* New York: Little, Brown and Company.

Shoffner, M., & Williamson, R. (2000). Facilitating student transitions into middle school. *Middle School Journal, 31,* 47–51.

Shore, S. (2004). *Ask and tell: Self-advocacy and disclosure for people on the autism spectrum.* Shawnee-Mission, KS: Autism Asperger Publishing Co.

Simpson, R. L. (2005). Evidence-based practices and students with autism spectrum disorders. *Focus on Autism and Other Developmental Disorders, 20*(3), 140–149.

Sinclair, J. (1993). Don't mourn for us. *Our Voice, 1*(3), Autism Network International. Retrieved from http://www.autreat.com/dont_mourn.html

Siperstein, G. N., Parker, R. C., Bardon, J. N., & Widaman, K. F. (2007). A national study of youth attitudes toward the inclusion of students with intellectual disabilities. *Exceptional Children, 73,* 435–455.

Snow, K. (2003). *People first language document.* Self-published at 250 Sunnywood Lane, Woodland Park, CO 80863.

Staub, D., & Peck, C. A. (1994–1995). What are the outcomes for non-disabled students? *Educational Leadership, 52*(4), 36–40.

Strain, P. S. (2008, May). *Key ingredients to effective inclusive early intervention for children with autism.* Opening address presented at the 3rd Annual General/Special Education Collaborative: Evidence Based Practice. Sponsored by California State University, Fullerton. Brea, California.

Strain, P. S., & Schwartz, I. (2001). ABA and the development of meaningful social relationships for young children with autism. *Focus on Autism and Other Developmental Disorders, 16,* 120–128.

Swedo, S. (2009). *Report of the DSM-V Neurodevelopmental Disorders Work Group, American Psychiatric Association.* Retrieved May 23, 2010, from http://www.dsm5.org/ProposedRevisions/Pages/InfancyChildhoodAdolescence.aspx

Tashie, C., & Rossetti, Z. (2004). Friendship: What's the real problem? *TASH Connections, 30*(1–2), 35–37.

Taylor, B., Miller, E., Farrington, C., Petropoulos, M.-C., Favot-Mayaud, I., Li, J., et al. (1999, June 12). Autism and measles, mumps, and rubella vaccine: No epidemiological evidence for a causal association. *Lancet, 353*(9169), 2026–2029.

Thousand, J., Villa, R. A., & Nevin, A. I. (Eds.). (2002). *Creativity and collaborative learning.* Baltimore, MD: Paul H. Brookes.

Tryon, P. A., Mayes, S. D., Rhodes, R. L., & Waldo, M. (2006). Can Asperger's disorder be differentiated from autism using DSM-IV criteria? *Focus on Autism and Other Developmental Disabilities, 21*(1), 2–6.

University of Wisconsin–Madison. (2005, March 10). Eye contact triggers threat signals in autistic children's brains. *Science Daily.* Retrieved April 20, 2008, from http://www.sciencedaily.com/releases/2005/03/050309151153.htm

Van der Klift, E., & Kunc, N. (1994). Hell-bent on helping: Benevolence, friendship, and the politics of help. In J. Thousand, R. Villa, & A. Nevin (Eds.), *Creativity and collaborative learning: A practical guide to empowering students and teachers.* Baltimore, MD: Paul H. Brookes.

Van der Klift, E., & Kunc, N. (1995). *Learning to stand still: Non-coercive responses to puzzling behavior.* Nanaimo, BC, Canada: Axis Consultation & Training Ltd.

Volkmar, F. R., & Lord, C. (2007). Diagnosis and definition of autism and other pervasive developmental disorders. In F. R. Volkmar (Ed.), *Autism and pervasive developmental disorders* (2nd ed., pp. 1–32). Cambridge, UK: Cambridge University Press.

White, E. (2002). *Fast girls: Teenage tribes and the myth of the slut.* New York: Scribner.

Will, M. C. (1986). Educating children with learning problems: A shared responsibility [the December 1985 Wingspread Conference address as published]. *Exceptional Children, 53,* 411–415.

Willey, L. H. (1999). *Pretending to be normal: Living with Asperger's syndrome.* London: Jessica Kingsley.

Wiseman, R. (2002). *Queen bees and wannabes: Helping your daughter survive cliques, gossip, boyfriends and other realities of adolescence.* New York: Crown Publishers.

Zemelman, S., Daniels, H., & Hyde, A. (2005). *Best practice: Today's standards for teaching and learning in America's schools* (3rd ed.). Portsmouth, NH: Heinemann.

Index

CORWIN
A SAGE Company

The Corwin logo—a raven striding across an open book—represents the union of courage and learning. Corwin is committed to improving education for all learners by publishing books and other professional development resources for those serving the field of PreK–12 education. By providing practical, hands-on materials, Corwin continues to carry out the promise of its motto: **"Helping Educators Do Their Work Better."**